SAMUEL JOHNSON
& THE
IMPACT OF PRINT

SAMUEL JOHNSON

& THE

IMPACT OF PRINT

———

ALVIN KERNAN

PRINCETON, NEW JERSEY

PRINCETON UNIVERSITY PRESS

MCM·LXXXVII

THIS BOOK WAS FIRST PUBLISHED AS PRINTING TECHNOLOGY,
LETTERS, AND SAMUEL JOHNSON, AND IS
COPYRIGHT © 1987 BY PRINCETON UNIVERSITY PRESS
PUBLISHED BY PRINCETON UNIVERSITY PRESS, 41 WILLIAM STREET
PRINCETON, NEW JERSEY 08540
IN THE UNITED KINGDOM: PRINCETON UNIVERSITY
PRESS, OXFORD

*Library of Congress Cataloging in Pub-
lication Data will be found on the last
printed page of this book. Publication
of this book has been aided by a grant
from the Harold W. McGraw, Jr., Fund
of Princeton University Press. ❧ Cloth-
bound editions of Princeton University
Press books are printed on acid-free paper,
and binding materials are chosen for
strength and durability. This book
has been composed in Linotron
Baskerville*

ISBN 0-691-06692-2
ISBN 0-691-01475-2, PBK.

FIRST PRINCETON PAPERBACK PRINTING,
WITH NEW TITLE, 1989

PRINTED IN THE UNITED STATES
OF AMERICA BY PRINCETON UNIVERSITY PRESS
PRINCETON, NEW JERSEY

CONTENTS

LIST OF ILLUSTRATIONS

BIBLIOGRAPHICAL NOTE AND
ACKNOWLEDGMENTS

A bibliography of works referred to, with citations attached to each item, appears at the end of this volume. Very short and very familiar quotes are not referenced, nor are quotes from a relatively short piece, e.g., *Rambler* 23, which has been identified in the text. All other quotes are cited under the appropriate work in the bibliography. The particular work from which quotes are taken will always be indicated in the body of the text, except when, as was just said, the quote is very short or well known, or when it is from the work cited most frequently in these pages, the Hill-Powell edition of Boswell's *Life of Johnson*. To locate the point in the original work where a particular quote appears, the reader need only turn to the entry of the book involved in the bibliography. There, the page number *on which the quote begins in my text* will be followed by a parenthesis, then the volume number (where applicable) and the first page number of the original. Thus: 4 (4:107) would indicate that the quote beginning on page 4 of this book is taken from the fourth volume and the 107th page of, say, Boswell's *Life of Johnson*. It is hoped that this arrangement will satisfy the needs of scholars and meet the responsibility to cite sources in a work of this type, while at the same time making for a more readable book.

No scholar working on Johnson today can do so without being aware of an enormous debt to a long line of Johnsonians, particularly in this century, who have edited the Johnson and Boswell texts, made some order of the complicated Johnsonian bibliography, biography, and chronology, and, in general, reconstructed Johnson's social circumstances and psychology. As a scholar who has not written on Johnson before, I am particularly aware of how much I owe to the great scholars who have made my work possible. I want formally to acknowledge this general indebtedness here, but furthermore, since in an attempt to make my text as readable as possible, I have minimized notes and bibliographic information there, I also need to record specifically some of my many scholarly debts. A great many books, of course, have contributed to our understanding of Johnson's involvement in the literary and print world of the late eighteenth century, but I am first and inescapably aware of debts to the textual work of G. B. Hill, L. F. Powell, J. D. Fleeman, R. W. Chapman, E. L. McAdam, Jr., Arthur Sherbo, and the many other editors presently involved in the ongoing Yale edition of Johnson's own works, planned and begun by, among others, F. W. Hilles and Donald and Mary Hyde. Since my argument involves, as it must, the relationship of Boswell to Johnson as a writer, the long line of Boswellians and their editions of his works have also been crucial to my studies. I want particularly to thank that remarkable literary scholar and historian, Frederick W. Pottle, as well as many of those who worked with him in continuing Geoffrey Scott's pioneering Boswell publications, especially Frank Brady and Marshall Waingrow.

There have been a number of remarkable biographies of Johnson in our time, and I have particularly found Joseph Wood Krutch's pioneering book and George Irwin's psychoanalytic interpretation, as well as Hugo Reichard's several articles, of special value; but I, like everyone else, owe the heaviest debts for an understanding of the life to two very recent and very different biographies by James Clifford and W. J. Bate. Clifford's work, most sadly interrupted by his death before the third volume of his biography, ordered all the facts and authenticated them in a newly authoritative way. Bate's *Samuel Johnson* is the magisterial Johnsonian work of our time, giving us not only the details of the life but a deep interpretation of Johnson as a man and writer which will continue to explain Johnson's life and writing for many years to come.

Macaulay and the nineteenth century left us with an image of Johnson as a John Bull conservative, quirky, self-satisfied, and dogmatic. The criticism and scholarship of the last fifty years have, however, constructed an image of the very different Johnson of radical fears and doubts who is at the center of the present book. Donald Greene's great book on Johnson's politics, as well as his numerous other contributions to Johnson studies; Bate on the psychology and the "achievement"; Bertrand Bronson, Leopold Damrosch, and Max Byrd on the tragic sense of life, "Johnson Agonistes" in Bronson's famous formulation; and Jean Hagstrum, W. R. Keast, and Damrosch on the criticism: these are only a few of the many distinguished works that have in various areas established the complexity of Johnson's thought and the unstable ground on which it rested. Besides these more general works on Johnson, I am also deeply indebted to a host of special studies which have made it possible to understand in detail what Johnson believed and did: W. K. Wimsatt on the style, for example, Claude Rawson on the scene of writing, Paul Korshin on patronage, Howard Weinbrot, James Sledd, and Gwin Kolb on the dictionary, Greene, again, on the books, Fleeman on the income from writing, and on and on.

I also owe much to a group of investigators of the growth and development of printing during the eighteenth century. There is a general historical and theoretical book on the subject, Elizabeth Eisenstein's recent *The Printing Press as an Agent of Change*, but there are numerous more specific investigations of particular eighteenth-century scenes of writing such as Ian Watt and Terry Belanger on the development of a print society, Pat Rogers on Grub Street, Richard Altick on literacy. Biographies, too, have brought Johnson's age alive: Pottle and Brady on Boswell, Lonsdale on Charles Burney, Sells on Gray, J. A. Cochrane on Strahan, Johnson's printer, Maynard Mack on Pope, and Ralph Straus on Robert Dodsley, Johnson's publisher. In a more general way I have been greatly and continuously aided by Father Walter J. Ong's lifelong writings on the literary consequences of the shift from orality to literacy, as well as by other social-historical studies such as those of Marshall McLuhan, Raymond Williams, Marilyn Butler, Robert Darnton, and P. O. Kristeller which trace, in various ways, the primary relationship between literary and social things, which is the central subject of my book. Beyond these works, there is still a vast range of highly specialized writings on which I have drawn heavily for information and without which this book with its focus on actual social detail would have been impossible; descriptions of George III's library, of cataloguing systems in early libraries, of the number of eighteenth-century books in the British Library, of Grub Street. The titles of these numerous works I must leave to the bibliography, but I want here to express my gratitude to their authors and to record the pleasure I derived from working in the community of Johnsonian scholarship that they and other writers have created.

Beyond this general indebtedness to scholarship, there are specific scholarly and editorial helps that I want to acknowledge. My many debts to Yale over the years by no means end with that university's great line of Johnsonians and Boswellians mentioned and used in these pages. I have learned over the years from Martin Price, Sterling Professor of English at Yale, particularly from his aptly named book, *To the Palace of Wisdom*, a great deal of what I know about eighteenth-century literature, and his generous, learned, and skillful reading of the manuscript of this book provided encouragement at a critical time as well as a good deal of the most helpful kind of commentary. Whatever the book may be, he helped to make it, and it stands, if he agrees, as a memorial of our long friendship. A younger colleague here at Princeton, David Bromwich, provided me with the sensitive readings of a remarkable stylist and historian of letters at crucial points. It is also a pleasure to thank A. Walton Litz, an old and always helpful friend, and Thomas Edwards, one of the best social critics of literature in our time.

Both Princeton University and the National Endowment for the Humanities, as well as the Mellon and Avalon Foundations, have, as on other occasions, generously given the leave, research funds, and the other kinds of support that continue to make research, scholarship, and writing possible in the humanities.

Finally, I want to record my gratitude and thanks to the many very skilled and very helpful people at Princeton University Press, and particularly to my editor, Mrs. Arthur Sherwood. To her, Princeton owes a long series of distinguished literary books, edited and published in hard times, both professional and personal. Many scholars are deeply indebted to her, and I would like in this, one of her last books, to record my thanks to her for her help and to compliment her on her courage and good sense and literary taste. It is a pleasure, too, to thank Harold McGraw, Jr., that longtime friend of Princeton University Press, for the subsidy that made possible the printing of this book at a reasonable price.

Finally, a brief word about a key term. Historians of the book and of printing have indicated, particularly forcefully in reviews of Elizabeth Eisenstein's *The Printing Press as an Agent of Change*, that there is an important distinction to be made between the words "print" and "printing." The difference is specially important in the term "printing technology," which is preferred over "print technology." I have generally observed the distinction, using, for example, the preferred term in my title. At some places, however, in a calculated attempt to emphasize the McLuhan concept of the technology and its cultural consequences developing initially from the root fact of movable type, which in turn generated printing and its business arrangements, I have made use of "print technology" and variant forms of this term.

Princeton, New Jersey
March 1986

SAMUEL JOHNSON
& THE
IMPACT OF PRINT

PRINT AND LETTERS IN EIGHTEENTH-CENTURY ENGLAND

Technology and Culture

Technological change has always affected social life, but in recent years it has accelerated at a near geometrical rate, as, for
example, the computer, *the* pill, and television have not only
changed ways of living and doing things but have increasingly
pressured traditional conceptions of reality and of the self that
have long been taken for well-established facts. That the primary modes of production affect consciousness and shape the
superstructure of culture is, not since Marx, exactly news, but
the changes come now with such rapidity and accumulated
force as to have disturbing, sometimes bewildering, effects on
our institutions and even our sense of existence and meaning
in the world. In these highly pressured cultural circumstances,
both Whiggish theories of progress and Marxist historical dialectic have failed to satisfy the desire to understand the technologically generated changes or to provide much real help in
deciding what might be useful and meaningful responses to
such radical change. Disappointment with such abstract and
generalizing theory has set the stage for an increasing number
of empirical studies, most notably and successfully in science
and in medicine, that work out in close detail the actual ways in
which technological changes affect people and their ways of
living and thinking. These same studies offer understanding
of the complex ways in which people have actually adapted,
by both accommodation and assimilation, to the pressures. In
the largest collective sense, the response has regularly been an
adjustment of culture, taking culture to be the complex, al-

ways-changing totality of activities and beliefs, never entirely coherent, never totally objective, through and in which people organize life meaningfully and make their values real.

The present book is another historical study of the technology-culture question, specifically as it worked out in one area of culture, literature, which is usually considered exempt from social and technological pressures, at a time, the mid-eighteenth century, when Europe was changing from an oral-scribal to a print society. That vast change, which had been building momentum since the invention of the printing press in the mid-fifteenth century, affected every area of social life, but nowhere was its force felt more directly and powerfully than in the world of writing and writers who lived hard by the printer's workroom and the bookseller's shop. An older system of polite or courtly letters—primarily oral, aristocratic, amateur, authoritarian, court-centered—was swept away at this time and gradually replaced by a new print-based, market-centered, democratic literary system in which the major conceptions and values of literature were, while not strictly determined by print ways, still indirectly in accordance with the actualities of the print situation.

Print exerted its pressure for change on the literary world at numerous social points and in ways that show very clearly how technology actually affects individual and social life. By changing their work and their writing, it forced the writer, the scholar, and the teacher—the standard literary roles—to redefine themselves, and if it did not entirely create, it noticeably increased the importance and the number of critics, editors, bibliographers, and literary historians. It transformed the literary audience, with profound consequences, from a small group of manuscript readers or listeners, such as we see in Dryden's *Essay on Dramatic Poesy*, to a group of readers, like those the author rather hopelessly if bravely tries to reach in *Tristram Shandy*, who bought books to read in the privacy of their homes. Print also made literature objectively real for the first time, and therefore subjectively conceivable as a universal fact, in great libraries of printed books containing large collections of the world's writings. The reality of "literature," thus collected, was authenticated and reinforced by various secondary legitimations—criticism, literary history and biography, standard editions, anthologies and collections—which the printers now found profitable to produce and sell. Print also rearranged the relationship of letters to other parts of the social world by, for example, freeing the writer from the need for patronage and the consequent subservience to wealth, by challenging and reducing established authority's control of writing by means of state censorship, and by pushing through a copyright law that made the writer the owner of his own writing, who for at least 28 years could sell it like any other piece of real property.

Because writers were so immediately and so personally involved in the changes print brought to writing, their lives provide the most moving record of the way in which human beings experience and react to technological change and the disturbances it forces upon them. In the lives of these writers—extensively and feelingly described, for example, in Boswell's *Life of Samuel Johnson* and Johnson's own *Life of Mr. Richard Savage*—we get some sense not only of the precise ways in which print affected letters and shaped the working life of writers for the printing press, but also of the complex and often agonizing ways in which a technology can be involved with human consciousness. The writers' active response to the pressures of print in an attempt to provide for their own existential needs not only makes clear the part that human beings play in cultural change but provides insight into the ways available to people to adjust and redirect technological pressure. Samuel Johnson, whose writing life provides the close focus of this study of print technology and literary culture, lived out, in an intense and dramatic manner, the social mutation of writers from an earlier role as gentlemen-amateurs to a new authorial self based on the realities of print and its conditions of mechanical reproduction. His struggle to create dignity for himself and his writing in new economic conditions that tended to make the writer only a paid worker in the print factory, and his work only a commodity—a struggle that has extended on into the romantic and modernist resistance to capitalist reality—shows in the most immediate terms the power of technology over life and belief, even as it dramatizes human resistance to absolute mechanical determinism. Furthermore, Johnson, as Carlyle (also a professional writer) saw and said, was a "culture hero," which means that his responses to the new situation of being a paid worker for the printing press, accepting print as the fact of writing but still actively shaping its tendencies to satisfy at least some part of his own needs for a worthwhile and meaningful life, are paradigmatic of the way in which people use culture to meet technological and other types of disruptive change.

Not so systematic as the law, not so central to society as the family, neither so coherent, nor so well objectified, as religion, literature paradoxically provides a somewhat more revealing model of how and why people construct the culture of which all of these institutions and ideologies are components. Literature reveals the culture-making activity more overtly than more stable institutions because of a historical vulnerability to change consequent on its failure as a secondary, loosely organized institution ever to achieve more than a semblance of objective existence and coherence. Inescapable conditions of the kind of socially constructed realities that make up culture, conditions that are more successfully hidden in such monumental cultural "realities" as, say, language, or the state, are more obvious in letters than they are elsewhere. "Weak" institutions, we could say, provide better sources for understanding the dynamics of culture than do "strong" institutions that more successfully manage to make themselves look like eternal facts of nature or the everlasting values of culture.

Literature and Letters

Before the nineteenth century, the word "literature" was used very broadly to refer to all kinds of serious and excellent writing, but after the print revolution, literature in time acquired a narrower meaning centering on a set of canonical literary texts displaying such qualities as creativity, imagination, and organicism. These qualities were assumed to distinguish literature categorically from types of discourse dealing with facts, such as history and science. These transcendental ideas have by now firmly attached themselves to the word "literature," obscuring, if not entirely excluding, all relationships of the world of writing to social realities like printing technology or copyright. Since my argument turns on the ways social events affect the writing world, I need a term that includes this aspect of literary activity, and I propose in the pages that follow to use the older and broader term "letters," in something reasonably close to its earlier eighteenth-century meaning, for the totality of literary things, social and aesthetic, reserving "literature" for the more restricted romantic meaning of verbal works of art made by the creative imagination. It is not my argument that "letters" is a more accurate term for literary activity than "literature." "Literature" is the correct historical term for the print-based romantic literary system centering on the individual creative self, that extended from the late eighteenth century to the present, passing through a succession of modes such as high romanticism, symbolism, modernism, and now, we are frequently told, a last "deconstructive" phase that is said to mark the death of literature, though not, presumably, the end of some kind of social system of letters. "Letters" as defined by the literary world Samuel Johnson creates in his *Lives of the Poets* is used to refer to the full social existence of the literary world and the ways it relates to social energies and change.

Partly objective construct, party subjective concept, letters, like the other socially constructed realities of culture, does not, and cannot, have the essence and the absolute coherence that are hypothetically attributed to the natural objects that are the study of science. Nevertheless, its components historically tend to aggregate in loosely organized literary systems, which theorists and critics are always, with only limited success, trying to tighten up. The point at which one of these literary systems breaks down and another begins to be cobbled together offers the best view available of the ways in which social change works on literary culture, and of the ways in which people respond in an effort to maintain letters and the life of writing as a meaningful activity in the face of new realities. We live in such a time when the by-now old romantic print-based order of letters is breaking down under the pressures of postindustrial society and a new electronic medium of communication. This "deconstruction," proceeding, but by no means finished, on both social and critical levels, which was the subject of an earlier book of mine, *The Imaginary Library*, increases our interest in earlier transformations, such as the point at which romantic "literature" began to appear in the eighteenth century when print destroyed the old oral and manuscript culture. A close look at this change and its literary consequences is the extended business of the following pages, and two books, Pope's *Dunciad* and Boswell's *Life of Johnson*, form gates of ivory and horn to its historical setting in the London literary scene in the eighteenth century.

THE DUNCIAD *and Print's Destruction* *of Courtly Letters*

Pope's *Dunciad* (written and rewritten over the years 1728–1743), portrays the apocalypse of an old courtly order of letters, in its last neoclassical mode, in England in the first half of the eighteenth century. Print is the destructive force, the instrument of Dulness, corrupting every area of traditional learning and letters until it brings at last "the Smithfield Muses to the Ear of Kings." As the expression of closely related new economic and social as well as technological orders, print during the course of *The Dunciad* replaces the literary arrangements of the old regime with those more in the spirit of its own mechanical, democratic, and capitalistic tendencies, creating a new world of writing, Grub Street, where writers became paid hacks, books print commodities, and the literary audience the reading public. These changes constituted in Pope's view the end of polite letters and ultimately of civilization.

Print, Pope shows in close and as unattractive detail as possible, had become by the early eighteenth century what it has continued to be until the electronic revolution of our own time, the basic, inescapable technological fact of letters, the medium in which writing must exist and communicate in the world. Print, of course, had affected Europe from the time Gutenberg set up his press in the mid-fifteenth century in the immediate ways that Natalie Davis, for example, portrays in her classic article, "Printing and the People"; but not until the end of the seventeenth and the beginning of the eighteenth century did it transform the more advanced countries of Europe from oral into print societies, reordering the entire social world, and restructuring rather than merely modifying letters. I shall explain this somewhat unfamiliar, but by now well-established, view of the length of time it took print fully to affect the social world, particularly letters, in more detail in later chapters.

"Books and the Man I sing," Pope began his first, anonymous, version of *The Dunciad* in 1728, and he was no stranger to the printing press, publishing all his works from his twenty-first year, when the *Pastorals* were printed, to 1743, the year before his death, when the last version of *The Dunciad* in four books appeared. He was probably, though he denied it, the first major author to arrange for his own letters to be printed, and his attitudes in many areas were characteristic of the author in an age of print. He rejected overt patronage, boasting, for example, in a letter to Lord Carteret, of 16 February 1723: "I take my self to be the only Scribler of my Time, of any degree of distinction, who never receiv'd any Places from the Establishment, any Pension from a Court, or any Presents from a Ministry." Able to scorn patronage because he so well understood the economics of the publishing business and how to profit from them, he has the deserved reputation of being, in Hugo Reichard's words, "the first business man among English poets," and Terry Belanger calls him the "watershed figure," the first English writer other than the Renaissance playwrights "who by careful management of his literary productions was able to earn a good deal of money from them." If in 1712 he naïvely sold the first version of *The Rape of the Lock* to Lintot for only £7, in following years, as Johnson recounts admiringly in his "Life of Pope," he got something like £5,300 for the six volumes of his translation of *The Iliad* by first signing up 575 subscribers at 6 guineas each, and then selling the rights to additional sales to Lintot for £200 per volume, requiring the publisher also to provide the original subscribers' volumes plus author's gift copies.

But however deep Pope's own involvement with the realities of publishing, he carefully cultivated an old-style image of the writer as a gentleman and man of means, living in his country home at Twickenham, mixing easily in the highest intellectual and social circles, advising kings and aristocrats on the use of wealth and learning. Pope's authoritative biographer, Maynard Mack, spends a good deal of time and learning on this question of Pope's "aristocratic attitudes toward the writer's profession," which, as he says, "crop out so incongrously . . . in his statements about his work—that he wrote only because it pleased him, gave up no serious calling for 'this idle trade,' lisped (as a child) in numbers 'for the numbers came' . . . ." "All this," Mack concludes, "seems laughable coming from one of the most painstaking of craftsmen, one who was also a canny publisher as well as a shrewd judge of timing and public taste. . . . Laughable, it may be, yet deeply felt. And while there is probably (it is difficult to be entirely sure) some element of snobbery in this claim to lofty self-sufficiency, there is plainly some clinging also to an ideal of serene detachment cherished by almost everyone in this age. . . ." However complex this "serene detachment," Pope's aristocratic attitudes to authorship extended to his public view of the effect of print on letters, and in his greatest poem, *The Dunciad*, he portrays the print world as monstrously dangerous to letters and to all civilized society. His attack on print is grounded in a metaphysical scheme, part pagan and part Christian, in which civilization is perpetually threatened by the goddess Dulness, "Daughter of Chaos and eternal Night," who is always trying to restore the ancient empire of primal stupidity and mental anarchy over which she reigned until the Creating Word ordered the world. Print, the pedantic mock-editor and commentator on the poem, Martin Scriblerus, tells us, now offers Dulness the means for reconquest "in those days, when (after providence had permitted the Invention of Printing as a scourge for the Sins of the learned) Paper also became so cheap, and printers so numerous, that a deluge of authors cover'd the land: . . ." In the poem itself, a multitude of printed books, a vast "Gothic Library" printed by Caxton, Wynkyn de Worde, and their successors, accumulates and bends the library shelves with dull, heavy, native authors such as Taylor, Benlowes, Holland, Quarles, Blackmore, and Shadwell. These are joined by an increasing flood of modern pamphlets and other printed materials—"Journals, Medleys, Merc'ries, Magazines: Sepulchral Lyes . . . New-year Odes"— and together they inundate in profusion and confusion both the ancient classics and the few English writers of true genius,

Shakespeare, Bacon, Locke, Newton, Milton, and Swift. As the number of printed books increases, truth becomes more obscure and understanding diminishes: "A Lumberhouse of books in ev'ry head, For ever reading, never to be read!"

Pope did not consider himself an enemy to all printed books, only to bad ones; but what he objects to and parodies in *The Dunciad* are the inevitable consequences of print. Not its perversion but the extrapolation of its inherent Gutenberg logic. A printing press is, for example, a machine with a potential for turning out, compared with scribe and scriptorium, large numbers of books, and it therefore necessarily produces what Pope describes as a bibliographic deluge. Print technology also tends toward what a historian of the printed book, Elizabeth Eisenstein, has called in her article "Conjectures" an *esprit de système*, "regularly numbered pages, punctuation marks, section breaks, running heads, indexes, and so forth. . . ." This systematic order imposed by print on its product, the printed book, was perceived by Pope as obscurantism, and he mocked it relentlessly in the format of *The Dunciad*. Advertisements, license, Scriblerus' prolegomena, remarks by various critics, letters to the publisher, testimonies by other authors, arguments for each book, extensive learned notes, and four different editions, including a variorum, accumulate grotesquely to bury the poem itself under the weight of the bibliographical apparatus made both possible and inevitable by print.

Dulness extends deeper than format into the printed book, for Pope understood well that the ability of the press to print many books, and the desire of printers, publishers, and writers to make money by doing so, called into being a vast number of new writers from all social classes who could now satisfy their vanity to see their names in print, or stave off hunger by providing the copy needed to feed the insatiable printing machine:

> An endless band
> Pours forth, and leaves unpeopled half the land.
> A motley mixture! in long wigs, in bags,
> In silks, in crapes, in Garters, and in rags,
> From drawing rooms, from colleges, from garrets,
> On horse, on foot, in hacks, and gilded chariots: . . .

"the Grub-street race," all those who "hunger, and who thirst for scribling sake," are, Pope perceived, as much the product of the press as printed books. Professional writers like the laureate Colley Cibber, whom Pope eventually made king of the dunces, and the numerous other hacks he names, some professional, some amateur, all foolish and inept, write out of vanity, poverty, desire for fame, mad fancy, and a variety of other debased motives. Lacking wit, skill, and learning, the hacks are still encouraged by the printing press to write vulgar books that embody the principal qualities of Dulness and spread her uncreating word throughout the nation. They plagiarize, not "imitate," the works of others; their styles are clumsy, disordered, and repetitive; their books are boring, long, fantastic, obscene, clichéd; they confuse tragedy and comedy, epic and farce, and break all civilized rules of decorum and good sense; and ultimately, for all their expansiveness, they are a frothy nothing:

> Prose swell'd to verse, verse loit'ring into prose:
> How random thoughts now meaning chance to find,
> Now leave all memory of sense behind:
> How Prologues into Prefaces decay,
> And these to Notes are fritter'd quite away. . . .

Print spreads through and eventually corrupts not only the book but all polite letters. It not only makes simple fools into hack writers, but it also turns honest mechanics into greedy printers and simple tradesmen into booksellers without scruples, taste, or morality, willing to steal and publish anything that will sell. The glut of books and authors soon creates keen competition for the patron, who, badly educated and unable in the flood of print to discriminate any longer between good writing and bad, can now be won only by obsequious flattery, or lower forms of service. "There march'd the bard and blockhead, side by side, Who rhym'd for hire, and patroniz'd for pride." The printing press makes the written word available and useful to party politics and generates propaganda writers, meanly skilled in lying and in slander, writing on any side of any question for pay. Books invade the schoolroom to a degree hitherto unknown in an education formerly oriented toward moral training and oral performance, and the master, now enforcing book learning, philology, with bloodstained rod, makes exact analysis of the word fixed in the printed text the only authority and substance of the students' education:

> We ply the Memory, we load the brain,
> Bind rebel Wit, and double chain on chain,
> Confine the thought, to exercise the breath;
> And keep them in the pale of Words till death.

Criticism and textual scholarship were encouraged at this time by the increasing availability of different printed texts and the ideals of accuracy that print technology and the comparison of a number of texts made possible. Pope, as usual, saw only the darker side of this print-based scholarship, the bookish pedantry that glosses every word, reduces all poetry to prose, and looking at the texts microscopically, sees only "hairs and pores, examines bit by bit." The subtle elaborations of meaning that can be teased out of a poem when the critics can endlessly analyze texts fixed by print, will only, Pope foresees,

> . . . dim the eyes, and stuff the head
> With all such reading as was never read:
> . . . explain a thing till all men doubt it,
> And write about it, Goddess, and about it: . . .

Meaning disappears not only downward into the depths of endless analysis, but outward as well, in the spread of a multiplicity of printed texts. That representative of civic humanism, Swift's king of Brobdingnag, restricted his library to about a thousand books, but the extensive world of books made available by print offers so many statements of so many different truths that all certainty and clarity are lost in endless contradictions. In the end, as a grotesque, mock-version of the most sacred texts of polite letters, *The Aeneid* and *Paradise Lost*, and its most prestigious genre, the heroic or epic poem, *The Dunciad* itself stands as the summary image of all the many different kinds of literary debasement that originate in print.

It was not Pope's view in *The Dunciad* that printing makes dunces out of people who otherwise have no dulness in them, for Dulness is always there, waiting. But print in his understanding is a dullish, mechanical, undiscriminating, repetitive, mass medium, a true instrument of Dulness that gives extraordinary opportunities to those already inclined that way, greedy booksellers, vain, dull gentlemen, poor scribblers, pedantic schoolmasters. Pope would not have found fault with Marshall McLuhan's generalization that print plunged "the human mind into the sludge of an unconscious engendered by the book." The kind of mental confusion that McLuhan refers to was, in fact, Pope's central satiric subject. But Pope also saw that even as the individual was confused and corrupted by print, the old aristocratic society and its system of letters was also being distorted and beginning to disintegrate under pressures from new print-fostered kinds of party politics, marketplace economics, rationalistic philosophy, and machine technology. Print was both the image and the instrument of these new ways of thinking and doing, and in Pope's apocalyptic vision, a flood of printer's ink was a darkness that spread across the land, staining, as in his memorable image of Fleet ditch running into the silver Thames, the white page, darkening the minds of the people and their rulers, obliterating polite letters, and finally extinguishing all light, to leave the land in ancient night and ignorance. Habitual print-readers like ourselves need not share Pope's elitist revulsion to the literary change involved in the larger change from an aristocratic to a democratic culture to appreciate how deeply he understood the power of print technology to remake literary culture and how exactly he as a direct observer of the advent of the high Gutenberg age perceived the specific and intricate ways in which print actually changed thought, letters, and the social world.

Boswell's LIFE OF JOHNSON: *Letters in Print Culture*

The responses of eighteenth-century men of letters to print were as various as their social circumstances. Pope made a fortune from the booksellers, prophesied the destruction of polite letters, and passed on, somewhat stained perhaps by print but still the last great writer of the old order. Writers who were protected by money and position from the full power of print to shape the life of writing, for example Horace Walpole with his art press at Strawberry Hill, the fastidious Thomas Gray at Cambridge, or the elegant Edward Gibbon writing in Lausanne about the decline and fall of an earlier aristocratic society, continued to maintain in their lives and writings the traditions of polite letters and the old role of the writer as gentleman-amateur, congenial to the mores of aristocratic society, and seemingly careless of fame and money. It must have been shocking to Gibbon to be thanked for a presentation of Volumes 2 and 3 of *Decline and Fall* by the Duke of Gloucester, with the words, "Another damned thick square book. Always scribble, scribble, scribble! Eh! Mr. Gibbon," as if he were only another hack. It was loftily obvious to Horace Walpole that Richardson's novels were "pictures of high life as conceived by a bookseller," while it was worth his noting that "Reynolds was a painter and Garrick a player."

The most moving and instructive records of the change in letters appear, however, in the lives of those writers like Defoe, Savage, Goldsmith, Smart, and Samuel Johnson who actually lived in the world of Grub Street and experienced without protection the full impact of print on the life of writing. If *The Dunciad* portrays the apocalypse of courtly letters, Johnson's *Life of Mr. Richard Savage* (1744) and Boswell's *Life of Johnson* (1791) are central statements of what it really meant and felt like to be a hack working in the new Grub Street print business—organized on the same principles, though not with the same efficiency, as Adam Smith's pin factory—where, as Goldsmith in "The Distresses of the Hired Writer" remarked, "writing is converted to a mechanic trade." Among the many who worked in the eighteenth-century print factory, Samuel Johnson stands out as perhaps the only writer of stature who fully understood, acknowledged, and consciously acted upon an awareness that print was now inescapably the primary fact of letters. He knew that his living as a man and his reputation as a writer had to be made in print terms, and he consequently accepted openly, rather than trying to conceal, the conditions of writing in print circumstances, such as his status as a paid professional writer, his need to develop a distinctive style that allowed him to write swiftly and effectively on any topic under deadline pressures, the power of the booksellers to dictate his subjects, and the necessity of pleasing those whom he was the first to call "common readers." So pervasive was print in Johnson's life that at times he seems to fulfill Pope's prediction that writers would soon become only another product of the printing press. The son of a bookseller, he grew up surrounded by the books in his father's shop. He read more books than any man of his time, and the pages he read were imprinted so exactly on his near-photographic memory that his mind was itself a great book, or a library, that furnished his writing and his conversation. That conversation itself was praised by Boswell as being always so "well-formed" that it could all have been printed without editing; another person remarked that his talk had the correctness of a second edition. In time, he took his name from a book, "Dictionary Johnson," and having no children, he left his books as progeny. His life was spent, his living earned, reading and writing books. In time he became the great cham of letters, as Boswell styled him, and in the end he inevitably has his existence in a book, Boswell's *Life of Johnson*.

Where Pope saw only disasters in print, Johnson found literary opportunities whenever possible. If, for example, the printing press made writers for pay, then Johnson capitalized on the situation by boasting openly of professionalism: "No man but a blockhead ever wrote except for money." When the printing business turned literary art into property by getting Parliament to pass a copyright law, Johnson extended the idea to the point where he argued that the author has "a stronger right of property than that by occupancy; a metaphysical right, a right as it were of creation, which should from its nature be perpetual." If the printing press produced a flood of books which threatened in their numbers to cheapen and ephemeralize all writing, then Johnson could also point out in *Rambler* 23 that a printed text has a peculiar fixity, in contrast to manuscripts, and hence a special ontological and epistemological authority: "When a book is once in the hands of the public, it is considered as permanent and unalterable; and the reader . . . accommodates his mind to the author's design." Such was the authority of printed texts that they could be used, he argued, to establish at long last a true scholarly text of the national poet, Shakespeare, by going back to and following the original printed plays without emendation by the editor—"It has been my settled principle, that the reading of the ancient books is probably true." And in his *Dictionary* he gave substantial print order to the flood of words Pope so feared, "the boundless chaos of a living speech," as Johnson called it, by deriving the existence and meaning of words from their appearance in certain printed texts, at the same time establishing the linguistic authority of writers by making their works the standard in all matters of language. If the printing press put books into the hands of ordinary people, both to read and to judge, making, as was often charged, "the vulgar rise above their humble sphere," then Johnson could point out in *Rambler* 52 that without printing, the "mass of every people must be barbarous," and go on to create out of the new mass audience for printed books his universal "common reader" whose judgments "uninstructed by precept, and unprejudiced by authority" are "in questions that relate to the heart of man . . . more decisive than learning. . . ."

Johnson in these new situations is a hard-pressed human being, finding ways to earn a living and, at the same time, to give himself some dignity and his work some value, in the midst of a radical change in English society and its system of letters. To watch him in these circumstances is to be reminded forcefully that writing is always a *human* activity, entered into and pursued to satisfy basic individual needs and desires. But Johnson's strategies for making the best of print ways are paradigmatic as well as personal. Such is the power of Johnson's personality, and Boswell's book, that it often appears that Johnson heroically and single-handedly invented a new poetic role and print-based system of letters in late eighteenth-century England. But Johnson was seldom an innovator in literary matters, preferring, whether in dictionaries or in critical theories, not to invent but to adapt, recombine, and expand traditional arrangements to fit and fill print circumstances. He was, nonetheless, central to the change in letters because in his experiences in the writing world from about 1738 to 1784, the major problems posed by print in his time appear in urgent personal terms; and, in an uncanny way, each of his personal efforts to establish the worth of his writings, and of himself as a writer, offers remarkable insights into the nature and function of letters in the age of print. Johnson, we might say simply, provides a model, both in motive and ways of working, of the social construction of letters in the age of print. Our sense of him as a true maker of letters is strengthened by the way he dramatized—and Boswell further emphasized—whatever he did in an outsized, emphatic manner that gives it more than ordinary meaning. The whole affair with Lord Chesterfield, for example, became, as a result of the way Johnson played it and Boswell reported it, not just, as it could have been in other hands, another dreary quarrel between a haughty peer and a truculent hack, but a great event in the history of letters and of print, the scene in which not just Samuel Johnson but *the author*, after centuries of subservience to the aristocracy, declares his democratic independence of patronage. This was the case with other events in Johnson's writing life which are analyzed in these pages. The meeting with the king, the confrontation with Macpherson, the irregular pattern of writing and correcting copy, the intense mode of reading and remembering, the battle with Osborne the bookseller over a library catalogue, sitting on his three-legged chair while writing the Dictionary, all these events might have been mere biographical trivia in another life, but his dramatic force makes them into the rituals and the typological scenes of letters in the age of print.

In no respect does he more accurately anticipate what is to come than in his construction of a new role for himself as the writer who can earn his living by writing for the marketplace and still assert his authorial dignity and social importance. The courtly connection no longer supplied writing and writer with the necessary authority, and if a writer like Johnson were to be anything more than a Grub Street scribbler who produced semifinished manuscript materials for the machine press to finish, then new ways had to be found to make the writer interesting and important. It was just this need for a new definition of the writer and his purpose that Johnson's remarkable personality provided, particularly after Boswell's *Life* gave him monumental form. In part, as we have already seen, Johnson's new authorial role was a matter of open, no-nonsense professional competence that wrote prodigiously and well about anything and everything—even the "life of a broomstick"—produced copy while the printer's boy waited at the door, and never corrected a piece once written. But this is only a small part of the remarkable and paradoxical figure whom we fondly called *Dr. Johnson*: quirky, compulsive, kindly, loveable and loving, brutal, ugly, brilliant, courageous, domineering, thanatophobic, ambitious, working with violent energy only to fall into lassitude and long immobilities, and on and on, the most contradictory and fantastic of men. It is obvious why as a man he has caught and held the world's eye, but at the same time, he was also what letters in the age of print needed, an intriguing personality who filled the writer's role in a way that made both him and what he wrote something more than mere utilitarian print products. There were no writers like Johnson before him, and none like him even afterward, but in the romantic system of literature that gradually developed after him, the authorial personality had to be, and continued in fact to be, like Johnson, in the respect of being strange and interesting enough to impart to writers and writing a psychological dignity and meaning they could no longer derive from a place and function in the social world of palace, great house, and cathedral. It is not likely that Johnson and Boswell consciously perceived and coolly constructed, in the manner of a modern political image maker, the kind of author that letters required in the Gutenberg era. It was rather that the moment was right for someone as complex as Johnson to become the type of the great writer, and that Samuel Johnson, with, as always, Boswell's help, capi-

talized on the situation to become the first of those titanic figures, the romantic poets, in whose deeps literature was henceforth to be forged, and by whose strange personalities and
struggles to make meaning it was henceforth to be authenticated.

Boswell understood the archetypal qualities of Johnson as a
writer in a print society—constructing a dictionary of the language almost single-handedly, reading more books than any
other Englishman of his time, denouncing Lord Chesterfield
and patronage—and, as if answering Pope's mock-epic of
print, he gave Johnson heroic stature in his true, not mock,
print epic, the *Life of Johnson*. Boswell compares his hero to
Odysseus, for obvious reasons, but he is really more an Aeneas
who as writer leaves behind the dying world of courtly letters
to found the beginnings of a new world of letters based on the
realities of print technology and its marketplace economics. In
the standard history of English literature, Johnson, of course,
plays a different part, that of a Roland, the last defender of the
old neoclassic literary values, while Collins, Gray, Cowper, and
the other pre-romantic poets, whom Johnson generally disliked, begin a new romantic literature, later to be firmly defined and established by Wordsworth and Coleridge. But Boswell's Johnson is a bearer of the new, an epic figure of the
Aeneas type in uneasy transition between two cultural worlds,
one dying and one trying to be born. There are struggles with
the old aristocratic literary system: an argument with Lord
Chesterfield over the matter of patronage; an expression of
scorn for noble lords who still circulate their poems in manuscript; and an exchange with King George III in the royal library in the royal palace, which will be the center of the next
chapter. But at times the struggle with the new world of print
is also open, even physical, as when Johnson knocks down the
monstrously ignorant bookseller Osborne with a mighty folio
and stands with his foot triumphantly on his chest; or when,

feeling himself to be a representative of writers, he endures severe discomfort at a party of booksellers and printers by sitting too near the fire in the place of honor rather than moving to a less honorable seat farther down the dinner table.

Pope was right about the effect of print on courtly letters, but he failed as a prophet of what would follow the destruction of the old oral-manuscript literary order in the new print society. Letters did not disappear into the apocalyptic darkness in which *The Dunciad* ends—"*Art* after *Art* goes out, and all is Night"—and Colley Cibber, laureate though he may have been, was not the writer who truly brought the Gutenberg message to the ear of kings. It was Samuel Johnson who told his monarch in the King's Library that the literary *ancien régime* was dead, and that in its place there was a new print-based letters ruled not by kings—or by printers—but by writers. The famous scene of the meeting with the king offers a point of high vantage from which to begin our detailed survey of how print and Samuel Johnson interacted in the social construction of a new literary system in eighteenth-century England.

CHAPTER I

THE KING OF ENGLAND MEETS THE
GREAT CHAM OF LITERATURE

The King's Library and the Meeting with Johnson

On February 10, a Tuesday, in 1767, Samuel Johnson went, as he often did, to read in the King's Library, a collection of fine books and manuscripts assembled by that dedicated royal collector of books, King George III, after his accession to the English throne in 1760. The library was located in the royal residence then known as the Queen's House, originally Buckingham House, on the site where Buckingham Palace was erected after 1825 by Nash. The plan of the entire library and engravings of its most impressive rooms, the Octagon Library and another gallery, appear following page 126. "The King's Great Library," says a historian of Buckingham Palace, John Harris, was built between "1762–66 as the first in a sequence of library compartments needed to quench the King's passion for books. Adjacent was the South Library, turned in an east-west direction and having its south wall broken by a segmental bay. On a gallery in this room the King kept his medals and drawings. On to the southern face of the Library was attached the Octagon, a most noble galleried apartment lit by seven Diocletian windows. One of the finest rooms in the palace, with a diameter of forty-two feet, in Chambers's *oeuvre* it compares to his Great Room for the Society of Arts (1759) or the Exhibition Room of the Royal Academy (1776). Finally, to absorb the glut of books the East Library was added about 1768 to lie parallel with the Great Library, and was raised another storey in 1774 to accommodate the King's Marine Gallery, where he kept his models of ships and harbours."

Richard Dalton was the librarian at the time that Johnson visited the collection. But Johnson was presented to the king by Frederick Augusta Barnard, a royal godson, as his name indicates, and a member of a family which had been royal pages for three generations. Barnard became the librarian in 1774 and built the collection, on which several thousand pounds a year was spent to make it reflect, like the king's palaces and his art collections, royal taste, power, and patronage of the arts. Johnson himself, in a letter of 1768, advised Barnard, who was then departing on a continental book-buying expedition, on how to go about procuring only the best books, first editions, perfect copies, and finest printings needed as "the great ornaments of a Library furnished for Magnificence as well as use." Ultimately the library contained over 65,000 volumes plus many pamphlets and manuscripts covering all areas of what was then called literature, or polite letters: classical learning, religion, philosophy, poetry, geography, history, mathematics, law, and many other subjects.

John Brooke in his close study of the King's Library argues that George III built a "universal library" which did "not reflect the interests of the collector but the interests of those who use it," and Esdaile remarks that "the King's policy was one of liberally admitting scholars" to his library. Ayling reports that he had also ordered his collectors "never to bid against a scholar, a professor, or any person of moderate means who desired a particular book for his own use," but in regards to his library, as in so many other matters, such as North America, George III was a curious mixture of modern sentiments and autocratic attitudes. Both the nature of the collection and a number of stories about it make it fairly certain that the king still considered his books not a national library, open to all, but a personal possession. When the politically radical chemist, Joseph Priestly, applied to use it in 1779, the king, according to Esdaile, grudgingly agreed that it should be open to him as to other scholars, but did not wish himself, he told Lord North regally, to give personal permission: "I can't think his [Priestly's] character as a Politician or Divine deserves my appearing at all in it." But Johnson was welcome, for by 1767, with his dictionary more than ten years behind him, he was the most distinguished man of letters in England, and Boswell tells us that when he visited "those splendid rooms and noble collection of books," Barnard "took care that he should have every accommodation that could contribute to his ease and convenience."

So great in fact was his reputation, Boswell goes on, that the king had expressed a desire to meet him, and on being notified on this day that Johnson had arrived and was reading at a table before the fire, George III, according to Boswell, but not the "Caldwell Minute," left his own affairs and went graciously to the great literary authority to question him about the state of letters in his kingdom. There then ensued a polite literary conversation, with many exchanges of graceful compliments, in which Johnson gave the king his views on such matters as the comparative states of the Oxford and Cambridge libraries, the writings of Warburton, Lyttleton, and Hill, and the quality of several literary journals being published at the time.

The real energy of the scene, however, is not to be found in this literary talk but in a persistent attempt by the king to urge Johnson to continue writing. His Majesty opens the subject by courteously enquiring if Johnson "was then writing anything," to which Johnson responds that "he was not, for he had pretty well told the world what he knew." Not to be put off, the king still urges him "to continue his labours," and at this point Johnson says rather abruptly that "he thought he had already done his part as a writer." King George still carries it off gracefully— "I should have thought so too . . . if you had not written so well"—and then drops the subject for a moment, only to return to it again at the end of the conversation when he "expressed a desire to have the literary biography of this country ably executed, and proposed to Dr. Johnson to undertake it." At this point, which is the end of the conversation as Boswell reports it, Johnson gave in and "signified his readiness to comply with his Majesty's wishes."

The setting, the action, and the parts played out in this library scene were shaped by a multitude of forces, not the least of which were the new young "patriot" king's determination to restore what he conceived of as the lost glory of his nation and its kings, and Johnson's exhaustion in the midst of his second critical period of mental depression. But whatever personal circumstances may have been involved, the library scene was a ritual in which a monarch struggling in all areas, including letters, to regain royal powers—"I will have no innovations in my time"—tries to enact once more the traditional royal authority over letters that had been maintained in Europe for four centuries. The extent and the force of this royal authority as it existed, or at least as it was conceived, in the court of James I has recently been analyzed and described by Jonathan Goldberg as a power that made the king "author" of all discourse, poems, pageants, masques, plays, sermons, personal correspondence, meditations, family portraits. "Under James, what is, is right; his is the time and the power, and in his state all time is one, all words are one," and the word is the king's.

It is this ancient power that George III reasserted in his noble library with its magnificent collection of books, the sacred objects that declared the king's ownership of all books through his possession of the best of them. The essential royal power over discourse is expressed actively by the king's command to one of his subjects to write, and the traditional royal control of writers and their writing is intensified by the subject of the proposed book, "the literary biography of this country," as if the king's prerogative to call writers into being extended beyond Samuel Johnson and the present moment into the past, from where older writers could be, at his commanding word, res-

cued from oblivion and given future life in biographies. Both
the setting and the brief drama enacted in the library ritualize
de facto powers exercised for centuries by the strong European
monarchies that had called art and artists into being by commissioning the architects who built palaces, great houses, and
churches, the painters and sculptors who decorated them, and
the writers who filled their libraries with books celebrating the
great princes and their courts, their kingdoms and their languages, legitimating and reinforcing the aristocratic ethos and
the hierarchical social structures that centered the entire political and artistic enterprise. In all the bastions of the established
order—palace, church, university, and great house—art existed to testify to and in turn be justified by the power, wealth,
authority, and grandeur of the king, the state religion, and the
court aristocracy.

Courtly Letters and the Old Regime

The *de facto* power of princes over art had been exercised
through a number of very practical and very forceful social arrangements that were all present just below the surface of the
ritual enactment of the royal authority over letters in the King's
Library. Most obviously, there was the legal power of the crown
to exercise censorship, establishing as fact the king's ownership
of all writing, actual and potential, by determining which books
could and could not be printed. This absolute authority over
the existence of books was extended by the traditional prerogative of the king to license presses and to give—in fact, to sell—
exclusive rights to print certain particularly sacred, and
thereby profitable, books—bibles, primers, law books—to a
printer or bookseller. Official censorship had ended legally in
England in 1694, except for stage plays, but the power remained very much an issue through the eighteenth century,
and governments continued to exercise authority in this re-

gard through various indirect methods such as the libel laws and taxation of printed paper. Defoe had stood in the pillory, with his ears at risk, for displeasing his queen by writing ironically on religious questions, and the century's crucial censorship case was still a center of controversy when Johnson and the king talked. John Wilkes, whom Johnson disliked on principle but found charming company when Boswell tricked them into having dinner together, had been imprisoned for seditious libel and an inflammatory issue of his paper, No. 45 of *The North Briton*, burned and suppressed for mocking the king's official address to Parliament. Print and speech once more at odds! In addition, a piece of pornography, the *Essay on Woman*, issued by a press Wilkes set up at his house, was declared "a most scandalous, impious and obscene libel" by the House of Lords. Later, in his "Life of Milton," Johnson was unable to make up his mind on the question of censorship, seeing both the "danger of . . . unbounded liberty and the danger of bounding it," and concluded that it is "a problem in the science of Government, which human understanding seems hitherto unable to solve." But when he first arrived in London, he had published anonymously a biting satire, *A Compleat Vindication of the Licensers of the Stage* (1739), attacking theatrical censorship in general, and specifically as it had been recently legalized in a 1737 statute and used to deny a license to Henry Brooke's play, *Gustavus Vasa*. If the censor, says Johnson's Swiftian persona, a defender of licensing, is allowed to extend his authority to everything published and at the same time close the schools where people are taught to read, then he will "in time, enjoy the title and the salary without the trouble of exercising his power, and the nation will rest at length, in ignorance and peace."

The king's authority in the library, however courteous, was also backed up by patronage, the elaborate system of rewards, operating on several levels and in complex ways, that the European courts and their churches had used for centuries to manage relationships with subjects, not only in the arts but in all areas of life, political, economic, and personal. Power was exercised, in an age before civil services and meritocracies, and subjects were tied to their rulers by gifts of many kinds—grants of money, titles, appointments to office, land, wardships, privileges, and many other various kinds of *quid pro quo*. The fortunate writers in an age before a living could be made by writing books for sale were those who managed to exchange their writing for some reward as substantial as Spenser's land grant and official position in Ireland, Donne's long-resisted appointment as Dean of St. Paul's, Jonson's as writer of the annual masque for the court, or Dryden's poet laureatship. The *quid* which rewarded the *quo* was not always so concrete, and courtiers such as Sidney, Lovelace, and Suckling found acceptable rewards for their poetry in reputations for cultured accomplishment and the consequent royal notice and favor. With a few obvious exceptions, notably Puritans like Bunyan and the later Milton (not the young writer of *Comus*), writers and writing from about 1300 to the early 1700s and beyond were closely tied to the court by the patronage system, although our romantic assumptions about poetic genius and self-expression regularly lead us to ignore the almost universal fact of patronage poetry during this time. Macaulay's brilliant description of patronage in the late seventeenth and early eighteenth centuries gives an excellent picture of how extensive patronage still was just before the time of Johnson's arrival in London to take up a life of writing. Never, Macaulay says, was there

> a time at which the rewards of literary merit were so splendid—at which men who could write well found such easy admittance into the most distinguished society and to the highest honours of the state. The chiefs of both the great parties into which the kingdom was divided patronized literature with emulous munificence.

Congreve, when he had scarcely attained his majority, was rewarded for his first comedy with places which made him independent for life. Smith, though his Hippolytus and Phoedra failed, would have been consoled with £300 a year, but for his own folly. Rowe was not only poet-laureate, but land-surveyor of the customs in the port of London, clerk of the council to the Prince of Wales, and secretary of the Presentations to the Lord Chancellor. Hughes was secretary to the Commissions of the Peace. Ambrose Phillips was judge of the Prerogative Court in Ireland. Locke was Commissioner of Appeals and of the Board of Trade. Newton was master of the Mint. Stepney and Prior were employed in embassies of high dignity and importance. Gay, who commenced life as apprentice to a silk-mercer, became a secretary of legation at five-and-twenty. It was to a poem on the death of Charles II, and to the City and Country Mouse, that Montague owed his introduction into public life, his earldom, his garter, and his auditorship of the Exchequer. Swift, but for the unconquerable prejudice of the queen, would have been a bishop. Oxford, with his white staff in his hand, passed through the crowd of his suitors to welcome Parnell, when that ingenious writer deserted the Whigs. Steele was a commissioner of stamps and a member of Parliament. Arthur Mainwaring was a commissioner of the customs and auditor of the imprest. Tickell was secretary to the Lords Justices of Ireland. Addison was secretary of state.

By 1760 when George III came to the throne, literary patronage was becoming increasingly antiquated, but with the aid of his mentor Lord Bute, the young king, says Collins, "gathered into his hands the reins of patronage in order to further his intention 'to be a king.' " Gibbon, Robertson, Hume, Home, the author of *Douglas*, and, somewhat surprisingly, J.-J. Rousseau were among the literary beneficiaries of a general patronage of the arts that founded the Royal Academy as well as supported numerous painters, musicians, scientists and, interestingly, instrument and clock makers. John Hill, the author of *Vegetable System*, got the appointment of royal gardener at Kensington for what seems the very large sum of £2,000 a year. Johnson himself was by no means free of the patronage system. He had, it is true, declared his independence of patronage in ringing terms in his famous letter to Lord Chesterfield in 1755. But he had been in possession of a pension from the crown of £300 a year since 1763. The pension was arranged by his friends but given by Lord Bute with assurance that it was for literary services to the nation already performed and would require no political writing in the future. It clearly did, however, and Johnson wrote several political pamphlets supporting government policies which ran contrary, at least to some degree, to earlier views of his that were openly professed and generally well known. "Inconsistencies," as Imlac says in *Rasselas*, "cannot both be right, but, imputed to man, they may both be true"; but what this particular inconsistency may have cost Johnson personally can be guessed from the force with which he expressed his view of patronage in his "Life of Dryden." This poet, he begins,

> had all the forms of excellence, intellectual and moral, combined in his mind, with endless variation; and when he had scattered on the hero of the day the golden shower of wit and virtue, he had ready for him, whom he wished to court on the morrow, new wit and virtue with another stamp. Of this kind of meanness he never seems to decline the practice, or lament the necessity: he considers the great as entitled to encomiastick homage, and brings praise rather as a tribute than a gift, more delighted with the fertility of his invention than mortified by the prostitution of his judgement. It is indeed not certain, that on these occasions his judgement much rebelled against his interest. There are minds which easily sink into submission, that look on grandeur with undistinguishing reverence, and discover no defect where there is elevation of rank and affluence of riches.

The most powerful actuality behind the king's command to write may well have been the established existence of a long po-

etic tradition acknowledging service to church and state. Dante
set for the Renaissance the archetypal role of the heroic poet
who, guided by the pagan classics (Virgil) and Christian love
and beauty (Beatrice), moved through and described in his poetry the highest realms of truth. The great line of heroic poets
who followed him—Petrarch, Ariosto, Tasso, Ronsard, Du Bel-
lay, Spenser and, in a different way, Milton, to mention only
the greatest—thought no less of their poetic powers, but all
conceived of their poetry as in various ways an art of service. If
Dante's poetic vision lifted him above earthly limits, what he
saw and taught as a poet were the established iconography and
ethics of his church: hell, purgatory, and heaven, all achieved
and suffered in doctrinally orthodox ways. Petrarch presented
himself in his coronation with laurels on the Capitoline Hill on
Easter Sunday, 1341, as a Christ figure redeeming with his poetry a fallen world; but he designed the ritual so that the civic
authorities of Rome crowned him, and afterward he crossed
the Tiber and laid his laurels on the altar of St. Peter's, the central shrine of the church he served and was supported by all his
life. Ariosto's *Orlando Furioso* exalted, though not without
chafe, the greatness of his patrons, the Este dukes and cardi-
nals of Ferarra, while Ronsard was the court poet of the monarchs of France and celebrated them in his *Franciade*. Spenser's
epic, *The Faerie Queene*, praised the great Queen of England as
the summit of all English history and all Reformation moral
virtue; and Milton, politically and philosophically the most radical of these heroic poets, after long service and an official position in the commonwealth government, still saw his poetic
task in *Paradise Lost* as the social work of explaining God's ways
to man and revealing beneath the confusion and distortion of
his historical moment the enduring order of human life in
mainly familiar terms of the biblical story and its traditional
elaborations.

These were the high moments of the old letters, the points at

which poetry's largest claims were made and its greatest services rendered to church and state. Ordinarily it had functioned
in less heroic but no less serviceable ways. Castiglione provided
in his *Courtier* (1528) a more modest and attainable model for
generations of amateur gentlemen-poets for whom writing was
only one social accomplishment, comparable and ancillary to
other courtly skills such as dancing, horsemanship, dress, manners, and speaking well. Poetry could be used by Castiglione's
aristocratic amateur to implement specific courtly interests,
praising a lady or tactfully advising a prince, but whatever the
subject, his poetry always served the courtly ethos by enacting
verbally the grace, skill, learning, wit, and good manners that
were the ethical ideals of courtly life in all spheres. This stylistic
identification with the court and its values was even more explicit in the poetic role itself. Whether the poet was of noble
family with something of an assured position in the courtly
world—Wyatt, Sidney, Lovelace, or Rochester, to give some
idea of the range of personal attitudes and variety of styles the
courtly tradition could contain—or a young man of less assured fortune and connections—Ben Jonson, say, or Jonathan
Swift—trying to make his way into the polite world and grasp
its political and economic rewards, he had to be or appear to be
a courtier and gentleman. "There were," says J. W. Saunders in
The Profession of English Letters, "very few writers who could not
have been said to be, in a very real sense, courtiers first and
writers second . . . half the writers of the age [1520–1659]
earned their living wholly at Court, . . . most of the others were
dependent for a major part of their income, in various ways,
upon courtly patronage, and . . . nearly all the great important
writers were either courtiers in their own right or satellites utterly dependent upon the courtly system." Maintaining the
necessary appearance of the gentleman-writer for whom poetry was only one of many courtly accomplishments was difficult for writers of limited means and high ability, like Donne,

necessity of appearing to be a
gentleman regardless of background

for example, and it was even more of a problem, while remaining apparently almost equally necessary, for the new professional writers who began to appear in England in the late sixteenth century, men like Nashe, Spenser, Marlowe, Shakespeare, and Jonson, who really earned their living by writing but tried in various ways, such as buying a coat of arms, to cultivate the appearance of gentility. Pope and Gray were still at the same game a century or more later, and even some of Johnson's Grub Street contemporaries who wrote for the printer, like Savage and Goldsmith, still tried to pretend in straitened circumstances that they were gentlemen who wrote poetry on occasion for amusement and circulation among friends.

This long-continued role of the poet as gentleman was reinforced in depth by a poetics that linked poetry *au fond* to the dominant social order of the courtly world. Classical or neoclassical aesthetic values, which during the Renaissance became increasingly fashionable and eventually replaced the old native or gothic traditions of folk art, were artistic transformations of the hierarchical principles central to the *ancien régime*. The idealization of classical texts, the obedience to the authority of the ancients, the maintenance of decorum, the emphasis on formal structures such as the unities, the elaboration of intricate style, imitation of traditional themes and traditional genres, and the teaching of official morality: these and other poetic expressions of literary piety, order, restraint, rules, tradition, and subordination tied poetry, and writing in general, as firmly to court values in the aesthetic realm as patronage linked it economically and censorship legally to the strong centralized monarchies.

Johnson Refuses to Write at the King's Command

The mismatch between this courtly tradition and Samuel Johnson must have been startlingly apparent in the King's Library in Johnson's failure as a person—huge, grotesque, scarred, with a ridiculous little wig, shabby clothes, compulsive tics and starts, a professional writer who made his living by selling his skills—to fill either of the poetic roles of gentleman-amateur or prophet and seer of monarchy. He was the first major writer to boast that he wrote for pay and to satisfy a wide reading public. His writings were largely of a practical informational nature—magazine articles, a series of general essays, an edition of the national poet, a dictionary, a set of biographies of poetic lives—designed to sell in the marketplace. As a critic, he was in the process of demolishing such antiquities as the rules and the unities in the name of a new common-sensical practical poetics. As a writer with a stake in the sales of his books, he was against censorship and any other official restraint on trade, and as the antagonist of Lord Chesterfield, he was the avowed enemy of patronage.

The literary old order was, however, still in place, though somewhat past its time, in the King's Library, symbolically represented in its architecture and the great collection, enacted ritually in a king's command to one of his subjects on when and what to write. But in the social history of letters, this scene between Johnson and King George in the library divides the old regime of courtly letters in the service of the established hierarchical order from a new kind of letters centered not on a king and his court but on print and the writer. The old order did not, of course, end precisely at this moment, no more than a new literary order entirely began here, and neither King George nor Johnson was aware that anything unusual was taking place. History, as has often been remarked, makes no right-angle turns. But Boswell's dramatic scene is like a painting encountered in a historically arranged art gallery that suddenly reveals that a crucial point has *somewhere* been passed. The formal subject may remain the same, the Annunciation, the Crucifixion, a royal portrait; but perspective, the elaboration of realistic detail, the increased importance of landscape, an emphasis on painterly techniques, perhaps the inclusion of an image of the artist, all accumulate to show that art has shifted its focus from service to church and state to a concern with itself, the artists who make it, and the fullness of the world.

A comparable assemblage of scenes where poets encounter the state and its rulers, both in fact and more obliquely in art, might begin with Petrarch on the Capitoline Hill, and move on to Castiglione's lords and ladies gathered by the duchess in the court of Urbino to talk of love and poetry. It would inevitably include the complex involvement of the poet in Shakespeare's *Sonnets* with an aristocratic patron, and the performance of a company of public players in the royal palace of Elsinore before a guilty king and his inattentive court. Milton's violent attacks on royalty in *The Tenure of Kings and Magistrates* and on the royal martyr himself in *Eikonoclastes* shortly after his death in 1649 would open up the growing antagonisms of poets and princes, which in subsequent years would be again somewhat concealed in, for example, the irony of a laureate's treatment of the succession question in *Absalom and Achitophel* and Pope's mocking instruction in "To Augustus" of a German king who disdained "boetry and bainting" in the uses of verse: "What better teach a Foreigner the tongue?" But Pope still did not see monarchy and poetry as institutions at inevitable odds, and so the insults are still slightly muted: "I mount on the Maeonian wing, Your Arms, your Actions, your repose to sing!" But after Johnson's meeting with George III in the library, the encounters of poets and kings become more openly antagonistic. Shelley in "England in 1819" openly derides the same monarch who had spoken to Johnson in his library as an "old, mad, blind, despised and dying king," and after that king's death, Byron, who died supporting a people's revolution in Greece, could in *The Vision of Judgment* (1822) parody the laureate Southey's sentimental description of the royal arrival in heaven and deification in terms so savage that the publisher was convicted and fined for caluminating majesty. Even the more cooly restrained Jane Austen, though she did accept in 1815 the invitation of the prince regent to dedicate *Emma* to him—she had been told that he had, rather surprisingly, "read and admired all your publications"—still could not resist burlesqueing the request of his surrogate, the royal librarian who handled the dedicatory transaction with her, James Stanier Clarke (surely one of the most fatuous and odious librarians of all time), that she include in her next novel an ideal English clergyman "of the present day," strong against tythes, interested in literature, and "the Friend of some distinguished Naval Character about a Court." (Letter of 21 December 1815.) Her burlesque, "Plan of a Novel, according to hints from various quarters," was, significantly, never printed, only circulated to amuse friends and family with descriptions of a dying clergyman in far "Kamschatka" expiring "in a fine burst of Literary Enthusiasm, intermingled with invectives again[st] Holders' of Tythes." But it still makes clear, in its clever way, the amusement of a professional writer for a bumbling amateur, even though he officially represents a prince. But during the nineteenth and twentieth centuries, defiance of all established authority, not of kings alone, became a *scène obligatoire* in the lives of artists. Ruskin remarked of Turner and the other painters of his time that "they can draw the poor, not the rich," and the poets, whether their politics were of the left or the right, have consistently enacted an equally strong prejudice by contriving scenes in which to defy the powers that rule modern society: Thoreau in jail asking Emerson why *he* is not, Baudelaire on the Paris barricades in 1848, Dostoevsky before the firing squad in Petersburg, Oscar Wilde in Reading Gaol, Pound broadcasting propaganda for Mussolini's Italy, Norman Mailer on the steps of the Pentagon, Lowell in the asylum, and on and on.

Staunch loyalists both, Johnson and Boswell were not conscious that a transfer of literary power from king to author was being symbolically enacted in the library. The scene "gratified [Johnson's] monarchical enthusiasm," Boswell believed, and to the king's final request for "the literary biography of this country . . . Johnson signified his readiness to comply with his Majesty's wishes." But Boswell depicts the entire scene from the perspective of Johnson, not the king, and he leaves no doubt about who, in the end, controlled it: "During the whole of this interview, Johnson talked to his Majesty with profound respect, but still in his firm manly manner, with a sonorous voice, and never in that subdued tone which is commonly used at the levee and in the drawing-room. After the King withdrew, Johnson shewed himself highly pleased with his Majesty's conversation and gracious behaviour." This shift of the center of the scene from the king to the writer appears in details of the scene as well. In the beginning, according to Boswell, it is the king who comes to Johnson, not the other way round, and during the conversation the king respectfully asks questions of Johnson about literary matters, rather than expressing royal wishes. And, most notably, the traditional power of kings to command writers to write is here rejected by the writer. Authorial independence is openly stated, politely but firmly, in the opening of the scene when Johnson responds to the king's urgings to write by saying that he thought he had already done his part as a writer. It is muted but still nonetheless there at the end of the scene if we remember that Johnson complied with his Majesty's wishes that he write "the literary biography of this country," only some ten years later, and then at the solicitation of a group of booksellers and printers who wanted short prefaces to the collected works of a group of poets in whom they were trying, futilely, to preserve copyright. Once started on the project, Johnson, out of his personal interests in literary biography and criticism, and out of a need to fill his declining days with some worthy and congenial work, extended it far beyond what had originally been requested, and finally made a free-standing work of *The Lives of the Poets* not by the command of king or bookseller but out of the interests of a writer in other writers.

The confrontation of king and writer in this scene had a technological base in the divergent literary values of oral and print cultures. The king's views on such literary questions as patronage, censorship, poetics, and the relation of the writer to the crown were those appropriate to the hierarchical and monarchical views of an essentially oral culture. Johnson's views on these and related questions were, however modified in practice they may have been, those appropriate to print circumstances and suitable for a professional writer working in the marketplace. The incompatibility, even antagonism, of these literary values was in some degree suppressed in the physical setting of the King's Library itself, where the King appears perfectly at home with printed books, and in the amiable meeting there between the genial king and the royalist, not Hanoverian, but Jacobite, author. But the barely concealed refusal to write at the king's gracious command reveals a deep and persistent antagonism between kings and print whose history is recapitulated in the fate of the King's Library.

Standing in their special bindings, gold titles on the spines, stamped with the royal arms, rank on glowing red rank along the shelves, upright as the king's soldiers, the books in this fine collection and their noble setting were symbols in the cult of courtly art centering on the king. But the relationship between absolute monarchs and printed books had never been easy, as the long, troubled history of censorship and efforts by the crown to control printers and limit the number of presses testifies. This antagonism between democratic print and absolute monarchs was open at the beginning of the age of print, and in Florence, E. B. Fryde tells us, "Authors in search of Medici patronage presented splendidly illuminated copies of their

works. But printed books were not welcome. Like his contemporary, Duke Federigo of Urbino, who did not possess a single
printed book in his library, Lorenzo had no use whatsoever for
this new technique." In an attempt to mask print and preserve
the mystique of the manuscript, type faces continued to imitate
scribal hands for many years, and even the great Venetian
printer and typographer, Aldus Manutius, boasted in the preface to one of his books that his letters were "as good, if not better, than any written with a pen." Aristocratic contempt for the
printed book gradually and inevitably gave way to attempts to
use and control it, but there was always a barely suppressed
conflict between a hierarchical society comfortable with oral situations and a technology that made numerous identical copies
of the same book, put them and their ideas, relatively cheaply,
in the hands of anyone who could read, and sought free markets in which to sell its products.

The old aristocratic antipathy for print lingered on longest,
and most openly, it is interesting to note, in poetry. Sir Philip
Sidney, who printed none of his own writings, speaks scorn-
fully in his *Apology* of "base men with servile wits . . . who think
it inough if they can be rewarded of the Printer," and he later
laughs at the writer whose "name shall florish in the Printers
Shoppe." It is difficult to discern any invariant pattern in the
social history of the publication of poetry in sixteenth- and seventeenth-century England, but it is reasonably correct to say
that the professional poets like Spenser, Chapman, Daniel,
Drayton, and, most scandalously, Ben Jonson, tended to print
and publish their own poetry, including dramatic poetry.
Shakespeare is a fascinating and complex mix: he printed the
long poems, but probably not the *Sonnets*, and about half of the
plays, but these, perhaps, unwillingly. And he died leaving no
provision for the publication of the remainder. Among those
who printed, a certain religious emphasis is noticeable—Cra-
shaw, Vaughan, Milton—but on the other hand, there were

some religious poets like Herbert and Traherne who did not publish. The latter was not printed until this century. A number of writers who were scrambling in the political world—Carew, Cowley, Samuel Butler, Waller, and Dryden, for example—did publish, but others like Marvell and Donne, who printed only four poems in his lifetime, were content to circulate their poems in manuscript. Donne was greatly distressed at the possibility of having to print some of his work in order to raise money a few years before his death. On the whole, those who did not print their own works but circulated them in manuscript were usually courtiers or writers making some pretenses to gentility. The list of these writers who did not print is instructively long, containing such names as Wyatt, Surrey, Sidney, Raleigh, Donne, Herbert, Suckling, and Lovelace. It is impossible to predict on social grounds exactly who would and who would not print in the late sixteenth and seventeenth centuries, but it is nonetheless clear that there was still during this time a fashionable and long-continuing, though not universally observed, antipathy to a medium that perverted the primary courtly literary values of privacy and rarity.

This aristocratic attitude toward what J. W. Saunders has described as "The Stigma of Print" remained widespread until well into the eighteenth century, and Samuel Johnson could observe that "Swift put his name to but two things, (after he had a name to put,) 'The Plan for the Improvement of the English Language,' and the last 'Drapier's Letter.'" The example of Swift is instructive, for he needed to and did print his works, like many another gentleman-writer, but by keeping his name off the title page, until the collected edition began to be printed in 1735, he continued to maintain at least during his early career the outward appearance of the gentleman-amateur which Sidney exemplified. So long as the court or the great house remained the social setting of poetry, print with its democratic associations of mechanic trade, money, and a vulgar public audience could never be accepted as the true medium of letters. In these circumstances it remained possible still to feel as vehemently about the printed book as did the French priest and theoretician of language Bernard Lamy: "The words on a page are like a dead body stretched out on the ground. In the mouth of the one who advances them, they are effective; on paper they are lifeless, incapable of producing the same effects." Not until the mid-eighteenth century could a professional writer openly laugh at the amateur poet circulating his writings in manuscript, as Johnson did when he remarked that "the highest praise" some bad poems "deserved was, that they were very well for a gentleman to hand about among his friends." Feelings about print and poetry died hard, and a poor young romantic poet like Keats could still feel that it was fashionable to be threatened by print: "I never expect to get anything by my Books: and moreover I wish to avoid publishing—I admire Human Nature but I do not like *Men*. I should like to compose things honourable to Man—but not fingerable over by *Men*."

Conservative courtly attitudes toward print may now seem only quaintly snobbish, but there was in them a real recognition that print was a democratic medium at odds in important ways with a courtly society and its system of polite letters. Avoidance of print publication was the gentlemanly poet's way of dealing with the problem, but the King's Library represented the more realistic and active political efforts by the old regime to control print through such devices as censorship, taxation, limiting the number of presses, and using patronage to ensure conformity. In France, as Robert Darnton has shown in *The Literary Underground of the Old Regime*, the bureaucracy was better organized than in England and efforts to control print more extensive and repressive; but while the results were somewhat different, in both countries books in the long run were, in ways the history of the King's Library shows, no more under a king's control than were Samuel Johnson and his many successors who

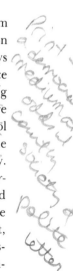

insisted that they wrote not for kings but only at the urgings of their own genius.

The fate of George's Library

When George IV "came to the throne," says Esdaile, "he employed Nash to remodel Buckingham Palace, and probably found the books in the way." The new king first tried to sell the library, and according to one story circulating at the time, offered it, appropriately, to the last of the great autocrats, the Czar of Russia. The sale was said to have been blocked by public indignation, and the king, saying that he was "by this means advancing the literature of my country," made the best he could of the situation by giving the collection to the national library of the British Museum, where, intact and still impressive, it can still be seen in a long gallery specially built for it to the right of the main entrance. Many other royal libraries and art collections, such as the Uffizi, the Louvre, and French royal library, and the Prado, underwent a similar change of setting and thereby of meaning, becoming national collections, open, at least ultimately, to all, where art and letters became the property of the nation, a manifestation of the national genius, and, in time, by expansion, a collection of the literary achievements of all mankind. The new national libraries at the British Museum and elsewhere became instances of and symbols of literature, the system of letters that print and capitalism created, even as the King's Library or, the Biblioteca Mediceo-Laurenziana, designed by Michelangelo and attached to the Medicis' church in Florence, represented the older courtly letters.

The "Caldwell Minute"

There is another description of the meeting between Johnson and King George that gives a very different interpretation of the scene than Boswell does. The "Caldwell Minute," which was probably dictated by Johnson to a copyist shortly after the event, describes some parts of the scene, such as the entrance of the monarch into the library, in a much more casual way. "The King came in and after having ~~walked by Mr. Johns~~ talked for some time to other persons in the Library, turned to Dr. Johnson and asked him if he were not lately come from Oxford." The conversation including the first of the urgings and refusals to write, is substantially the same in the Minute and in Boswell, who, in fact, used a copy of the Minute to construct his account, but changed the beginning to make the king come specifically and directly to see Johnson, centered the scene on Johnson, and added at the end the king's request that Johnson undertake "the literary biography of this country" to anticipate the writing of *The Lives of the Poets*. And instead of Boswell's magnificent conclusion in which the king withdraws leaving the great cham in serene possession of the library and of English letters, the Minute tells us that "~~the Princess Dowager came in and put an~~ a visit from the Princess Dowager put an end to the Conversation."

The passages with a line through them indicate early editing of the Minute, perhaps at Johnson's direction as he was dictating, in an effort, says Taylor, to save his "dignity by removing the possible implications that the King *deliberately* walked by him or that that Princess Dowager *deliberately* put an end to the conversation." Boswell saves even more of Johnson's dignity. He doesn't really change very much, dropping a deflating detail here and adding a proleptic reference to *The Lives of the Poets* there, pointing up the scene by showing it from the Johnsonian perspective and making it more dramatic by providing a more effective beginning and ending. The changes were slight, but in the end what was according to the Minute a fairly ordinary morning in the royal household became one of the great symbolic scenes of literary history in which control of writing passed from kings to writers.

That the epic dimensions of the scene are largely the invention and the art of James Boswell does not, I think, diminish its importance in the history of letters or qualify the truth of its portrayal of the writer, rather than the king, as the central figure in literary culture. The "Caldwell Minute" does, however, dramatize the complex and intricate manner by which the energies of print technology, and the values it assumed in the social world, were transmitted through people, and transformed by them, into the social facts, the received beliefs, of culture. That Johnson was the spokesman in his meeting with the king for print values, and that these same values both led and allowed him as a professional writer to resist the king's command to write, seems clear enough. But it was Boswell in his biography of Johnson who realized the full meaning of what took place in the library, and constructed an icon of sufficient power to establish as fact the growing reality of the dominance of the individual writer in the world of letters. It was not, I think, that Boswell as social historian perceived more clearly than Johnson, or the king, what was actually happening in the literary culture in the mid-eighteenth century. Considering his own adulation of kings and courts, he is most unlikely to have consciously understood the basic literary change of the time or his own portrayal of it. But, as the subsequent history of literature makes clear, he did get it right, whatever may have actually happened in the library, partly because of his overwhelming high opinion of Johnson, partly because of his skill in writing lively human scenes, and partly because of his own neurotic, obsessive involvement with writing and writers. Boswell's motives, here as elsewhere, are numerous and tangled, and probably ultimately undecipherable, but they are of continuing interest to us because it was and is his biography, more than any other document, that made Johnson the great author of the age of print and established as real and believable print-based changes in the literary system that were only partially or faintly evident in actual events. The *Life of Johnson* is not simply a description of what actually happened in the English literary scene in the middle years of the eighteenth century; it is, in ways that the "Caldwell Minute" exemplifies, a reworking of given facts in ways that do not so much falsify them as adjust them in a fashion that brings out their full meaning in the contemporary print revolution and for literary culture. Boswell's book is thus not simply a historical record of Samuel Johnson—though this is the way Boswell presents it—but is itself, complete with all its own complex background, a part, and an important, even crucial, part, of the numerous events through which a new print-based, author-centered literary system was constructed and made real enough to become an accepted part of culture. That we most often see Johnson and his literary scene through Boswell, and that his lens is to some degree distorting, might at first appear only an awkward inconvenience to be ignored, as it has regularly been in the past, as resolutely as possible. Instead, this complicated process of cultural change, involving both Johnson and Boswell, serves not only as an insight into the social world of letters in the eighteenth century, but as a remarkable paradigm—as does so much else connected with Johnson—of the way in which cultural changes of this magnitude come about and how much of human existence they ultimately involve.

CHAPTER II

PRINTING, BOOKSELLING, READERS, AND WRITERS IN EIGHTEENTH-CENTURY LONDON

Print Logic

We do not as yet have a detailed history of print in eighteenth-century England, but there are a great many specialized studies of different aspects of the printing and publishing trades, and in a survey of this material, Terry Belanger concludes that all the evidence points toward a transformation during the century from an oral-scribal society to a print society: "England in the 1790s was a well-developed print society; in the 1690s, especially once we leave London, we find relatively little evidence of one." The point requires some emphasis, for the standard historical view has assumed that England became and remained a print society after about 1500. There is, of course, no question that the national life was deeply affected in the 200 years between 1500 and 1700 by printed books, such as, by way of obvious example, vernacular bibles or the propaganda pamphlets of the civil war, but the weight of evidence increasingly suggests that it was not until about 1700 that printing began to affect the structure of social life at every level. Belanger lists many print products that became common for the first time in the eighteenth century, and in their very ordinariness they suggest how extensively print during this period expanded into and affected social and institutional life: posters, theater bills, newspapers and magazines, handbills, bill-headings, labels, tickets, "printed forms meant to be completed by hand . . . marriage certificates, printed indentures or receipts." In time, simple usefulness acquired an aura of authority as, for example, permanent records began to be printed, accurate information conveyed in newspapers, and the society's privileged texts—legal, sacred, instructional—stabilized and stored in print. Gradually this kind of authority grew into the authenticity that is probably the absolute mark of print culture, a generally accepted view that what is printed is true, or at least truer than any other type of record.

In this general transformation to a print culture, letters and the entire world of writing, which were directly and continuously involved with printing, inevitably underwent radical, even revolutionary, changes. To mention only some of the most familiar print-related changes in letters at this time, the novel became the major literary form, and prose challenged poetry as the most prestigious medium; the author's copyright was legalized and censorship was nearly abolished; enormous numbers of literary works, both new and old, were printed and made available to readers; large public and private libraries became common; criticism became a standard literary genre; patronage nearly disappeared as authors began to be able to live by selling their writing; literacy increased and a new public audience of readers appeared; literary histories were written for the first time. Changes of this magnitude were cumulatively as revolutionary in the world of letters as the events of 1688 and 1789, with which they were socially co-ordinate, were in the political world, and like the related political changes, the literary changes were not random but followed a particular logic.

The "logic" of a technology, an idea, or an institution is its tendency consistently to shape whatever it affects in a limited number of definite forms or directions. Peter Berger, in *The Sacred Canopy*, describes, for example, the logic of tools such as the plow, and of language, and the way that their logics press on and impress both social activity and human consciousness:

Once produced, the tool has a being of its own that cannot be readily changed by those who employ it. Indeed, the tool (say, an agricultural implement) may even enforce the logic of its being upon its users, sometimes in a way that may not be particularly agreeable to them. For instance, a plow, though obviously a human product, is an external object not only in the sense that its users may fall over it and hurt themselves as a result, just as they may by falling over a rock or a stump or any other natural object. More interestingly, the plow may compel its users to arrange their agricultural activity, and perhaps also other aspects of their lives, in a way that conforms to *its* own logic and that may have been neither intended nor foreseen by those who originally devised it. The same objectivity, however, characterizes the non-material elements of culture as well. Man invents a language and then finds that both his speaking and his thinking are dominated by its grammar. Man produces values and discovers that he feels guilt when he contravenes them. Man concocts institutions, which come to confront him as powerfully controlling and even menacing constellations of the external world.

Marshall McLuhan in *The Gutenberg Galaxy* traces the logic of print to the basic fact of the technology itself, "the mechanical spirit of movable types in precise lines." In a print culture, he argues, where what is printed is intensely true and the printed text is ultimately composed of the pieces of type in the printer's cases, texts and truth are therefore structured by the principal characteristics of type, which he lists as abstraction, uniformity, repeatability, visuality, and quantification. The printed book, with its potential infinity of abstract words, its standardized spellings, punctuation, and grammatical rules, its regular lines, numbered pages, and orderly format is the visible world of print logic or of the "spirit of movable types." Through the book, by the process McLuhan calls "the interiorization of technology," type extends its reality into the consciousness of readers: "Gutenberg typography filled the world the human voice

closed down. People began to read silently and passively as con-
sumers." And as they did so, print logic began to shape mental
structures, imparting a sense of the world as a set of abstract
ideas rather than immediate facts, a fixed point of view organizing all subject matter into an equivalent of perspective in
painting, and the visual homogenization of experience. It also
encouraged individualism, even solipsism, by the silent privacy
in which the printed book is read: "The unconscious is a direct
creation of print technology, the ever-mounting slag-heap of
rejected awareness." And inevitably, McLuhan relentlessly
goes on, as print logic changed mental structures, the social
world was also changed by the increasing numbers of people
whose minds were programmed by print logic. Rationalism,
idealistic philosophy, consumerism, individualism, capitalism,
and nationalism—"by print a people *sees* itself for the first
time"—are all, in McLuhan's view, the inevitable consequences
of movable type, the workings out in psychological and social
life of print logic.

"It is quite easy," McLuhan states flatly, "to test the universal
effects of print on Western thought after the sixteenth century,
simply by examining the most extraordinary developments in
any art or science whatever." In his applications of this hypothesis to modern western consciousness and society, McLuhan
also applies it to letters and argues that some of the principal
features of romantic and modern literature are closely related
to the type which has been its primary medium for the last two
hundred years or so. Print, he shows, for example, fixed the literary text, by giving it an objective and unchanging reality in
its own right. In earlier oral cultures there could be no such
thing as an exact text, since the particular form something took
at any given moment always depended, as Parry and Lord in
their studies of oral poetry have demonstrated, on performance. Even in a manuscript culture a work was seldom or never
reproduced *exactly* the same way twice running, and so re-

mained always a process, never becoming a completed, static object. But in a print culture, type makes it possible for the work to exist as a fixed object, infinitely and accurately reproducible, controlling, even "being" as it were, its own form independent of perception or accidents. Print thus makes poems into literary works of art and encourages thereby "a new hypnotic superstition of the book as independent of and uncontaminated by human agency." Printed books like the Bible, *Paradise Lost*, or Johnson's *Dictionary* have acquired enormous validity and transcendental authority in their own right. Even as print made the works of literature, so it also, McLuhan argues, made authors. In the words of E.P. Goldschmidt, "the Middle Ages for various reasons and from various causes did not possess the concept of 'authorship' in exactly the same significance as we have it now," but the factual, solid external existence of the printed book in numerous copies "told" the writer he was an author, identified him as such on the title page, and offered him permanent existence in eternal fame.

Many of the formal properties considered central to romantic and modern literature are also, according to McLuhan, aesthetic expressions of print logic. The crucial literary concepts of a central plot and a single structure are extensions of the movement of type in precise lines, which generates "the notion of moving steadily along on single planes of narrative awareness . . . totally alien to the nature of language and consciousness." Even those ideal fictional worlds created by the imagination that are the fundamental assumption of romantic literature derive from "the power of print to install the reader in a subjective universe of limitless freedom and spontaneity." McLuhan's point is not that these leading ideas of romantic and modern literature, such as ideal text, author, and imagination, were unheard of in preprint cultures, but rather that when print became the dominant literary medium, it intensified these and other print-related values, while diminishing those manuscript qualities, such as rarity, with which it was not co-ordinate.

In her summary book, *The Printing Press as an Agent of Change*, Elizabeth Eisenstein has, in effect, tested McLuhan's brilliant insights—for they are little more or less than that—by looking at the historical effects of print on European culture of the Renaissance and Reformation. As a historian, Eisenstein is less concerned with nonobjective states of mind than Mc-Luhan, and much more concerned with such solid details as, for example, print runs, costs and prices, the proportion of new books printed to old books reprinted, the accumulation of books on various subjects, and the growth of libraries. Her historical work tends to bear McLuhan out, however, and Eisenstein's leading "features of print culture" are very close to some of his basic principles of movable type. Eisenstein's subheadings in her second chapter provide a good scheme of her findings about the primary social effects of print logic: dissemination, standardization, reorganization, data collection, preservation, and amplification and reinforcement. Very briefly, these leading characteristics of print manifested themselves socially as: (1) the spread of knowledge as a result of the large number of printed books; (2) standardized printed texts which replaced the indeterminacy of oral performance and manuscript drift, and continued to replace imperfect printed copies with more accurate editions; (3) a rational organization of knowledge fostered by the inherent *esprit de système* of work in the printing house and its product, the printed book: "regularly numbered pages, punctuation marks, section breaks, running heads, indices"; and (4) "typographical fixity," the ability of printed books to give to the words and ideas they print a substantial and durable form, and to amplify this objectified verbal reality by the distribution of numerous identical copies of the same organization of words on the page.

In a print culture, McLuhan and Eisenstein, as well as other

historians of print and writing, particularly Walter Ong and
Eric Havelock, have shown us that everything that is affected
by print—and almost everything eventually is—will reveal in
some way and to some degree, depending on always complex
circumstances, its leading characteristics, the impress of its
logic. The basic elements of print logic as they have been variously defined interconnect and overlap, but writings on the
subject like those of McLuhan and Eisenstein regularly emphasize three leading characteristics that for convenience can in
our present discussion be called multiplicity, systematization,
and fixity. The way in which these print qualities manifest
themselves in the world can be illustrated most immediately
and obviously with print's most characteristic product, the
book: multiplicity—the printing press makes many different
books and many copies of the same book; systematization—a
book is systematically produced and internally ordered, and its
existence forces the systematic structuring of knowledge; fixity—the book is objectively, durably, there, always the same or
moving toward a "true" form.

These primary tendencies of print logic—multiplicity, systematization, and fixity—can provide a focus for the broad effects of print on letters in eighteenth-century England as we
look in the remainder of this chapter at the interlinking chain
that extended from the print shop, to the publishers—or booksellers, as they were then known—to the marketplace and the
Grub Street writers. To concentrate on the "logic" of the historical process is, of course, to simplify for the sake of clarity,
and something of the actual complexity of what happened is
suggested by the fact that although multiplicity and systematization are both openly and immediately at work in the Grub
Street world of writing, the full effects of fixity appear only
over a longer period of time and in more indirect ways. In fact,
one of print's first effects on its products, whether books or authors, was, because of its tendency toward large numbers, to

make them into common and therefore ephemeral commodities or even consumables. It was only cumulatively and gradually that the effects of fixity appeared. That is to say, there is at least some tension, if not downright contradiction, between two of the primary energies of print logic, multiplicity and fixity—what we might call the "remainder-house" and the "library" effects—which, as we shall see in the final chapter, has never entirely been resolved.

The Printing Business

The old-style hand-press print shop, and the ways a bookseller-publisher conducted his business, are too well known to require detailed recounting, but a quick description of the print shop of William Strahan, Johnson's chief printer, and the bookselling business of his major publisher, Robert Dodsley, will reveal something of the complex and multifold ways print logic expressed itself in life, work, thought, and society.

At the center of the print shop of William Strahan, a young Scot who came to London to earn his fortune after learning the printing trade in Edinburgh, stood several of the old wooden hand-pulled presses, costing 15 guineas each, which had changed little since Gutenberg's time. In the 1750s, Strahan's printing house was located at 10 Little New Street, off Shoe Lane, in premises for which he paid a rent of £200 a year. Basic working materials for his presses were paper, which cost 12 to 20 shillings a ream of crown sheets, sized 15 by 20 inches, or 12 by 16 inches; a supply of good quality printer's ink; a number of cases of type, which cost 7s, 6d. a pair; and an assortment of relatively inexpensive ordering and locking devices (systematization and fixity at the mechanical level) such as composing sticks, galley trays, chases, and quoins. Strahan's account books still exist, and his biographer, J. A. Cochrane, has used them to study carefully the economics of Strahan's printing business.

He estimates that in the 1750s a capital investment of a few hundred pounds would set up a basic print shop.

The organization of labor in Strahan's shop, as in printing houses for the preceding three centuries, was an extension of print's logic of systematization to human activity. Strahan, who ran a large and active shop, remained the master printer and supervised operations; however, he hired a manager, whom he paid 30 shillings a week, and increased his income further by allowing him several apprentices. The shop was worked by these few apprentices and a number of journeymen whose weekly wage could rise as high as 1 guinea, good pay for that time. These journeymen were specialized, but the main divisions of labor were few. The compositor who set the type was paid on a piece-work basis, 8 shillings for an octavo sheet of 16 pages, or sometimes, after 1744, 4 pence per thousand letters. The proofreader or corrector got 2 pence for every shilling paid the compositor. The two men who worked the press itself, one to ink and one to pull, were together paid 1s. 2d. for every 250 perfected sheets, that is, printed on both sides. Their average rate of work has been computed by Cochrane at four impressions per minute, or about 250 perfected sheets in two hours, and average pay for a long workweek was therefore, Cochrane says, 15 to 17 shillings. In a large shop such as Strahan's, there were also other less skilled workers who hung the printed sheets up for drying, and later, stacked, folded, and bundled them in proper order, before sending them to the bookseller or the binder, binding ordinarily being done outside the printing shop.

In 1759 Strahan employed over 50 men in his shop and therefore when he operated continuously had a payroll of £40 to £50 a week. In computing his charges to his customers, Strahan used the standard method of adding one half of his wage costs to the actual wages paid for a job to cover material, overhead, and profit. For example, if his wage costs for 1,000 sheets of octavo came to 14 shillings he would add 7 shillings and bill 21 shillings total. Paper was the most expensive item in the entire process, and it was usually supplied by the bookseller, author, or whoever ordered the printing; but if Strahan supplied the paper, he would add its cost to his charges.

Strahan eventually became rich enough to take a seat as an M.P. and keep a coach—which was unusual enough for a printer to be remarked on favorably by Johnson, who sometimes had the use of it—and he did so not only by organizing his shop efficiently and keeping an eye on the pennies, but by adapting successfully to other economic realities of his situation. He eventually ran the largest print shop in London, with nine presses, and his combined fixed costs were high enough to make it very expensive for him to let his machinery stand idle or operate at less than full capacity. He did not pay his workers when there was no work for them, since he paid by the piece, but there was a strong incentive for him to keep his workforce adequately employed, and his capital investment, rent, and the money tied up in work completed but not yet paid for exerted a constant pressure on him, and in turn on those, including writers, who worked for him, to provide a steady flow of work to and through the presses. A little story Johnson told Boswell illustrates well how closely and carefully Strahan calculated these matters. While working on his *Dictionary*, which was printed in sections by Strahan, Johnson neglected to return at once some proof pages which had been sent him for correction. Strahan's boy was at the door immediately, and Strahan later explained patiently but forcefully to Johnson that his type—which cost money and was always short in the printing house—was tied up and his entire operations disrupted, until such time as the corrected proof was returned, corrections made in the set type, and the presses at work again. In view of this exemplary story of print, there is more than a little irony in the recent discovery that a number of authorial

58PRINTING AND BOOKSELLING

changes marked on *Dictionary* proofs that still exist were not made in the type.

Perhaps the proofs came too late, or perhaps it seemed too expensive to make changes which seemed unnecessary and delaying to a printer who always sought in all ways he could find, large and small, a steady flow of work for his presses. He was the friend and helper, sometimes the banker, of a number of authors who wrote books he printed; he sought and got various government printing contracts; he functioned as a publisher and bought copyrights—which was where the big money was—of books he would then print; and he entered into "congers" (joint venture groups) such as the combination that shared the financial risk for Johnson's *Dictionary*. All this effort to provide work for his presses made sense only if there were a ready market for the printed products, and though sales and distribution were primarily the realm of bookseller and wholesaler, Strahan inevitably became involved in this end of business as well, dealing directly with authors and books that were likely to sell, and serving as an agent and wholesaler to booksellers, particularly in North America.

Logical organization (system) and continuous, high-volume production (multiplicity) are the most prominent characteristics of Strahan's printing operation. Even at this handicraft stage, printing, if done efficiently, was capable of producing large numbers of printed products, and profits could be increased greatly by taking full advantage of this production potential and finding ready markets for the printed products. More presses, more printed materials, and more customers equaled more profits, and since the number of books produced had such important effects for letters, it will be worthwhile to try to summarize what we know about the bibliographic flood produced by Strahan and other printers in eighteenth-century England.

It is clear from the entry in *The Journal of The House of Com-*

mons for 17 April 1695 that Parliament allowed the Licensing Act, the statute that legalized official censorship and limited the number of presses, to lapse in that year not because it infringed on the liberties of Englishmen but because it conferred a monopoly on the crown and a very limited number of booksellers to print, sell, import, and bind books and pamphlets. The main arguments for allowing the Act to lapse were commercial, not constitutional: the Act, it was argued, operated as a restraint on trade, as all forms of censorship do, by retarding the progress of imported books through customs, permitting only 20 printing houses in all England, and limiting the number of presses in each shop, usually to no more than two. After the lapse of the Licensing Act, the number of printers grew steadily, and by 1724 there were 75 printers in London, plus at least 28 more in the provinces. By 1785 there were 124 printers in London alone, and many more presses, since as many as nine were now concentrated in one shop. By 1713, two thirds of the paper used in printing, which earlier had mostly been imported, was being produced in England, and with the opening of Caslon's type foundry in 1720, well-designed, high-quality English type became increasingly available. Counts of the number of printers and booksellers are notoriously imprecise and usually disagree with one another, but in his survey of the London book trade, Ian Maxted offers figures as hard as we are likely to get. His tables show that in 1668 there were 198 men employed in all the printing trades, working 65 presses—considerably more than the 40 the law strictly allowed—while in 1818 there were approximately 625 active presses worked by 3,365 masters, journeymen, and apprentices, a huge increase (multiplicity) over the 150-year period. The number of bookseller-publishers doubled during a somewhat shorter period, going from 151 in 1735 to 308 in 1802, though the number dropped in intervening years, to 72 in 1763, before rising again to 111 by 1772.

We lack, and probably will continue to lack, precise information about the number of books the printers produced in the eighteenth century. A number of recent scholarly projects have, however, given us more accurate estimations than we once seemed likely to have. The compilers of the *Eighteenth-Century British Books Author Union Catalogue (AUC)* have found that the holdings of books printed in English in the eighteenth century, including translations into English and books in English printed abroad, in the collections of the British Library, the Bodleian, and the Cambridge University library approximate 250,000. This figure, which contains an unspecified number of duplications, the compilers estimate to be 65 per cent of the total of all eighteenth-century English books. This would give us about 337,000 individual eighteenth-century titles of books in English or, with some adjustment downward for duplicates, an average of, say, 3,000 titles annually.

But an annual average is, we have recently learned, a misleading figure. The work of assembling the *Eighteenth-Century Short-Title Catalogue (ESTC)* has been moving steadily toward completion in the British Library—though, ironically, it will never be recorded entirely in print but kept on computer to allow for easier change. (Print fixity has its disadvantages when facts begin to soften.) But even so extensive a project as this will never tell us either the exact number of titles printed or the number in each printing. As C. J. Mitchell puts it, "since there is no single catalogue of eighteenth-century works compiled from all existing library catalogues, and since even if such a union catalogue did exist it would lack the uncatalogued material, it follows that we know neither what nor how many works were printed during the eighteenth century." Here, as in so many other places in our time, the more we pursue exact objective knowledge, the faster it seems to recede; but the *ESTC* has, by using several samples, yielded important information about eighteenth-century books and printing. The most surprising discovery has been that across Europe and in England, in Mitchell's words again, "printing did not increase steadily during the century but almost everywhere suffered during the middle decades of the century a contraction so severe that the level of output achieved during the first third of the century was not regained, if at all, until near the end of the century." Our traditional assumption has been that growth was continuous, but Mitchell's figures, derived from the sample, of the number of titles printed in London alone show a drop from 8,836 in the decade ending 1710, to 7,605 in the decade ending 1750, but a rise to 16,243 by 1800. The total for London during the entire eighteenth century is estimated at 98,360, which rises for England as a whole, not Scotland or Ireland, only to 109,547.

The very large difference between the *ESTC* figures for the number of eighteenth-century English books and those of the *Author Union Catalogue*—approximately 1,100 compared to 3,000 annually—can partly be accounted for by the fact that the *AUC* counts *all* books printed in English, in England, Scotland, Ireland, and elsewhere, while the *ESTC* counts only those books printed in England. The discrepancy is too large to be explained entirely in this way, however, and it is clear that the two projects defined differently the printed items to be counted. The *ESTC* numbers are the most conservative, and since they are based on what we are most directly concerned with—the number of substantial monographs printed in England during the eighteenth century—these figures of an average of about 1,100 books annually printed in all England and 980 in London, will be used. But the *ESTC* figures show that an average figure is misleading since a sharp rise at the beginning of the century was followed by a deep slump and then a strong recovery. No obvious explanation presents itself for the steep decline in the book trade in the middle years of the century, as measured by the number of titles published, and by the earlier-mentioned decrease in the number of booksellers. This evidence is, however, extremely interesting since the figures show that the major attack on print in the first 1728 version of *The Dunciad* came at the end of a period of great expansion in printing activity, and that the crucial beginning and central years of Johnson's writing life, the late 1730s through the 1760s, corresponded to a period of depression in the book business.

The long-range trend, all the figures agree, was a large increase in the number of presses, booksellers, and book titles printed in England and in London during the eighteenth century. The numbers, therefore, while telling us something extremely interesting about the ups and downs of the book publishing business during that time, provide in the end statistical support for, and additional explanation of, Belanger's thesis that it was during this time that Britain, along with the rest of western Europe, became a print culture; and they also show in specific terms how print's logical tendencies toward system and numbers were objectified in the social world.

Bookselling, Readers, and the Marketplace

The booksellers were the other, the more public, half of the book business, and during the eighteenth century they, and particularly a small influential group known as "the trade," dominated the book publishing business, controlling both printers and writers. Many of them not only ran bookstores but functioned as publishers as well. As Strahan, along with being in part a publisher, was Johnson's chief printer, so Robert Dodsley in his shop at Tully's Head in Pall Mall was Johnson's primary publisher, bringing out *London, Irene, The Vanity of Human Wishes, Rasselas*, and other of his works, as well as being involved in Johnson's *Dictionary*. Located in the fashionable West End, Dodsley was the prestige publisher of his day and a remarkable man. Beginning as a servant in aristocratic households, he wrote his way out of service by means of a number of poems which were read and praised by his employers and their distinguished friends. His most notable early work, an instructional manual for servants titled *Servitude, A Poem* (1729), brought him to the attention of Alexander Pope, and Pope's friendship, along with that of other notables, was instrumental in getting Dodsley started in the book trade. Johnson always spoke very warmly of Dodsley, considering, he told Langton in a letter of 9 January 1758, that "Doddy . . . is my patron"; and Dodsley, with literary interests of his own, ran his business in a way that deserved Johnson's respect. He himself continued to write, turning out plays, poems, and poetic textbooks, and he encouraged a number of writers who were better than he. Dodsley was noted for the quality of the books he published and remained deeply interested throughout his life in the paper and type used in his publications, supporting, for example, John Baskerville (a former footman turned typefounder) in the manufacture of the elegant fonts Baskerville was developing at this time, one of which bearing his name is used in the present book. His literary reputation was further enhanced by the salon he maintained in his back rooms, of which Johnson could say, "The true *Noctes Atticae* are revived at honest Dodsley's house." The way in which Dodsley conducted his business justifies his own cautious suggestion to Joseph Spence, in a letter quoted by Straus, that publishing too might be an art, "I don't know but I may sometimes be as entertain'd in planning a book, as you are in laying out the plan of a Garden."

But along with his literary interests, Dodsley remained what he had to be, a shrewd businessman, who constantly looked for manuscripts, edited them to some degree, and arranged with a printer for the manufacture of books to be sold, sometimes exclusively in his shop, occasionally in those of other booksellers as well. He got his manuscripts in various ways. Because of

Dodsley's reputation as a genial and literate man, and because of the quality of his books, excellent manuscripts sometimes found their way into his shop without solicitation. Samuel Johnson, aware of Dodsley's reputation, sent him his first poem, *London*, for which Dodsley gave the writer the generous sum of ten guineas. Laurence Sterne wrote offering the first two volumes of *Tristram Shandy* for £50, but when Dodsley, by then formally retired but still active in the publishing decisions of his firm, refused on the grounds that this was too much money to risk on an unknown author, Sterne replied with a plan to print at his own expense in York, but to sell the printed books in London through Dodsley. If the first two volumes sold well, Sterne proposed, he and Dodsley would then set a fair price for the subsequent volumes, which would be published by Dodsley. Young's *Night Thoughts* also came to Dodsley without solicitation for a price somewhat over £200, and Akenside's *Pleasures of the Imagination* for £120. Perhaps his greatest windfall, the most famous poem of the eighteenth century, Thomas Gray's *Elegy Written in a Country Churchyard*, came to him through the offices of Horace Walpole, who much favored Dodsley. Gray had learned that his poem was about to be pirated by the editors of a periodical, and in order to make the best of what he still considered the unseemly and tasteless act of printing his poetry, he wrote to his friend Walpole on 11 February 1751 in terms which show how long the courtly tradition of anonymity and preference for manuscript circulation endured:

> I have but one bad Way left to escape the Honour they would inflict upon me, & therefore am obliged to desire you would make Dodsley print it immediately (which may be done in less than a Week's time) from your Copy, but without my Name, in what Form is most convenient for him, but in his best Paper & Character. he must correct the Press himself, & print it without Interval between the Stanza's, because the Sense is in some Places contin-

ued beyond them; & the Title must be, Elegy, wrote in a Country Church-yard. if he would add a Line or two to say it came into his Hands by Accident, I should like it better.

Gray's aristocratic disdain for print extended to asking Dodsley for no copy money for this, or for subsequent works of his that Dodsley printed. Dodsley was said to have made over £1,000 altogether out of Gray's poems.

Dodsley was not always so lucky or so perceptive. He advised his brother James, who took over the shop after Dodsley's retirement to a country house as a rich man in 1759, that copy money of £100 for the three volumes of Bishop Percy's collection of old ballads, the *Reliques*, was too large an amount, though a deal was later struck. James Dodsley on his own turned down some of Chatterton's Rowley poems for publication, which probably had something to do with Chatterton's suicide soon after at age seventeen.

But Dodsley, like most successful bookseller-publishers in his time, did not merely sit in his shop and wait for attractive manuscripts to come to him; he sought them out and he made them. He made them in the most literal sense by writing a number of works, even as the printer Samuel Richardson wrote *Pamela* to satisfy what he perceived to be both a moral and a marketplace need. Dodsley's *Chronicle of the Kings of England, Pain and Patience, The Art of Preaching, Public Virtue*, and a collection of *Select Fables* designed as a school text were as much the staples of his business as the "hot-pressed" fine quality paper he sold or the "methodical memorandum book," the pocket diary systematizing an individual's time that he was the first to sell. Dodsley also encouraged a number of writers to produce work he thought would be both prestigious and saleable. The poet Shenstone, a particular friend of Dodsley, was urged throughout his life to write and publish, and Edmund Burke, while still an unknown young man, was commissioned by Dodsley in 1758 to write for £100 the first of many *Annual Registers* containing a variety of material dealing with the most notable events—literary, political, and social—of the preceding year. Magazines sold well at this time, and Dodsley underwrote at least three, persuading various writers to collect the material and handle the editorial work. He gathered and published a number of collections of material which he considered to be of value and interest. The most familiar of these is his multivolumed *Old Plays*, a reprinting, excluding Shakespeare, Jonson, and Beaumont and Fletcher, of older English plays which were in danger of passing into oblivion as a result of not having been printed for some time. He was more famous in his own time, Straus points out, for the several volumes of *Collections*, anthologies of recent poetry, which he brought together "to preserve to the Public those poetical performances which seem to merit a longer remembrance than what would probably be secured to them by the manner wherein they were originally published." Print's logic of fixity is at work in these preserving activities, while the logic of multiplicity appears in the bookseller's world as a continual search for more manuscripts, to make more books, to sell to more customers. Using the listing of Dodsley's publications in Straus's biography, we can calculate that in the late 1750s this one bookseller published annually between 42 and 55 different titles, both new books and reprints. At the average print run for the time of 1,000 copies, this means that Dodsley was handling about 50,000 copies of his own books a year, and this figure does not include his magazines and other periodical publications.

The acquisition and publication of manuscripts and their sale in large numbers also required system in the form of orderly planning and time schedules at all levels of the book business. We can get some sense of why system and deadlines were so important to a bookseller from a letter, quoted by Straus, to the poet Shenstone of 21 January 1758 in which Dodsley tries politely to explain to the poet why he so desperately needs the few poems from Shenstone required to finish out one of his *Collections*. "The Season is wasting, and I have between 6 and 7 hundred pounds bury'd in the Paper & print of this Edition, which I want to pay and can not 'til I publish. I fear it is impossible You should read or understand what I have writ." What the bookseller, but only the rare writer like Johnson, understood was that publishing was a capital-intensive business. Although the original investments in a bookshop might be relatively small, and the labor costs for printing relatively cheap, paper was still very expensive, and none of the total cost of printing a book could be recovered until the printed books were sold to customers and they, usually after a considerable and fashionable delay, paid their bills. The bookseller Knapton, for example, owned stock valued at £30,000, but failed when he was unable to meet debts of £20,000. Johnson's fee for writing the *Dictionary* was, by way of another example, £1,575, paid to him in installments during the course of his work. Strahan printed the book in sections as batches of manuscript became available, and his total printing bill to the consortium which undertook the *Dictionary* was £1,262. 10s.6d. Add the cost of paper and other expenses, and the capital outlay for the *Dictionary* was somewhere between £4,000 and £5,000, without a penny of return until the two completed volumes could be sold.

Books remained very expensive in relation to other commodities during the eighteenth century, because of capital, not labor, costs. Under the constant pressure of a cash-flow problem, printers like Strahan and publishers like Dodsley had to organize their businesses as efficiently as possible to control investment costs and speed returns. This brought pressure in turn on literary activities. Authors like Shenstone and Johnson had to meet deadlines for copy. Congers were formed to raise capital and share the financial risks of expensive projects like

Subscription

Johnson's *Dictionary*. Subscription publication, like Johnson's edition of Shakespeare, was regularly used to get subscribers, whose names were printed in the finished book, to pay some portion of the costs beforehand, and guarantee a certain number of sales after publication. A network of middlemen, warehousers, and wholesalers, operating on a system of discounts of the kind Johnson describes in explicit detail and recommends to the Oxford University Press in his letter of 12 March 1776, was set up to provide for wider, quicker, more efficient distribution of books. Better methods of advertising books and of making them known to prospective buyers through criticism and reviews had to be and were arranged. Advertising became at this time a large item in a book's budget. When, for example, Johnson's collected *Idler* was published in 1761 at 5 shillings sewn, or 6 shillings bound, Marjorie Plant reckons that "the total expenses for the 1500 copies were £113.16s. 6d., of which advertising accounted for £20.0s. 6d., printing £41.13s., and paper £52.3s." Above all, of course, books had to be made interesting and attractive to prospective buyers, and, to take the most sensational example among many, the success of the novel at this time represents the effort to cater to wider audiences. The novel is the characteristic print genre—lyric, epic, and drama being the inventions of oral culture—even to the extent that long, particularized prose narratives were economically more advantageous than poetry to both writers and publishers since book prices were set and copy paid for by the number of words. But the novel was also, as Ian Watt has shown in detail in his classic *Rise of the Novel*, an expression in form and subject of middle-class values, and world-view, which were, inevitably, closely identified with, even extensions into reading of, print logic, and as such most likely to interest the mass of literate middle-class people with enough money to buy books.

the Novel's success

These economic realities and marketing strategies make

clear how print multiplicity destroyed Milton's old "fit audience . . . though few," or the small group of gentlemen who discuss poetry in Dryden's "Essay," and created a new and much
larger and more various audience for letters by centering readers in the literary scene as buyers of books in the marketplace
for whom all writing and publication was designed, the final
judges of what was written, printed, read, and preserved. It is
not certain that print increased significantly the number of actual readers in eighteenth-century England, though its logic of
multiplicity surely worked in this direction. One historian of
the subject, Richard Altick, has concluded that, "by 1780 the
national literacy rate was scarcely higher than it had been during the Elizabethan period." But the hard evidence for this
conclusion is very slight, if not nonexistent. More recent analyses that include such evidence as subscription lists to lending
libraries, book clubs, serial publications, newspapers and their
advertisements for books have created what Paul Kaufman
summarizes in his study of eighteenth-century libraries as "a
picture of far more widespread reading than has been conven-
tionally described."

To the statistical evidence I can add nothing certain, but it is
worth remarking that to Johnson and his contemporaries it did
appear that the number of readers increased greatly in their
time, which is what print logic and the increase of printed
books during the period would also suggest. Johnson once
measured the change, about which he frequently spoke, in
terms of the first sales, 1,300 in the first two years, of *Paradise
Lost*. The sale of what seemed so few copies of so great a poem
was taken by Johnson's time to be a sign of earlier indifference
and neglect, but he argues in his "Life of Milton" that it was
really the consequence of the few people who read then, in
contrast to the greatly increased numbers who did so by his
time:

The sale, if it be considered, will justify the publick. Those who have no power to judge of past times but by their own, should always doubt their conclusions. The call for books was not in Milton's age what it is in the present. To read was not then a general amusement; neither traders, nor often gentlemen thought themselves disgraced by ignorance. The women had not then aspired to literature, nor was every house supplied with a closet of knowledge. Those, indeed, who professed learning were not less learned than at any other time; but of that middle race of students who read for pleasure or accomplishment and who buy the numerous products of modern typography, the number was then comparatively small. To prove the paucity of readers, it may be sufficient to remark that the nation had been satisfied, from 1623 to 1664, that is, forty-one years, with only two editions of the works of Shakespeare, which probably did not together make one thousand copies.

Johnson was by no means alone in believing that his time had seen a great increase in reading, for his society perceived a "literacy crisis" that was the exact reverse of the "literacy crisis" of our own time. Rightly or wrongly, it was widely believed that the spread of reading, and writing, particularly among the lower classes, endangered the established order in polite letters, as well as in the more critical areas of politics and religion. As we might expect, Johnson, who always well understood the identity of his interests as an author, up to a point at least, with those of the printers and booksellers, uncompromisingly defended literacy in his pronouncements on the question. Whatever the facts may be about the increase of literacy, it is nonetheless clear that an increasingly numerous and democratic audience of readers, rather than a few listeners with shared tastes, was one of the most profound effects, as we shall see in detail in later chapters, of print logic on letters. These effects were not, however, so immediately obvious or so deeply felt at first as the effects of print on writers.

Writers in a Print Culture

H. J. Chaytor remarks that "association with printed matter has changed our views of literary art and style, has introduced ideas concerning originality and literary property of which the age of manuscript knew little or nothing." One of the most important of these print-created literary ideas has been a firm conception of the existence of the author, which print established with such substantial factuality that it has largely obliterated even the memory of an older tradition of literary anonymity extending in the European postclassical period from the oral singers of tales, through medieval manuscript culture, well into the Renaissance. Anonymity began to wane when writers like Dante, Petrarch, and Chaucer appeared in their authorial roles in their poetry; but Chaucer's palinodes and the irony with which he treats his poetic persona may suggest that some psychological and social difficulty was still involved in being an author in the late Middle Ages. The difficulty lingered on for a long time, as if manuscripts could never quite make authors real, and a large number of Renaissance writings were still attributed to "anon.," published under a pseudonym, or with some formulaic protestation that the work had been printed without the writer's knowledge or only at the continued insistence of friends. During this time the courtly role of the poet as a gentleman-amateur for whom poetry was only one of many secondary accomplishments also continued to suppress the author as a primary identity. Indeed, authorial anonymity in the genteel tradition of polite letters lasted on until well into the eighteenth century, when Swift, who put his name on the title page of very few of his works, still played elaborate ironic games with the authorship of *Gulliver's Travels*, and Johnson himself published a number of his works, such as *London*, *Rasselas*, and the *Ramblers* anonymously.

Preprint writers like Dante and Petrarch, who had a strong sense of their identity as poets, make it clear that the social existence of the writer does not entirely depend on the printed book with a title page carrying his name. But the fact of the book, solidly and durably "out there," objectified the writer, making him real to himself and to others to a degree impossible in a world of oral performance or a few "drifting" manuscripts. As Lionel Gossman puts it, "In all probability, it was only gradually, and in combination with a variety of historical circumstances, that the identification of works with individual graphically recorded utterances led to a conception of literary creation as absolutely original production, arising out of and in some way embodying a unique, substantial and autonomous self." One small but telling actual instance of the way in which the book objectified authors is noted by Arber in a 1641 order of the House of Commons that probably had as its primary purpose only the restraint of seditious writings but also had the effect of making the author existent: "It is ordered that the Master and Wardens of the Company of Stationers shall be required to take especiall Order, that the Printers doe neither print, nor reprint any thing without the name and consent of the Author. . . ."

Gossman's "variety of historical circumstances" that combined with print to create the author is specified by Roland Barthes in the following way: "The author is a modern figure, a product of our society insofar as, emerging from the Middle Ages with English empiricism, French rationalism and the personal faith of the Reformation, it discovered the prestige of the individual, of, as it is more nobly put, the 'human person.'" In the essay in which these words appear, "The Death of the Author," Barthes removes the author from the center of our literary system and replaces him with the reader. If the idea that so seemingly natural a figure as the author can die, and therefore can also be created, seems strange, we need only consider another medium, film, which in our time has unmade authors as surely as print once made them. Literary people like Edmund Wilson have seen in the disastrous Hollywood experiences of established writers like F. Scott Fitzgerald, William Faulkner, Nathanael West, and Aldous Huxley only the "appalling record of talent depraved and wasted," which has been depicted in many Hollywood novels like West's *The Day of the Locust*. Great literary artists, the creators of imaginative works of art, so the standard story goes, encountered in the film studios a vulgar medium and its even more vulgar owners and business executives, who ignored their genius and treated them as mere technicians, forcing them to collaborate with other writers or to work in succession on a story, used their writing as only an outline for production scripts, and listed their names deep down in the credits, if at all, below the director, the stars, the producer, among the cutters and makeup men. One studio head, Jack Warner, put the Hollywood attitude toward writers bluntly but not inaccurately when he defined them in a well-turned *mot* as "schmucks with Underwoods." But, as Leslie Fiedler explains, this attitude toward authors was not mere envy or vulgarity, though there was plenty of both in Hollywood, so much as the inevitable logic, however crudely expressed, of a visual medium that defined writers and their wordcraft as supporting, not central, to pictures: "What was involved in the flight of writers to Hollywood and their inevitable defeat there was not so much a series of betrayals and appropriate punishments as the first stage in a revolution—only recently defined by such commentators as Marshall McLuhan—which would make print obsolete, and the first panicked attempts of those committed to the old regime of words to come to terms with the future."

The pre-eminence in letters of the author, it would appear, may be closely connected with print—"Flourished 1750–1950?"—for with the dominance of print in England during the eighteenth century authors became very numerous. The book business, even in its relatively primitive technological stages, was capable, as we have seen, of producing and marketing large numbers of books, and that potential had to be fully exploited to meet the constant need for working capital and to maximize profits. Full production required a steady supply of copy for the printer. In part this need could be and was met by reprinting old books, Shakespeare, Milton, Pope, or classics like Dodsley's editions of Horace, or his collections of old plays. But reprints were not enough, and there was an increasing need for new manuscripts as well. To supply these manuscripts, writers were needed, and while we ordinarily assume that they were there already, simply waiting to take advantage of the opportunities to publish that print now offered, contemporary evidence suggests that it was mostly the other way round—that it was the need of print for copy that created writers like Tom Brown, Ned Ward, Oldmixon, Defoe, Smart, Savage, Thomson, Goldsmith, Johnson, and many others whose names have by now nearly disappeared in time. *The Dunciad* shows polite letters being destroyed by what Pope saw as a swarming rabble of these talentless Grub Street hacks who were made writers only by the appetite of the printing press for copy. Johnson, in *Adventurer* 115, described, though with a different tone, the rage for print that made this mob of writers:

> The present age, if we consider chiefly the state of our own country, may be styled, with great propriety, *The Age of Authours*; for, perhaps, there never was a time in which men of all degrees of ability, of every kind of education, of every profession and employment, were posting with ardour so general to the press . . . but though it may, perhaps, be true, that at all times more have been willing than have been able to write, yet there is no reason for believing, that the dogmatical legions of the present race were ever equalled in number by any former period: . . .

He goes on to explain that it is "the itch of literary praise" that turned "our nobles and our peasants, our soldiers and traders, our men and women, all into wits, philosophers and writers."

But the existence and identity that print gave to the writer with one hand it took away with the other, for if widely circulated printed books made authors real to themselves and others, and made the *idea* of the author a social fact, then the very number of books published guaranteed, with rare exceptions like Johnson, that the individual writer would exist only momentarily. Oliver Goldsmith, himself a Grub Street hack, well understood how dependent writers were on print and how brief their existence was: "I consider an authour's literary reputation to be alive only while his name will ensure a good price for his copy from the booksellers." How very short a time that could be is brilliantly dramatized by Swift in the little bookshop scene in "Verses on the Death of Dr. Swift" (1731), which also makes clear that while print established the idea of the author, it did not guarantee anything more than momentary existence to any particular author:

> Some Country Squire to *Lintot* goes,
> Enquires for SWIFT in Verse and Prose:
> Says *Lintot*, 'I have heard the Name:
> 'He dy'd a Year ago.' The same.
> He searcheth all his Shop in vain;
> 'Sir you may find them in *Duck-lane*:
> 'I sent them with a Load of Books,
> 'Last *Monday* to the Pastry-cooks.
> 'To fancy they cou'd live a Year!
> 'I find you're but a Stranger here.
> 'The Dean was famous in his Time;
> 'And had a Kind of Knack at Rhyme:
> 'His way of Writing now is past;
> 'The Town hath got a better Taste:
> 'I keep no antiquated Stuff;

'But, spick and span I have enough.
'Pray, do but give me leave to shew 'em;
'Here's *Colley Cibber's* Birth-day Poem.
'This Ode you never yet have seen,
'By *Stephen Duck*, upon the Queen.'

There was for all writers, but particularly for the professionals who made up Grub Street—the name that Pope and Swift fixed upon this subworld of writing—an inbuilt contradiction in print, which gave them something of what was needed to live but denied them the dignity that was needed to make life meaningful. The writing life of at least the most interesting hacks, including Johnson, was a continuous effort to resolve this contradiction, which can best be understood by looking at the work patterns of writers in the age of print. What print did to the numerous writers who earned a living in Grub Street was defined in a coldly theoretical manner by Johnson's fellow Literary Club member, Adam Smith, in *The Wealth of Nations* (1776) in an analysis of the principles of efficient factory production. Smith's famous example was the pin factory, but the publishing business, though it remained in some ways a cottage industry in that all the operations were never brought under one roof, also tended to organize itself on factory principles. Smith classified "men of letters of all kinds," along with players, buffoons, churchmen, and kings, as nonproducers, who by his definition were those whose labor could not "afterwards purchase or procure an equal quantity of labour." But, he added, "the labour of the meanest of these has a certain value, regulated by the very same principles which regulate that of every other sort of labour." Those systematic economic principles—specialization, the wage-profit ratio, the open marketplace, and its constant pressure for increased efficiency and productivity—determined the life of the book worker, whether writer or printer, as rigidly as they did the coal miner or the weaver.

Goldsmith, always specially sensitive to his social status, understood clearly that "a fatal revolution" had taken place "whereby writing is converted to a mechanic trade." Hannah Arendt in her discussion of labor and work in *The Human Condition* provides the terms needed to define the profound cultural shock that writers-for-pay like Goldsmith experienced in the transformation that Smith treats as a matter-of-fact inevitability in any well-run business. Arendt sees all human activity against the background of nature, which is defined as a process of ceaseless mutability or "spoiling," in which things appear, only to rot and disappear, and people *labor* endlessly to satisfy their immediate biological necessities and maintain the existing social order. Labor produces no surplus, no durable objects, for its products are at once used up, even as the tilling of the fields produces food that immediately spoils or is consumed. To this endless round of disappearing labor, Arendt opposes *work* by which people make a human world, using tools for their own purpose rather than being used by them, choosing their own times of activity rather than being scheduled by some iron law of necessity, and producing durable objects like a legal code or a work of art. In ancient times, Arendt says, labor was assigned to slaves, while work was the activity of the free, but in the modern consumer society, labor has become the lot of everyone, and as such it has had to be, by Marx for example, romanticized and idealized. It did not yet appear, however, to be a basis for human dignity to the many writers in eighteenth-century London who found themselves laboring in the print business rather than working at the writer's art, and the stories of a number of the more bizarre Grub Street writers reveal both the way labor in the book factory affected the life of writing and the desperate need of these writers to improve upon the identity print offered them.

There is in Boswell's descriptions of Grub Street always a most touching quality of courage and humanity in the new laborers in the book factory, as when Floyd, homeless and wandering the streets at night, comes upon and wakes another hack, Derrick, sleeping on some pilings. "Derrick started up, 'My dear Floyd, I am sorry to see you in this destitute state; will you go home with me to *my lodgings?*' " The courtly gesture in the face of a wretched but resolutely ignored reality is not only touching but emblematic of Grub Street. Most of the hacks, driven by their pride, tried to pretend that they were still gentleman-authors of the courtly tradition rather than the poorly paid print laborers they in fact were. Their eccentric and often astoundingly ingenious efforts to create this aristocratic reality for themselves provide a good picture of how Grub Street was actually experienced by those who found themselves in it, and an instructive contrast to the way Johnson eventually made himself an author rather than a mere hack.

Richard Savage (1697–1743), Johnson's close friend and frequent companion during the hard years following his arrival in London, was, to judge from his rather conventional neoclassical imitations of Dryden and Pope, a writer of modest talents who drifted into writing only because he had no other means of support. His characteristic Grub Street background—poverty, leaving school early, apprenticeship to a shoemaker—was as dreary as the later circumstances so feelingly summed up by Johnson in his *Life of Mr. Richard Savage*:

> He lodged as much by accident as he dined. He composed his verses in his head while walking the streets, stopping in shops to cadge pencil and paper to jot them down. He passed the night sometimes in mean houses, which are set open at night to any casual wanderers, sometimes in cellars, among the riot and filth of the meanest and most profligate of the rabble; and sometimes, when he had not money to support even the expences of these receptacles, walked about the streets till he was weary, and lay down in the summer upon a bulk, or in the winter, with his associates in poverty, among the ashes of a glass-house.

The circumstances are familiar to Grub Street, but in their midst, Savage daringly created and lived out the role of the writer in an earlier age, that of the aristocratic rake and gentleman of fashion, the man of honor, the town wit, a Rochester or Wycherley writing solely for his own amusement. He wore his ragged clothing with an air, was fastidious in his tastes, drank and talked with ready authority in the taverns, which, Johnson tells us, he was never the first to leave. He borrowed money easily, spent it carelessly, and was deadly if repayment was mentioned. Ordinarily gravely courteous, sometimes insolent, he became quickly violent when restrained or reproached, and murdered a man, though he was not convicted, in an argument over a tavern room and a whore. Even his way of handling his proofs, as described by Johnson, gave a tone of elegance and refinement to this very practical print business. "A superstitious regard to the correction of his sheets was one of Mr. Savage's peculiarities: he often altered, revised, recurred to his first reading or punctuation, and again adopted the alteration; he was dubious and irresolute without end, as on a question of the last importance, and at last was seldom satisfied: the intrusion or omission of a comma was sufficient to discompose him, and he would lament an error of a single letter as a heavy calamity."

Savage's re-enactment of the old Castiglione, courtier tradition of the gentleman-writer was always just on the edge of the shabby and the ludicrous, as if Shakespeare's Pistol had somehow combined with a Restoration Lovewit, but Savage brought it off with a remarkable personal style and reinforced its reality with several breath-taking inventions. When Colley Cibber was made poet laureate in 1730, Savage expressed his belief that his own writing had entitled him to the post and that he had still once again been wronged by his many powerful enemies. Instead of merely grumbling in the tavern, however, he boldly proclaimed himself "volunteer laureate," wrote an annual birthday ode not to the king, as the official laureate did, but to the queen, and so flattered her vanity by this device that this intelligent woman entered into his fiction and gave him an annual allowance until her death.

But his greatest act of self-creation was a lived-out story, which the usually skeptical Johnson appears to have entirely believed, that he was the illegitimate child of the Countess of Macclesfield and Earl Rivers. She felt, Savage's version had it, an irrational and unnatural hatred for her child and put him into the hands of poor people to be raised as their own, but Savage later discovered his illustrious background. Fantasy at this point merged into reality, and Savage began to press his claims on his "mother" and her noble family. His efforts were first met with outrage, threats, and attempts to have him hanged and, that failing, transported to America; when these exertions of power did not silence him, various arrangements were made to provide him with a modest living, all of which foundered because of Savage's dissolute way of life.

The responses of the family to Savage's claims were for him, and for Johnson, who had a considerable emotional investment in Savage, proof that they were true. But while the absolute truth can never be known, it seems rather more probable to recent scholars that the whole story was Savage's invention, brilliantly and brazenly acted out, to reinforce his role as a gentleman-writer with an aristocratic background. This interpretation squares with Savage's lifelong efforts to make himself a gentleman in defiance of other facts, and it explains, at least as well as any other theory, the actions of the countess and her family as understandable attempts first to silence and then to buy off a troublesome wretch who was bringing scandal on a noble house. Indeed, probably without intending to, Johnson himself encourages this suspicion with frequent remarks to the effect that it is nearly impossible to understand how a mother could act in so malicious and unnatural a way toward her own child. If Savage were not her child, however, her behavior seems very natural and Savage's vicious treatment of her becomes more understandable as the action of a blackmailer rather than the disappointment of a rejected child: "He . . . threatened to harass her with lampoons, and to publish a copious narrative of her conduct, unless she consented to purchase an exemption from infamy, by allowing him a pension." Savage maintained the truth of his claims until the end of his life in a Bristol jail, where his outraged creditors were determined to keep him even though it cost them money to do so. He died there, still playing the grand gentleman fallen on evil days: "The last time that the keeper saw him was on July the 31st, 1743, when Savage, seeing him at his bed-side, said, with an uncommon earnestness, 'I have something to say to you, Sir'; but, after a pause, moved his hand in a melancholy manner, and, finding himself unable to recollect what he was going to communicate, said,' 'Tis gone!' "

The old image of the gentleman-poet died hard, and even Oliver Goldsmith (1730–1774), along with Johnson probably the greatest of the Grub Street hacks, tried to live out this role, often with results more comic than tragic. Boswell, who did not really like him because he was a competitor for Johnson's affection, describes succinctly the obvious gap between what Goldsmith was and what he tried to be: "His person was short, his countenance coarse and vulgar, his deportment that of a scholar awkwardly affecting the easy gentleman." When he had money he dressed himself in extravagant, brightly colored clothing and strutted about in his finery only to make himself look ridiculous. As his situation improved, he moved to fashionable quarters and squandered money on rich draperies, china, and stylish blue furniture. Learned, kindly, and the master of a beautiful literary style, he was unusually awkward and inept in conversation, but talked loudly and boasted outrageously in order to appear a man of parts, frequently telling easily discovered lies, such as bragging that his brother was Dean of Durham, in his eagerness to shine. The author of *The Good Natured Man*, noted for the kindness and gentleness of his writings, beat a bookseller named Evans "on account of a paragraph in a news-paper published by him, which Goldsmith thought impertinent to him and to a lady of his acquaintance." He then published an apology in order to advertise his fashionable anger, only to earn Johnson's deflating comment, "I believe it is the first time he has *beat*; he may have *been beaten* before. This, Sir, is a new plume to him." But the enormity of his desire to be something more than a poor, awkward hack appears perhaps best in the anecdote of his visit to a puppet show: "when those who sat next him observed with what dexterity a puppet was made to toss a pike, he could not bear that it should have such praise, and exclaimed with some warmth, 'Pshaw! I can do it better myself.' " But there was a happy ending of sorts, a formal vindication of worth, for "Goldy"—the hated undignified nickname Johnson fixed on him—did not die like Savage in debtors' prison, but, deeply and fashionably in debt, was buried in the poet's corner of Westminster Abbey, not because he was a gentleman but because he was a great writer.

Christopher Smart (1722–1771) offers a more desperate instance of poet-making than either Savage or Goldsmith, both of whom merely elaborated the ancient role of gentleman-poet. Smart's father was steward to the wealthy and prominent Vane family, and, impressed by his early poetic efforts, they sent him to Cambridge, where he won poetry prizes and attracted the attention of Thomas Gray, who unkindly predicted the jail or asylum for him unless he mended his ways. Smart took his degree at Cambridge, but instead of entering the church, he appeared in London in the late 1740s as a hack, writing magazine articles and vaudeville entertainments under the pseudonym "Mrs. Midnight." An amorous disposition, the usual Grub Street love of drink and talk, an unfortunate marriage, and pronounced neurotic tendencies intensified his financial problems and forced him into ridiculous arrangements such as the contract described by Johnson: "Old Gardner the bookseller employed Rolt and Smart to write a monthly miscellany, called 'The Universal Visitor.' There was a formal written contract, which Allen the printer saw. . . . They were bound to write nothing else; they were to have, I think, a third of the profits of this sixpenny pamphlet; and the contract was for ninety-nine years." Under this kind of pressure, Smart began to break and "shewed the disturbance of his mind, by falling upon his knees, and saying his prayers in the street, or in any other unusual place." Until he discovered the terms of the contract, Johnson fulfilled Smart's writing commitments for "The Universal Visitor" after Smart had been put in the madhouse, where he lived in a manner Johnson and Burney discussed with more wit than sympathy:

> BURNEY. 'How does poor Smart do, Sir; is he likely to recover?' JOHNSON. 'It seems as if his mind had ceased to struggle with the disease; for he grows fat upon it.' BURNEY. 'Perhaps, Sir, that may be from want of exercise.' JOHNSON. 'No, Sir; he has partly as much exercise as he used to have, for he digs in the garden. Indeed, before his confinement, he used for exercise to walk to the alehouse; but he was *carried* back again. I did not think he ought to be shut up. His infirmities were not noxious to society. He insisted on people praying with him; and I'd as lief pray with Kit Smart as any one else. Another charge was, that he did not love clean linen; and I have no passion for it.'

This might be only another pitiful but familiar Grub Street story of hard times and unstable character, but in his madness Smart created for himself an authorial role which was totally beyond his grasp in the actual world where he was only a hack and a joke. Committed to an asylum in 1756, where he remained until 1763, Smart began to write the very great poetry in a prophetic, visionary mode that his earlier work had only suggested: *The Song to David*, published in 1763, and the *Jubilate Agno*, not discovered and printed until 1939. The myth has it that these poems were written on the walls of his cell, with charcoal in one version, with a key in another. The key is more suggestive, for in his poetry of madness Smart unlocked the intolerable actualities of Mrs. Midnight and 99-year contracts with booksellers like Old Gardner by making himself as poet the central figure in a highly charged symbolic world where divine energies shine through his famous cat Jeoffrey and all his day-to-day reality. Here, the poet is, as Boccaccio, Sidney, and earlier poetic tradition had frequently imaged him, King David, interpreting God to the world, and in the midst of all human weakness and sin praying in his poetic psalms for the rest of creation. As David, Smart is all the things "poor Kitty" was not:

> Great, valiant, pious, good, and clean,
> Sublime, contemplative, serene,
>   Strong, constant, pleasant, wise!
> Bright effluence of exceeding grace;
> Best man!—the swiftness and the race,
>   The peril, and the prize!

Perhaps the most interesting and revealing acts of authormaking in Johnson's time took place outside Grub Street proper but very much within a print-made anxiety about writing. The fictitious poets, Chatterton's Rowley and Macpherson's Ossian, usually seem only curiosities of literary history, but when seen in the context of the breakdown of traditional poetic roles and eighteenth-century writers' efforts to make themselves something other than laborers in the book factory—the role printing was imposing on them—they become extreme, dramatic instances of the kind of poet-making that we have already seen in Savage claiming that he was a noble changeling, in Smart scribbling his poetic prayer on the walls of the madhouse, or in Goldsmith boasting that he belonged to the nobility of the sword and could handle martial weapons better than a puppet.

Thomas Chatterton (1752–1770) wrote a number of pseudo-archaic poems that he claimed were transcriptions of original manuscripts, found in a belfry, written by a fifteenth-century Bristol monk, Thomas Rowley. The imposture was exposed a few years after Chatterton's suicide at seventeen, apparently in despair over his poverty, but the high quality of his verse has continued to guarantee it a place in literature. He also left us with the instructive irony that so talented a poet felt at this time that worth and fame as a writer could be achieved not in his own person but only through a fictitious medieval persona. Bertrand Bronson explains Rowley in psychological terms as "a projected embodiment of the child's innermost life, an essential personification emerging from the earliest years, of the dreams and wishes of his secret being." But that "secret being" could not find its satisfaction in the writer's role offered by print, and Chatterton's attempts to establish a more satisfactory poetic personality in the public world were blocked by the refusals of the bookseller Dodsley and the art-printer, Horace Walpole, to publish the poems of Rowley.

The Scot, James Macpherson (1736-1796), was made of considerably sterner stuff than "the marvelous boy," but he too, though a poet of merit in his own right, also tried to establish himself as a writer by offering his own poems as translations of a legendary figure, the third-century Gaelic bard, Ossian. Claiming to be recovering ancient Celtic poetry, Macpherson published a number of his own artificially aged poems as *Fragments of Ancient Poetry Collected in the Highlands of Scotland* (1760), *Fingal, an Ancient Epic Poem, in Eight Books* (1761), and *Temora* (1763). Macpherson's "decision to become an ancient," as Robert Folkenflik calls this choice of a poetic role, was, he continues, an attempt to deal with the most pressing issue for writers in his time: "The chief question consciously or unconsciously asked by the ambitious was, 'How can I be a great poet now?'" For Folkenflik this question and its attendant anxiety was a matter largely of Bloomian literary belatedness and Bate's burden of past writing, but that psychological and cultural sense of being too weak and too late to write heroic poetry was surely in large part engendered by the overwhelming presence of print-produced texts of the great writing of the past, a condition made even more tense by the confusion about the writer's role that print had forced on the contemporary writer. Macpherson seems both to relieve his conscience by secretly confessing his forgery and to explain its necessity in terms of his own felt inadequacy when he writes in the preface to *Fingal*: "Poetry, like virtue, receives its reward after death. . . . This consideration might induce a man diffident of his abilities, to ascribe his own compositions to a person, whose remote antiquity and whose situation, when alive, might well answer for faults which would be inexcusable in a writer of this age." Controversy about the authenticity and quality of the Ossian poems can scarcely be said still to rage, but it does still bubble, and in his lifetime Macpherson achieved great acclaim as a poet, found his way into Parliament, and eventually was buried in Westminster Abbey.

The urgency and ingenuity of such poetic lives as those of Savage, Smart, Goldsmith, Chatterton, and Macpherson tell us not only that the eighteenth century was a literary watershed when the poetic role was no longer fixed, but also that there was an enormous concern about the form the poetic role should take. Print may have determined that henceforth all writers would be some kind of, to put it most crudely, Grub Street hack, but this life of *labor* rather than *work* was obviously unacceptable to the most intense writers of the day; and though they had to accept print realities to some degree, they also expended large amounts of energy and undertook great risks that threatened reputation, sanity, and even life to carve for themselves an acceptable poetic mask, a mask that was for them a realization of being itself. The extreme intensity and imagination these poets expended to make an acceptable, a liveable, poetic role for themselves, however mad the actions may now seem, serve to suggest, startlingly, the degree to which human feelings and existential values are involved in a radical change in the social arrangements of letters. That involvement is, of course, noticeably there in the activities of printers who buy coaches with their profits and booksellers who make an art of book design, but it is the hack writers violently determined to be something more than laborers for the book factory who make it obvious that the social construction of a new print-based system of letters was not a technologically determined process. Technology in the form of print plays a critical, perhaps even a primary, part in literary change in eighteenth-century England, but the new print-based literary system that was ultimately constructed was an interaction of print logic and human needs.

Both the technology and the humanity appear fully in the life of Samuel Johnson, and subsequent chapters of this book explore, in turn, the ways he and print interacted to remake the basic, what we may call, the structural components of letters: the poetic role, the definition of the true literary text, the conception of the new audience of readers, and the establishment of a meaningful place for letters in modern society and its conception of knowledge. It is not my argument, as I have said earlier, that his solution to certain crucial literary questions determined what happened later—though his influence has been great—but I do argue that his encounters with and ways of handling these structural problems are paradigmatic of the way these same critical issues have been worked and reworked over the last two centuries of romantic and modern literature.

In the end, wonderfully, zanily inventive as they surely were, the writers we have just looked at all chose, in their different ways, to become ancients: gentlemen-amateurs of the old regime like Sidney, David the king who sang to Saul and God, an old Bristol monk, or a Celtic tribal bard. Johnson alone chose to be openly a modern. Seen under the aspect of eternity, Dr. Samuel Johnson, the great cham of literature, is perhaps no more or less a fiction than Ossian, but his poetic image was constructed in hard ways out of hard stuff, the facts of the print world. Instead of trying to act out some dream of a courtly or mythic past, Johnson took exactly the opposite course. Participating fully in the life of the laborer in the print factory, he slowly made himself an author, a professional whose writings were literary work, by taking full advantage of all the opportunities that print offered a hack writer to achieve some dignity for himself, his skills, and his writings. The role of professional writer he made for himself became a meaningful part of the actual world of letters being constructed by print in his time, because, to put it simply, it seemed real and made sense in the print world and the new industrial democratic society of which print was so important a component. Success in role-making of this kind required personal commitment and emphatic, dense, hard, continuous effort. It also required, in this case, the kind of mythological monumentalization of Dr. Johnson supplied by Boswell's great biography. Of Boswell's part in making Johnson's life the model of the poetic role in the age of print we will say more later, but we can begin to get some idea of what had to be done to make a social role credible as a "fact" of human nature and of culture from Johnson's confrontation with Macpherson.

Macpherson's one mistake, and a big one which brought him into conflict with Samuel Johnson, was to claim that the Ossian poems were translated from ancient manuscripts rather than recorded from the memory of oral performances. The latter position would have been defensible despite suspiciously modern elements of style and sentiment in the poems. Johnson, the perspicacious reader, did not like the romantic qualities of the verse and suspected when the poems were first printed that they were spurious. But he did not attack Macpherson until the publication in 1775 of his *Journey to the Western Isles of Scotland*, where, after having investigated the matter in his recent visit to the Highlands, he declared flatly that the poems of Ossian "never existed in any other form than we have seen," namely, in Macpherson's own printed versions. "Where are the manuscripts?" he thundered at Macpherson, and answered himself, "A nation that cannot write, or a language that was never written, has no manuscripts." The eye of the professional writer and reader had unerringly found the sensitive literary areas, the style, the sentiments, the absence of copy texts, that print foregrounded. Johnson and Macpherson were both extremely combative individuals, and Macpherson tried to force Johnson to retract his charges. When this, of course, failed, he threatened physical violence. Johnson responded by buying a large oak stick and writing a letter, the original of which, only recently discovered, is reprinted by Bate in his *Johnson*: "I received your foolish and impudent note. Whatever insult is offered me I will do my best to repel, and what I cannot do for myself the law will do for me. I will not desist from detecting what I think a cheat, from any fear of the menaces of a Ruffian."

The Macpherson-Johnson battle dramatizes, like so many other Johnsonian scenes, the struggle between the old oral and the new print cultures, and it centers one of the critical issues in this struggle, the definition of the poet or the true writer. Though Johnson may have hammered Macpherson down in the 1770s, it should not be forgotten that Ossian was in fact the poet eventually needed and used by a nostalgic romanticism to project its literary theory of the creative imagination, its primitivism, and its nationalism. In many ways, it can be argued, the visible features of the type of the poet in romantic and modern literature have more often resembled Ossian than they have Samuel Johnson, the professional man of print. But in putting his finger exactly on what was wrong in the original situation, Johnson located fatal weaknesses that have followed romantic poets throughout the age of print. First, print is inescapable, for though Ossian was conceived as a primitive oral bard, composing his songs in his head and singing them to his people, Macpherson, in order to make him believable and real, had to invent written manuscript versions of the poems and then put them into print, where their authenticity could be challenged and their style and sentiments rationally analyzed and dated by comparison with other printed works. Second, Ossian was not Ossian but only old Macpherson pretending to be Ossian, intriguing but always suspect of mere pomposity and self-interest, and never quite entirely real. The situation catches perfectly, at their beginning, some of romanticism's continuing problems with authenticity in the modern print world.

It might well seem, however, that Johnson's victory is only negative, for while discrediting Macpherson-Ossian, he in his clear rational sense of things and his stout determination to expose humbug does not seem to project any recognizable image of a type of poet who has been historically important. But his character in the exchange does, I want to argue, reveal, in fact, at least the outline of the basic drives and energies that have been the true center of our conception of the writer, romantic or professional, in a print culture. It was this image of a writer whose whole effort and skill are directed to making sense of elusive, deceiving, conflicting and complex, perhaps even evanescent and ultimately meaningless, things that Johnson, and Boswell, constructed and made real, in ways we shall see in close focus in the next two chapters, over their lifetimes.

CHAPTER III

MAKING THE WRITER'S ROLE
IN A PRINT CULTURE

Print Makes Johnson a Writer

Johnson always argued that all particular occupations, including that of the writer, were "accidentally determined." For example, after recounting in the "Life of Cowley" the story of how reading Spenser at an early age made Cowley "irrecoverably a poet," Johnson goes on, "Such are the accidents, which, sometimes remembered, and perhaps sometimes forgotten, produce that particular designation of mind and propensity for some certain science or employment, which is commonly called Genius. The true Genius is a mind of large general powers, accidentally determined to some particular direction." But the accident which made Samuel Johnson a writer was neither so charming nor so accidental as that which made Cowley a poet. When he arrived in London in the late 1730s, a few pennies in his pocket, having walked from Lichfield with his pupil David Garrick, his entry into the life of writing seems far more fateful than accidental. His immediate and real needs were for work, money, a place in the world; and only print, with its reciprocal need for copy, was ready to supply what he had to have in exchange for the only thing that he could really do. Despite being advised because of his size to take work as a porter, he soon found employment as an editor and writer for the printer and magazine publisher Edward Cave, approaching him in response to an advertisement for writers: "Having observed in your papers very uncommon offers of encouragement to men of letters. . . ." But shortly afterward, hesitating before committing himself finally to the occupation of writer, he made a major effort to extricate himself. "He could not expect," Boswell tells us, "to produce many such works as his LONDON, and he felt the hardship of writing for bread; he was, therefore, willing to resume the office of a schoolmaster, so as to have a sure, though moderate income for his life." But in order to get a respectable teaching position, he needed a university degree, and attempts to procure the degree, first at Oxford and then, through Pope's effort to get Swift to help, at Trinity College, Dublin, failed. Blocked in this direction, "he made one other effort to emancipate himself from the drudgery of authourship" by trying to enter the legal profession, but was again rebuffed for want of a degree. Describing this crucial point in Johnson's life, Boswell writes one of his simplest but most intense sentences: "He was, therefore, under the necessity of persevering in that course, into which he had been forced; and we find, that his proposal from Greenwich to Mr. Cave, for a translation of Father Paul Sarpi's History, was accepted." Johnson himself provides a more laconic version of the identical situation in the life of his alter ego, Richard Savage, who after a series of reverses was "obliged to seek some other means of support; and, having no profession, became by necessity an author."

We usually think of Johnson as enormously self-possessed and relentlessly self-directing, always in command of the situation, but Hugo Reichard has recently called our attention to a deep strain of passivity in him.

> Boswell's Johnson is generally recognized as a character who, despite great obstacles, does well in several spheres, does so often in a long lifetime, and does so famously. Standard grounds for his success—his vast "powers" and "particularities"—have always been noted. Yet something vitally nonstandard has not been reckoned with, though it has been felt. Although men making their mark have often had to confront obstacles outside and inside themselves, with and without aid, the helps and hindrances af-

fecting Johnson's career prove unwontedly polar: it is mainly inner resistances that hold the man back, chiefly outside forces that start him, route him, and keep him going. He is grandly endowed, the world knows, for stagnation—by indolence and torpor, delays and glooms, breaches of resolutions as well as of manners, a lack both of short-run initiative and long-run ambitious drive. What he badly needs, others come prepared to give; and what he massively takes from them amounts not merely to help but also to guidance.

Reichard goes on to show how regularly Boswell, the Thrales, Langton, Dodsley, and other friends had to "start" Johnson, in conversation, on journeys, to dinners, and on writing; and it can be said with equal truth that printers, booksellers, and printing also motivated him again and again. Not only Johnson's many occasional pieces, but all the great Johnsonian writing projects, excluding only the very personal writings like the poems and the prayers and meditations, have a standard history in which print is involved at several levels. The catalogue of the Harleian library, the *Dictionary*, the Shakespeare edition, the *Ramblers* and *Adventurers*, *The Lives of the Poets* were all either commissioned by the printers and publishers, or planned by Johnson himself as commercial publishing ventures. For example, *Rasselas*, that most Johnsonian of works, was written, to pay—at least so Johnson said—his mother's funeral expenses. Furthermore, the works were themselves typical print projects, made conceivable and possible by print, and distinctly bearing the impress of print logic: a printed catalogue of printed books, a set of poets' biographies designed as introductions to a collection of poems intended to maintain publishers' copyrights, a dictionary in which all words printed in books of a certain period are systematically listed and objectively defined by their usage in printed books, and an authoritative edition of Shakespeare constructed by comparing the earliest printed texts.

Print made Johnson a writer, first of all, by shaping and publishing his writings, but it also reached deep into his life to
structure his identity as a writer as well. A few examples—his
patterns of work, the consequences of author's copyright, the
end of patronage—will show how print actually determined
the writer's identity in direct, objective ways. But as we watch a
print-based authorial identity taking shape, we will also begin
to see how Johnson, working with and within print realities,
also adjusted and extended these same realities in ways that
maximized the dignity and social importance of the writer.

The Writer's Work Patterns

In the life of the professional writer, print's logical tendencies
of multiplicity and system were experienced as the need to
write a great deal by laboring long and regularly to produce a
steady flow of copy to meet the deadlines of printer and bookseller. Johnson, over his lifetime, wrote so much that Johnsonian scholars, notably Donald Greene and John Abbott, are still
attempting with great difficulties to assemble a catalogue of all
he wrote. He wrote for the most part whatever he and his employers thought would sell or help to sell books: introductions,
prefaces, advertisements, translations, articles on Amazons or
taxation, reports of parliamentary debates or library sale catalogues, a dictionary, an edition of Shakespeare, short biographies, and on and on. He may even have written a famous series of lectures on the law and volumes of sermons that appear
under the names of other writers. Subdued to what he worked
in, he accepted and could even praise the orderly labor and the
structured time that printing projects and their deadlines imposed on his daily life. His *Prayers and Meditations* constantly de-
plore wasted time and sinful sloth and reveal that the Weber-
Tawney thesis of the close connection of Protestantism and
Capitalism was never lived out more painfully than it was by
Samuel Johnson. He always met his commitments, eventually,

to provide the printers with the copy they had to have to keep the presses running, and he learned from them the hard lessons of why steady labor was necessary. We have seen him, for example, promising Strahan that he would instantly correct his *Dictionary* proofs after it had been pointed out to him that the printer was losing time and money by keeping his press standing idle and his type locked up while waiting for the author's corrections.

But while Johnson may have bragged that "a man may write at any time if he will set himself doggedly to it," accepting writing as labor, rather than the more noble activity Arendt calls "work," he always had extraordinary difficulties in setting himself to it, and many of his major writings, like the edition of Shakespeare and the *Dictionary*, were notorious for their long delays. When the last sheet of the *Dictionary* copy was finally delivered to the bookseller in charge of the project, Andrew Millar's exclamation, "thank GOD I have done with him," suggests just how difficult working with Johnson could be for a businessman with schedules to meet. Johnson constantly reproached himself for his habitual lack of punctuality, remarking sadly in 1781, for example, that he had "finished the 'Lives of the Poets,' which I wrote in my usual way, dilatorily and hastily, unwilling to work, and working with vigour and haste." This seems to have been his pattern: long periods in which nothing was done, followed by bursts of intense activity in which a very great deal was done quickly and efficiently because he had, like the professional writer he was, trained himself to think clearly and developed a reliable first-draft style: "he had early laid it down as a fixed rule . . . to impart whatever he knew in the most forcible language he could put it in; and . . . by constant practice, and never suffering any careless expressions to escape him, or attempting to deliver his thoughts without arranging them in the clearest manner, it became habitual to him." Even his conversation, Boswell tells us, was so "clear and perspicuous; and his language was so accurate, and his sentences so neatly constructed," that it "might have been all printed without any correction."

In this and other ways, the laborer in the book factory accepted the necessities of his print situation but managed them in such a way as to transform writing into a profession, and taking pride in the skill, speed, and certainty with which he performed his work. He laughed at Lord Lyttleton's "extreme anxiety as an authour" and at the thirty years that amateur spent preparing his book for publication, remarking proudly that he and his friend Murphy as professional writers "never felt that anxiety, but sent what we wrote to the press, and let it take its chance." He wrote his *Ramblers*, he said, "just as they were wanted for the press," sending off "a certain portion of the copy of an essay" and writing "the remainder, while the former part of it was printing. When it was wanted, and he had fairly sat down to it, he was sure it would be done." And when it was done, Johnson, confident of his ability as a writer, expended little or no labor in revision:

> Mr. Langton remembers Johnson, when on a visit at Oxford, asking him one evening how long it was till the post went out; and on being told about half an hour, he exclaimed, 'then we shall do very well.' He upon this instantly sat down and finished an Idler, which it was necessary should be in London the next day. Mr. Langton having signified a wish to read it, 'Sir, (said he) you shall not do more than I have done myself.' He then folded it up and sent it off.

He not only accepted but boasted that his writing often had little to do with inspiration, remarking that it might always be done at any place or time, on any subject, if the writer set himself "doggedly" to it. He did not invent his subjects, he said with pride, but wrote what was needed, adding bravely that if necessary, "he could write the Life of a Broomstick." He also openly acknowledged, even flaunted, his status as a wage-earner: "No man but a blockhead ever wrote, except for money."

In making the labor of writing into professional work, Johnson did not escape into Savage's romances or Smart's fictions, but accepted and arranged the real situation that print offered in the most attractive manner possible. Print made him a writer and defined his subjects, his workload, even to some degree the way he wrote and spoke. Johnson fulfilled his commitments by providing over his lifetime an enormous amount of copy for finishing by the printer and distribution by the bookseller, but he did so not as a drudge but as a proud and efficient professional. Furthermore, the irregularity of his working patterns allowed him to escape being simply a hired writer who regularly sent his copy to the printer on time, and made him into an author who did not work to the factory whistle but freely determined when and how he would write. It was an ingenious and characteristically Johnsonian compromise, a way of saying indirectly to the printers and to the world what he had said privately to his king, that the writer controls writing. In the end his work habits, whatever their cause, even restored to his writing a touch of mystery and suspense, perhaps for himself as well as others. Boswell fixed the image: "I never could discover," he tells us, "how he found time for his compositions. He declaimed all the morning, then went to dinner at a tavern, where he commonly staid late, and then drank his tea at some friend's house, over which he loitered a great while, but seldom took supper. I fancy he must have read and wrote chiefly in the night, for I can scarcely recollect that he ever refused going with me to a tavern, and he often went to Ranelagh, which he deemed a place of innocent recreation."

Copyright and the Writer's Identity

In western society there is no firmer way to authenticate an identity than to give it status in law, and writers were legally objectified by the English copyright act of 1709, the first in the world, though there were earlier special arrangements, in Venice for example, for protecting the ownership of texts. Copyright did not come to France until 1777, and then only in an ineffective form, and still later in Prussia. The full title of the statute, "An Act for the Encouragement of Learning by Vesting the Copies of Printed Books in the Authors or Purchasers of Such Copies," makes clear the intent of the act. The spread of knowledge is the stated aim, and it is to be achieved by defining books as property owned by those who write them or purchase them from the writers. After the Act of 1709, an author was in law a person who owns the books he or she writes, and books were, as Frye says, "an invention distinctive enough to be patented." The creation of this reciprocal legal identity for writers and their work was the product of print at a number of levels. First, the printing press had made writing into books, solid fixed objects with a real marketplace value, and therefore property to be bought and sold in a way that an oral poem or the few copies of a manuscript never could be. Secondly, as if to declare print's interest in the matter, it was the publishing industry which lobbied for and brought about the copyright act, with consequences which, as we shall see, no one quite anticipated.

Until about 1700, the right to print was a royal prerogative, exercised negatively by the crown as censorship, and positively as the right to license presses and confer exclusive permission to print certain categories of books, such as law texts or prayer books. No book could legally be printed unless it had been passed by the censor and entered by a licensed printer in the register of the Company of Stationers, the booksellers' guild. Once entered and printed, however, *perpetual* rights under common law were vested in the bookseller or printer who made the entry, and any unregistered manuscript or book that fell into the hands of a member of the Company could be claimed by him as his property by entering and printing. This kind of legalized piracy seems to have troubled almost no one, for while a few writers, notably and oddly, George Wither, protested that authors should own their writing, the majority do not seem to have conceived of their work as property of which they were the legal owners. Johnson was aware of this earlier attitude and contrasted it to that of his own time: "consider how long it was before writing came to be considered in a pecuniary view. Baretti says, he is the first man that ever received copy-money in Italy."

In 1695 the Licensing Act, which had legalized censorship, was allowed to lapse—largely because of resentment of the monopoly rights it conferred on certain powerful printers and booksellers. As one consequence, all existing copyrights were voided, which left the printing business in a state of anarchy and deprived the Stationers' members of valuable copyrights in which they had a great deal of capital invested. Their agonized reaction eventually brought about the 1709 Act, making authors, not publishers, the primary proprietors of their works, which could now legally be assigned to a publisher for only two separate fourteen-year periods before entering public domain. Why copyright ended up in the hands of writers instead of publishers is suggested by the petition of a group of booksellers recorded in the *Journal of the House of Commons* (26 February 1706, o.s.) when the matter was being considered; it reads in part: "many learned Men have spent much Time, and been at great Charges, in composing Books, who used to dispose of their Copies upon valuable Considerations, to be printed by the Purchasers . . . but of late Years such Properties have been much invaded, by other Persons printing the same Books. . . ." It seems a likely inference that while it was the booksellers who were pushing the issue, they were using the author's rights as a blind for their own interests. No one, however, seems to have recognized the radical change of ownership from printer to writer that had occurred in the statute, and after its passage all went on, as they had before, selling and purchasing what the booksellers and authors still assumed to be perpetual rights in books old and new. Serious challenges to these practices, which remained at odds with the 1709 statute, came later along in the century when the Scotch printer Donaldson began to publish cheap editions, notably of Thomson's *Seasons*, of writing by then in the public domain under the 1709 statute. He was successfully challenged by the proprietors of the copyright in the lower courts, which held that the common-law doctrine of perpetual right in property legally owned was applicable to the texts of books as to land or houses; but Donaldson then appealed to the House of Lords, which in 1774 affirmed the earlier statute and thereby ruled in his favor.

As we might expect in a matter so central to letters as the legal definition of authors and their rights in their writing, Johnson was deeply concerned. Boswell in an earlier case had defended Donaldson in the Scottish courts, and Arthur Murphy drew up "the plea against the perpetual right" in Lords. The central issue as Johnson first perceived it was a shared interest of authors and booksellers in defending literary property against piratical printers and an unreasonable view of the public benefit to be derived from cheap, readily available books. He was, Boswell says, very angry when in 1763 Donaldson opened a shop and began to sell his books at low prices in London, and he was much concerned "that the Booksellers of London, for whom he uniformly professed much regard, should suffer from an invasion of what they had ever considered to be secure. . . ." When it was pointed out to him that Donaldson made books available to poor students who could not otherwise afford them, Johnson responded truculently that he was still "no better than Robin Hood, who robbed the rich in order to give to the poor."

While he continued throughout his life to support the

printer and bookseller in what he considered just claims to protection of investments in copyright, Johnson also gradually developed the particular possibilities for the profit and dignity of authors latent in authors' owning their work. At first he was content merely to begin to think of the writer as a man whose ideas were income-producing property, cautioning Thomas Warton in a letter of 27 October 1757, for example, to keep confidential several plans for books Johnson had outlined to him, because "the schemes of a writer are his property and revenue, and therefore they must not be made common." But then the Donaldson case forced deeper thought about how long the writer should retain rights in his work, and Johnson began to consider that written work might be quite different from the products of a laborer worthy of his hire, or even, perhaps, the lands that a gentleman purchased or inherited. Since the writer "created," not just made, bought, or received, his property, authors, he concluded, had "a stronger right of property than that by occupancy; a metaphysical right, a right, as it were, of creation, which should from its nature be perpetual." Copyright, we might say, encouraged Johnson to think of the writer as the *author* of his work in the fullest and most explicit sense of that word. But perpetuity, he wrote Strahan, was not realizable, or perhaps even desirable, in actuality, and so Johnson without surrendering any of the author's metaphysical status as creator, has him enter into a social contract in which he yields so much of his rights as will benefit society in return for its protection: "The Authour has a natural and peculiar right to the profits of his own work. But as every Man who claims the protection of Society, must purchase it by resigning some part of his natural right, the authour must recede from so much of his claim, as shall be deemed injurious or inconvenient to Society."

The history of the development of Johnson's writer into an author with "a natural and peculiar right" to his writing, while making it available to all, provides a perfect small-scale example of how literary reality was socially made. The components are complexly related and numerous—the lapsing of the Licensing Act, the booksellers' need to protect their property, the copyright law of 1709 vesting copyright in the author, Donaldson's perception of the possibility of quick profits, the Enlightenment's interest in the spread of knowledge, and the desire of poor writers like Samuel Johnson, who worked for the printing press, to claim dignity wherever they could find it. Beyond these social and psychic immediacies, it is possible to perceive many other ideas at work, such as the traditional importance claimed for the poet by earlier writers like Milton and Pope, and the growing democratic tendencies of the age heard in the words "natural and peculiar right." The line leading indirectly but continuously through all these events, men, institutions, and ideas to Johnson's conception of the writer as the creator of his work, with metaphysical rights validated now by the majesty of law, is a concrete instance of what Gossman describes more abstractly as "the identification of works with individual graphically recorded utterances [that] led to a conception of literary creation as absolutely original production, arising out of and in some way embodying a unique, substantial and autonomous self." The movement is long, complex and roundabout, in the way of history rather than philosophy; but in the end, the author stands out sharply real against the social background, as a creator and as a valuable and cooperative member of a society.

Patronage and the Independent Writer

The development of the author can be traced by another path leading through the relationship of the professional writer and the patron. It was, of course, print that created the conditions that eventually separated the writer from the patron, and the

social order he represented, by providing writers with a new
way of earning a living—writing for a reading public. No great
writer before Johnson, it can be argued with considerable assurance, either made or fully accepted that he made his living
from the sale of his writing to the bookseller and through him
to the public to the extent that Johnson did. Shakespeare
earned most of his wealth from the theater and appears to have
avoided publication. Milton sold *Paradise Lost* for £5 simply to
get it printed. Dryden published his works and made most of
his money from plays but he was still deeply involved in patronage and derived income from land. Pope made a considerable
amount of money from publication, but he carefully avoided
the attitudes and appearance of a writer for hire. Johnson
could, therefore, rightly boast to Boswell that "No man . . . who
ever lived by literature, has lived more independently than I
have done." But it would also be possible to say with justice that
few writers worried the question of patronage so persistently as
did Johnson. Jacob Leed estimates that more than one-fifth of
the *Ramblers* deal fairly directly with the matter, and that many
others take up the central issues involved in patronage. Johnson, as Boswell often points out, never made a fortune from his
writing, and his famous generosity to other writers and to numerous poor friends and dependents constantly depleted his
resources. But he did earn a living by his writing, and in the last
twenty years of his life, as J. D. Fleeman points out in an analysis of Johnson's writing income, he did fairly well. "In very
rough terms it can be said that Johnson's income after 1762 was
nominally in excess of £300 p.a., and it was perhaps as much as
£400 for perhaps a quarter of that period. Over a twenty-one-
year period therefore the pension and his other earnings
would have produced £6800, perhaps even £7000, and Johnson died worth little less than £3000. This means that he was
able to save over 40 percent of his income, despite his carelessness of money." His income derived mainly from the "gener-

ous, liberal-minded men," as he sometimes called the booksellers, who were now, he rightly understood and said, "the
patrons of literature." They could confer independence and
therefore dignity on even so poor a writer as the hack Derrick:
"consider that his being a literary man has got for him all that
he has. It has made him King of Bath. Sir, he has nothing to say
for himself but that he is a writer. Had he not been a writer, he
must have been sweeping the crossings in the street, and asking
halfpence from every body that past."

Most of Grub Street made little or nothing of its freedom
from the patron, merely exchanging one kind of servitude for
another; but Johnson perceived and realized its full potential
for writers in the famous exchange with Lord Chesterfield. In
1746 Johnson had grudgingly addressed his plan for a dictionary to Chesterfield, the official *arbiter elegantiarum* of language
in Hanoverian England, who signified his acceptance of the patron's role by giving Johnson £10. But in the nine years between the plan and its fulfillment in 1755, Chesterfield expressed no interest and gave no help, though he may not have
treated Johnson as badly as appears in the popular story of the
humble drudge left to wait in the anteroom while the noble
lord conversed at length with Pope's king of dunces, Colley
Cibber. But in 1754, when the *Dictionary* was about to appear,
Chesterfield was willing to play the part of the patron again in
order to gratify his noted vanity and explicitly assert once again
the implicit claim of the patronage system that letters derived
their greatness and language its standards from the manners,
tastes, and values of the ruling class. And so he smoothly, without, I believe, any sense of what was really happening, gave the
work his imprimatur in a published article—"I therefore recommend the previous perusal of [the *Plan*] to all those who in-
tend to buy the Dictionary, and who, I suppose, are all those
who can afford it"—and sat back graciously to wait for a gift
copy with its expected subservient, flattering dedicatory letter

of the type that had prefaced most printed works for three hundred years. Even after the explosion, he still tried to carry it off. Dodsley, who had a large financial stake in the *Dictionary*, and perhaps something still of the servant's reverence for a noble lord, but no understanding that he and print had made Johnson's actions possible, rushed at once to Chesterfield to smooth things over. He found that Chesterfield had laid the letter "upon his table, where any body might see it. He read it to me; said, 'this man has great powers,' pointed out the severest passages, and observed how well they were expressed."

The letter on the table was, of course, Johnson's famous Letter to Lord Chesterfield, a short but powerful document that still stands as the Magna Carta of the modern author, the public announcement that the days of courtly letters were at last ended, that the author was the true source of his work, and that he and it were no longer dependent on the patron or the social system he represented: "Seven years, my Lord, have now past, since I waited in your outward rooms, or was repulsed from your door; during which time I have been pushing on my work through difficulties, of which it is useless to complain, and have brought it, at last, to the verge of publication, without one act of assistance, one word of encouragement, or one smile of favour."

Here as so often in his writing life, Johnson was not entirely clear of the old literary arrangements, even as he enacted the new. He had accepted in 1762 a pension of £300 a year from the crown, at a time when he was exhausted, on the edge of mental breakdown, and the to him munificent sum seemed at long last an escape from "the hardship of writing for bread." The pension was elaborately hedged about with civilities on both sides, and George III's minister, Lord Bute, assured Johnson that "It is not given you for any thing you are to do, but for what you have done." Throughout his life Johnson heatedly maintained that the pension was for literary merit alone—"Here, Sir, was a man avowedly no friend to Government at the time, who got a pension without asking for it. I never courted the great; they sent for me." When the administration did approach him in 1775 "to write political pamphlets . . . he was even so much irritated, that he declared his resolution to resign his pension." But he did not resign it, he may even have done some political writing for it, and he was involved in the government patronage system throughout his life. His friends, Thomas Sheridan, Arthur Murphy, and Sir Joshua Reynolds had labored mightily, and probably with his knowledge, to obtain the pension for him in the first place; Strahan tried to get him a seat in Commons by promising that he would show stability and support the administration; Lord North was said to have paid him £200 for political pamphlets; and even as Johnson lay dying, Boswell and Reynolds were, unsuccessfully, trying to get the government to provide funds to send him to Italy where it was hoped he might recover.

Just what services he may have provided in return for his pension will never be known for certain. Donald Greene in his magisterial book, *The Politics of Samuel Johnson*, has argued convincingly that none of Johnson's political writings violates his lifelong principles, but some of his contemporary admirers were amazed and disturbed when he wrote in the 1760s and '70s a number of strident polemical pamphlets defending government policy in North America and elsewhere. Like other social institutions, "our Poetical Church and State," as Dryden once called it, did not change all at once, and Johnson perhaps puts the patronage matter about as satisfactorily as possible for an author who earned his living and thought about his writing somewhere between the old and the new conceptions of the writer's place in society: "I think that the pleasure of cursing the House of Hanover, and drinking King James's health, are amply overbalanced by three hundred pounds a year."

Social Identities and Cultural Roles

"To look at cultural events," Thomas McFarland perceptively remarks, "is like looking at stars in the night sky," and the dark Johnsonian sky was dotted with a multitude of lights: rhetoric, languages, Christian theology, the politics of Walpole and the Hanoverian kings, the profits of Thrale's brewery, the satires of Juvenal, the great city of London, the paintings of Sir Joshua Reynolds, the Drury Lane theater where David Garrick acted, the conversation of Edmund Burke, Topham Beauclerk, and Bennet Langton, and the extensive literary galaxy of eighteenth-century London, the studies and libraries, the editorial offices of magazines, the print shops, Grub-Street garrets, and booksellers' back rooms, a swarm of books, pamphlets, journals, and newspapers. In this area, Johnson made for himself a literary identity of considerable magnitude and brightness as a professional writer for the marketplace, skilled and capable, extremely knowledgeable, the hard-headed intellectual of independent mind and habits, writing in a powerful and distinguished style. He fitted into, understood, and worked well within the new print circumstances of letters, the world of booksellers, large libraries, copyrights and common readers, printers' deadlines and cash flow, literary criticism and book-markets. And, as we have already seen, using print facts such as work schedules, copyright, and independence from patronage, he made a reputation for himself as an important writer in the age of print. In subsequent chapters we will see further major examples of the various ways that Johnson used print circumstances to enhance his own reputation, which gradually grew to that of a literary dictator, and to establish new values for letters in language, criticism, bibliography, and literary history.

Johnson would have been a considerable person and an English writer of note even without Boswell; but the somewhat odd and limited nature of even that part of his *oeuvre* that stands out from the great mass of his occasional writing—a dictionary, an edition of Shakespeare, a few imitative poems, a series of essays, a collection of biographies of the English poets, an oriental tale—would by itself have given him a less archetypical place than he presently enjoys. Without Boswell, to put it another way, Johnson would surely have been an important writer, and an interesting, powerful personality, but probably not the literary type that he is, the towering and highly charged image of the first writer in the industrial, democratic, rationalistic age of print. Nor would the many other Johnson biographies have fixed him as the type of the writer in literary history and cultural consciousness so vividly and lastingly as Boswell's *Life of Johnson*. That is, I suppose, a truism, scarcely worth saying, but its consequences seem seldom to have been either fully accepted or followed out along the track of the strange Johnson-Boswell relationship.

The power to make not just an individual literary identity, such as Johnson made for himself, but a poetic role of the first magnitude that blazes in the cultural sky and orients the lives of other writers is as rare as the great writers who have achieved it, Dante, for example, or Milton, Wordsworth, Byron, Eliot, Frost, or Joyce. Or Johnson, after Boswell. There is always at least something of a mystery about this transformation of writers into the type of the poet. How did Castiglione in *The Courtier* put his amateur aristocratic poet so at ease in the Renaissance court that he remained the *beau idéal* of writers for two hundred years? Why did Byron, or Hemingway, by way of modern example, succeed in making their lives, as much as, perhaps more than, their works, an image of the poetic sensibility? What made Wordsworth's romantic visionary, leaving behind the urban industrial world and returning to nature, childhood, and the rural past in *The Prelude*, the cynosure of the scene of writing throughout the nineteenth century? What was Joyce's power to shape in the inward and isolated figure of Stephen Dedalus wandering the modern wasteland of *Ulysses* the image of art and sensitivity in our time? It is not only a matter of getting the social conditions and the conceptual interests of a time and place just right—though these are important components of the poetic role. A kind of human energy or power of being is also critically involved in poet-making (using "poet" as the most prestigious generic name for the writer) which is much illuminated, both negatively and positively, by the Boswell-Johnson relationship.

Johnson seems to us totally real, almost overwhelmingly so, forcing his literary personality and his absolute authority on people and on society by the vigor of his style, the range of his knowledge, the incontrovertibility of his judgments, the clarity and force of his mind, the monumentality of his writings, the eccentricity of his appearance and manner, and the violence of his argument, to achieve, at last, the gigantic self of Dr. Johnson. His potency as an author-maker extends even beyond himself to the making of many other writers, both his predecessors and his contemporaries, as well as his successors, strengthening their reality by talking about and praising them, editing and criticizing their works, providing explanatory introductions to their books, and, above all, writing their lives. "The biographical part of literature . . . is what I love most," Johnson observed, and *The Lives of the Poets* realized both that love and Johnson's ability to make writers real in the world. Cowley, Milton, Dryden, Savage, and Pope were not made by Johnson in the same way that he made his own identity as professional writer, but once Johnson had written their lives, isolated them from other kinds of lives not involved with poetry, and linked them to one another in the stabilizing context of literary history, their reality as writers, as well as that of the writer in general, was strongly reinforced. Lawrence Lipking points precisely to what it means to make poets and the poetic role real in this way in society, and to the emptiness thus filled, when he says that *The Lives* ask "not only whether men can be happy, but whether a literary vocation can be successful . . . *The Lives of the Poets* records the professional histories of men who have tried to do something worthy of a man's attention, and thus implies that a literary vocation may do much to fill the vacuity of human life."

But for all Johnson's power as a maker of poets, his own reality as a poetic type was finally the work of Boswell. Johnson himself suffered a surprising deficiency in regard to himself in this kind of reality-making. On the surface a man known for his aggressive self-confidence and certainty of his Tory convictions, Johnson had an ego problem that Reichard identifies as a need to be "started" by others, and that appears in a classic double-bind form in his biography of Richard Savage, who is in many places a thinly disguised version of himself as a Grub Street hack and as a person. Savage's lack of real talent and success as a writer obliquely reflects Johnson's deep and endless concerns about his own literary failure, while Savage's successes, his high personal style and aristocratically careless way of life, condemn by contrast what Johnson felt to be his own personal ugliness and clumsiness.

This social deficiency takes on more nihilistic dimensions in the great biographer's inability to keep his own journal or write an autobiography. He could write about others but not about himself. Boswell tells us that although Johnson "at different times, in a desultory manner, committed to writing many particulars of the progress of his mind and fortunes, he never had persevering diligence enough to form them into a regular composition. Of these memorials a few have been preserved; but the greater part was consigned by him to the flames, a few days before his death." This is the required Virgilian gesture of the great writer, and its authenticity therefore somewhat suspect, but in Johnson's case it corresponds with genuine doubts about his own being. The few fragments of Johnson's autobiographical writings that were preserved give us a relatively direct glimpse of Johnson as an oftentimes guilt-ridden, terrified man, ailing, unhappy, uncertain, oppressed by a sense of sin and laziness, and fearful that his life was utterly meaningless, coming from and going nowhere. Goldsmith once remarked to Johnson that the Literary Club should admit some new members since the old members had by now pretty well "travelled over one another's minds." Johnson's angry retort, "Sir, you have not travelled over *my* mind, I promise you," suggests how vigorously he guarded his profoundest feelings.

But there was something deeper at work than a pronounced sense of privacy. When Boswell asked him what he would have done had he discovered that some of his journals that Boswell had surreptitiously read were missing, Johnson replied simply and immediately, "I believe I should have gone mad." Johnson apparently lived always in acute terror that his most personal experiences might be known to others, including his official biographer. He often told Boswell that if a writer "professes to write *A Life*, he must represent it really as it was," but despite this repeated view of biography as the full truth, including peculiarities and vices, he continued to avoid talking with Boswell about even the ordinary open facts of his life, notwithstanding his awareness, even satisfaction, that Boswell was writing his biography. Whenever Boswell pressed him, as he frequently did, for more detail, Johnson, though he was sometimes amiable, would often put him off, as he did at a dinner party at General Paoli's on 31 March 1772: "He did not disapprove of my curiosity as to these particulars; but said, 'They'll come out by degrees as we talk together.' "

Indolence, forgetfulness, unwillingness to recall a painful past, shame, desire to protect inmost feelings, these were obvious impediments to putting the full truth of his life into the "regular composition" of an autobiography, or even a biography. Nothing very unusual about this, but it does point to a kind of modesty, perhaps even ego deficiency, that was something less than helpful in realizing the self in the world and fell far short of the levels of energy needed to make the self real as an institutional role of the writer. We take the kind of personal reality that biography records for granted, but absence rather than presence is the norm in human life. However passionately existence may be felt by individuals, the achievement of a *life*, let alone a cultural role like that of the king, the judge, the priest, or the poet, is an enormous, nearly impossible, undertaking. Johnson's understanding of the existential deficiency in most lives appears openly in some of his remarks about biography.

As Boswell and Johnson talked of biography, and they often did, they found blanks in the lives of those people they discussed, gaps which quickly opened on still emptier spaces. Johnson tells of questioning the chaplain of a late bishop, whose memoirs he was to assist in writing, only to discover that though "They only who live with a man can write his life with any genuine exactness and discrimination, . . . few people who have lived with a man know what to remark about him." Not only, the remark suggests, are people not very observant of others, nor do they remember them very distinctly, but an actual life may not itself have the kind of solidity and coherence that biography takes for granted and offers in its pages as the given human reality. The emptiness of life can be even emptier when a few details are present but these are utterly trivial and meaningless. When Johnson, trying to write a life of Dryden, questions the two living persons who had seen him, old Swinney and old Cibber, "Swinney's information was no more than this, 'That at Will's coffee-house Dryden had a particular chair for himself, which was set by the fire in winter, and was then called his winter-chair; and that it was carried out for him to the balcony in summer, and was then called his summer-chair.'

Cibber could tell no more but 'That he remembered him a de-
cent old man, arbiter of critical disputes at Will's.' " Even when
a few seemingly pertinent details do emerge, they may still be
unsuitable for biographical reality, as in the case of a nobleman
who reconverted from Catholicism simply because "he found
the rigid fasting prescribed by the church very severe upon
him." Mrs. Thrale felt strongly that such a petty motive in a
matter of such importance was unworthy of biography, and
should be suppressed. But Johnson responded with more understanding of existence: "How often are the primary motives
of our greatest actions as small as Sibbald's, for his reconver-
sion."

Being, Johnson both felt and understood, is not up to the
ontological standards of biography, and whatever fire is there, as
he remarks in a powerful passage in his life of Addison, soon
dies away: "Lives can only be written from personal knowledge, which is growing every day less, and in a short time is lost
for ever. What is known can seldom be immediately told, and
when it might be told it is no longer known. The delicate features of the mind, the nice discriminations of character, and
the minute peculiarities of conduct are soon obliterated; . . . As
the process of these narratives [*The Lives of the Poets*] is now
bringing me among my contemporaries I begin to feel myself
'walking upon ashes under which the fire is not extin-
guished. . . .' " As to achieving the status of a cultural role, the
impossibility of being *the poet* finds voice in Johnson's oriental
tale, *Rasselas*. There, in Chapter X, an idealized image of the
great poet is drawn:

> His character requires that he estimate the happiness and misery
> of every condition, observe the power of all the passions in all
> their combinations, and trace the changes of the human mind as
> they are modified by various institutions and accidental influences
> of climate or custom, from the sprightliness of infancy to the des-

pondence of decrepitude. He must divest himself of the prejudices of his age and country; he must consider right and wrong in
their abstracted and invariable state; he must disregard present
laws and opinions, and rise to general and transcendental truths,
which will always be the same.

Upon hearing these requirements, the Prince of Abyssinia concludes, practically, that "no human being can ever be a poet,"
nor can Johnson's imaginary poet, Imlac, rise to the heights of
this ideal. He accompanies Rasselas on his journeys as a tutor,
and offers quiet instruction on the melancholy realities of life,
but in the end he and his scientific companion, the astronomer,
"were contented to be driven along the stream of life, without
directing their course to any particular port." Johnson did,
however, eventually become the writer in the age of print, not
so much from his own ontological energies, which were intermittent, but out of the needs and art of James Boswell.

The Hero as Man-of-Letters

In the long portrait gallery of western writers, Boswell's "Flemish" picture of Johnson stands out sharply in size, detail, energy, colorful intensity. Many writers before Johnson may
have, certainly did, write greater books, but even the most in-
dividualized of them, a Petrarch or a Milton, let alone the
anonymous Shakespeare, seem alongside him pale, fading, a
few thin lines without much depth, shading, or emotional
color. His intense personality, in a way the first romantic artist,
appears at exactly the right point in literary history in several
ways, the kind of poor, strange, troubled person that the print
business could attract and use as a Grub Street hack, and, at the
same time, the type of individual who needed and could use
print to satisfy certain existential needs of his own for bread,
for status, for meaning. But it went beyond this, and in the end,
out of their own needs, Johnson and Boswell together created

a social role that transcended individual needs, giving writers
an important social function and making books, even in the
vast numbers now produced by the printing press, something
more than mere information, amusement, and commodity.
Johnson and Boswell, in my opinion, worked in the same general directions in making the writer, and there is no need,
though it would be possible, to identify, as William McCarthy
has, a "Piozzi's Johnson," or even a "Johnson's Johnson" who
was different in some ways from Boswell's Johnson. In the following pages I therefore freely mix evidence from the *Life*,
from other biographical writings, and from Johnson's own
works. But without Boswell, Johnson would slip away from us,
for it is the *Life* that fixes him in time, highlights what is crucial,
and structures the material in memorable form, in ways that
the "Caldwell Minute" clearly exemplifies.

Thomas Carlyle, though he badly underestimated the writer
he familiarly and inevitably called Bozzy, did understand very
well what he had wrought. As a writer for the printing press
who earned his living by that means, Carlyle recognized how
profoundly print had changed the writer's world: "Never, till
about a hundred years ago, was there seen any figure of a
Great Soul living apart in that anomalous manner; endeavour-
ing to speak-forth the inspiration that was in him by Printed
Books, and find place and subsistence by what the world would
please to give him for doing that." Nor did he miss what he also
felt in himself, the emptiness and hunger for meaning in Johnson "with his scrofulous diseases, with his great greedy heart,
and unspeakable chaos of thoughts; stalking mournful as a
stranger in this Earth; eagerly devouring what spiritual thing
he could come at: school-languages and other merely grammatical stuff. . . ." Carlyle also saw sympathetically how little of
a hero Johnson was to himself: "A hard-struggling, weary-
hearted man, or 'scholar' as he calls himself, trying hard to get
some honest livelihood in the world, not to starve, but to live—

without stealing! . . . He does not 'engrave *Truth* on his watch-seal'; no, but he stands by truth, speaks by it, works and lives by it."

In the end Carlyle recognizes in Boswell's Johnson the culture hero as Man-of-Letters: "He, with his copy-rights and copy-wrongs, in his squalid garret, in his rusty coat; ruling . . . from his grave, after death, whole nations and generations who would, or would not, give him bread while living—is a rather curious spectacle! " This figure has to be understood, Carlyle perceived, in his historical setting, "the *spiritual paralysis*, so we may name it, of the Age in which his life lay; whereby his life too, do what he might, was half-paralysed! " "The Eighteenth," Carlyle goes on, "was a *Sceptical* Century," and as he warms to his work the great romantic declares the Enlightenment to have been "boundless bottomless abysses of Doubt, of wretched god-forgetting Unbelief; . . ." Against this emotionally overstated but not intellectually inaccurate view of the eighteenth century, Carlyle found Boswell's Johnson to be the writer as a romantic hero, "speaking still in some sort from the heart of Nature," with a gnostic certainty of transcendent truth which it is his work to make known to the world: "To his large, open, deep-feeling heart Nature is a Fact: all hearsay is hearsay; the unspeakable greatness of this Mystery of Life, let him acknowledge it or not, nay even though he seem to forget it or deny it, is ever present to *him*—fearful and wonderful. . . ."

Subsequent writers have disagreed with Carlyle's picture of Johnson as the struggler against meaninglessness and hopelessness only in their understanding of the mode in which he opposed them. For Macaulay and most of the nineteenth and early twentieth centuries, he became the great Tory, the rational defender of the old order, the last voice, quirky and eccentric, but authoritative, of neoclassical values in a time of radical skepticism and social change. This remains still today pretty much the public's received standard view of Johnson, but the last two generations of Johnsonian scholars, re-examining the evidence, have gradually replaced the authoritarian Johnson with a much more complex Johnson, skeptical, deeply troubled in mind, mad at times, neurotic nearly always, radically doubtful of himself and of the social values he at the same time so stoutly defended. The evidence was always there, in Boswell and in Johnson's own writings, but recent scholarship has brought this darker Johnson into the foreground and put him into play with the more traditional Johnson with his firm grasp on reality and definite opinions—"The truth of the matter is, Sir"—on all subjects. As a result, Johnson has become more interestingly complex and the characteristic Johnsonian scene more dramatic. The famous incident at Harwich, for example, where he kicks the stone to refute Berkeley's idealism no longer demonstrates just his sure common sense, or Carlyle's gnostic certainty, but becomes a complicated gesture in which the very violence of the action both asserts that what the senses perceive is obviously real *and* expresses at the same time a powerful need to prove it in a conclusive way. This existential Johnson is still a voice of truth, as Carlyle and Macaulay saw, in a time of grave doubts, but the very force with which his truths are stated in speech or in writing, now directs attention to the near desperation of the effort and the unstable foundations on which the statements of truth are constructed. This is a modern Johnson who accords with the needs of our own time, and may be somewhat suspect for this reason, but he has always been there in the *Life*, where he became the image of the writer needed to authenticate letters and the life of writing in the age of print.

CHAPTER IV

THE WRITER AS CULTURE HERO:
BOSWELL'S JOHNSON

Boswell's Writing and the LIFE OF JOHNSON

Unlike Johnson, Boswell was consciously troubled by few philosophical or practical doubts about the possibility or the truth of biography. His life of Johnson was for him an exact report of the real life of an actual man, Samuel Johnson, who, he confidently boasts, "will be seen in this work more completely than any man who has ever yet lived. And he will be seen as he really was; . . ." To support this claim to literal truth, Boswell offers a great deal of evidence for the accuracy of his record: his intimate acquaintance with Johnson, scrupulous on-the-spot copies of conversations and his ability to record information precisely by means of an abbreviated but accurate method of taking notes. His biographical method, he argues, allows him to reproduce reality exactly by including in his "Flemish" picture the small details of Johnson's life, faults in the character, conversations which reveal the real truth of the man, and excerpts from Johnson's own letters and writing. Furthermore, Boswell tells us, he took great pains in assembling the materials when he came to the actual writing of the biography, questioning friends, ascertaining dates, and collecting letters and scattered writings.

By and large, history has accepted Boswell's claims to have given us Johnson in all his depth and fullness, and the *Life* has been enshrined as the first true biography and a model for those written since. Scholars such as Geoffrey Scott, Frederick Pottle, and Marshall Waingrow, who have examined the relation of Boswell's other papers to the *Life*, and the *Life* to other contemporary accounts of Johnson, have concluded that Boswell achieved a high standard of accuracy in his description of Johnson. Nor did Johnson on the occasion when he read Boswell's journal during their trip through the Hebrides object to any distortion or inaccuracy. Rather, as Brady makes clear in his discussion of this matter, Johnson was on the whole well pleased with what Boswell had written, and in a letter (19 June 1775) to Mrs. Thrale, who had also read the journal at Boswell's invitation, Johnson expatiated, "He moralised, and found my faults, and laid them up to reproach me. Boswell's narrative is very natural, and therefore very entertaining. . . ."

But there is still some considerable distance between Boswell's printed pages and the historical Johnson. We have already seen one important example of the problem in the contrast of the "Caldwell Minute" and Boswell's description of Johnson's meeting with the king. But it is not just a simple matter of Boswell adjusting the perspective, or getting a few facts wrong, or disagreeing in significant ways with the earlier biographies by his rivals, Sir John Hawkins and Mrs. Piozzi. There are more radical questions about how well Boswell really knew Johnson, not only in some deep psychological sense, but also in the most literal sense of the amount of time they were actually together. It is easy to read Boswell's book and get the impression that they were in constant contact throughout their lives, but they did not meet until 1763, when Boswell was twenty-two and Johnson was already fifty-four, past the years of greatest struggle and well established as a public figure. It has been estimated that in subsequent years they saw each other on only 425 days, of which 100 were concentrated in the tour of the Hebrides. The distance between Johnson and Boswell's *Life* increases further still when we remember that Boswell's plan to write the biography was first recorded in 1772—Johnson was probably told and approved only in 1773—and the writing did not begin, though plans were made earlier, until well after Johnson's death in 1784.

The space between Boswell's book and reality opened even wider in this century when the discovery and examination of Boswell's unpublished papers, particularly his intimate journals, revealed how little Boswell had told us of the truth about himself in the *Life*. He may have told as much about Johnson as he actually knew, but his veracity in general becomes less certain when we learn, for example, from his *London Journal* that the sober, serious, morally earnest young Scot who meets Johnson in 1763 in the *Life* is, if not an outright fiction, only one small part of a very odd and complex man who was writing freely in his journal about picking up whores in the park, the large size of his sexual apparatus, and attacks of venereal disease; who was fawning on the great in order to get a commission in a guards regiment, struggling with fundamental religious doubts, engaging in a violent authority conflict with his father, and trying to deal with strong opposing feelings of radical inferiority and superiority as a Scot and as an individual.

As the enormous cache of Boswell papers has been discovered in old Scottish houses and Irish castles, sorted out, and gradually published, it has become possible to understand a great deal about how the *Life* was written; and almost all that we have learned further increases the distance between the actual man Samuel Johnson and the written biography. Boswell first wrote notes in his version of shorthand about his meetings and conversations with Johnson either at the time, or, more often, some time after the recorded occasion. Then, sometimes sooner and sometimes later, these notes were used as the basis for entries, not copied verbatim, in one of the journals Boswell kept fairly consistently throughout his life. The notes were then destroyed, though a few survive. Years later, after Johnson's death in 1784 and when Boswell was working on the *Life* in the later '80s, the journals, already several removes from

Johnson, and unverifiable by comparison with the destroyed notes which were the first record of events, provided basic materials—they were not reprinted exactly or in chronological order—for the biography.

But Boswell was a careful and zealous researcher, and he solicited information from and questioned many of Johnson's old friends and acquaintances. This material has recently been assembled and printed by the Johnson scholar, Marshall Waingrow, in preparation for writing the definitive book on the subject, and in the aggregate it makes it clear how very hard and thoroughly Boswell worked to collect and verify his material. He, for example, invented an early form of questionnaire for Francis Barber, Johnson's black servant and, in some ways, almost his adopted child:

1. Where was you born? When did you come to England? How was you introduced to Dr. Johnson? At what age did you become his servant? Was you then free?
2. How long was you at sea? In what year did he send you to school in the country? How long did you continue there? Under whose care was you? What were you taught?
3. Where did your Master and Mistress live when you first came to Dr. Johnson? If in London in what part?

He actively pursued and used such trivia as that provided by William Bowles (*not* the poet Coleridge admired) in a letter of 9 November 1787: "It is very singular that Dr. Johnson had no idea of the use of a Barometer and that he even obstinately maintained that no man living that he knew thought it of any use. To the variations of the Thurmometer [*sic*] he was pretty constantly attentive. The Dr. valued himself a good deal on being able to do every thing for himself. He visited without a servant when he went to stay at the houses of his friends, and found few or no occasions to employ the servants belonging to the family. He knew how to mend his own stockings to darn his linen or to sew on a button on his cloaths. 'I am not (he would often say) an helpless man.' "

But the Waingrow collection also makes it very clear how selective and diverse Boswell's materials were, how dependent the *Life* finally was on weak memories, on chance, on circumstance, on personality and other random factors. Some of his inquiries were not answered; others, like Bowles's, yielded unexpected treasure. Bishop Percy delayed and edited his comments to be sure that he and others were treated fairly; Hector, Johnson's old Birmingham chum, idealized his friend and obviously fantasized their youth to increase Johnson's reputation; Frederick Barnard refused on unspecified personal grounds to allow Johnson's letter to him, quoted earlier, on buying books for the King's Library to be printed. When it came to selecting among and assembling all this aggregate, Boswell, who had always been a compulsive if erratic writer, began to have a great deal of difficulty. The period following Johnson's death and Boswell's remove to London to escape the tedium of Edinburgh and Auchinleck and write the *Life* was a very bad time for him. His lifelong tendency to depression worsened, family troubles, particularly the death of his wife, overwhelmed him, his career as a lawyer—never so distinguished as his father's—and his attempts at politics failed, and his drinking became an increasingly serious problem. In these circumstances, what he always called his "Magnum Opus" understandably faltered, and it now appears that it probably would not have been written without the help of the great literary scholar and Shakespearean, Edmond Malone. That Malone helped with the *Life* has long been known, but the Waingrow collection makes it possible to see how far that help extended. Boswell came to depend on Malone, was lost, in fact, without him, regularly dining and then working with him for several hours. The extent of Malone's involvement, even dominance, is suggested by the superior tone of master to the pupil used in a letter to Boswell of 23 December 1790: ". . . I am very glad to hear the Opus Magnum goes on so well. Pray take care of colloquialisms and vulgarisms of all sorts. Condense as much as possible, always preserving perspicuity and do not imagine the *only* defect of stile, is repetition of words. . . ." Malone's improvements were not stylistic alone but also extended to content, as is recorded— in a way that makes him sound like Jane Austen's Mr. Collins— in his letter of 8 July 1790, when he was, significantly, reading the proofs of the *Life* for Boswell: "Your compositor has gone on very smartly; and has not been delayed by me, though I am so busy. I have never seen more than two proofs. . . . I took but one liberty more than I have mentioned, which, I think, upon reflection you will approve. It was to strike out two lines in which you mention an expression which you have heard Johnson used originally in *The False Alarm*, and struck out. Why raise up against him a host of enemies, by telling a thing that need not be told, and in which perhaps your information may have been inaccurate? I do sincerely believe that my friend Lord Charlemont, if he had read that passage in your book, would have thrown it into the fire. . . ."

Somewhere in the long and complex line of transmission that leads from the man, Samuel Johnson, who actually lived, to the public role of the great writer in the age of print fixed in Boswell's biography and perceived by Carlyle—which is *the* Johnsonian reality for all except a few scholars—we begin to lose a firm grasp on any simple positivistic belief that what we have in the *Life* is a roughly accurate record of a historical figure. Expert opinion agrees that there is no question that Boswell tried very hard to depict Johnson as he and others knew him, and that he got it right in many important ways. But when we take into account the circumstances that I have just sketched of the composition of the *Life*—rather than conveniently ignoring them as we usually do—Johnson the actual man inevitably recedes from us, even as Addison did from him, carrying his own long-extinguished, intensely private fires into some deeper vagueness where, as he knew and said, existence is neither very firm nor very extensive, and in which the bits of a life that do manage to float in some form down the historical stream seem to have been a part of no very definite pattern of meaning.

The complicated and chancy nature of the long series of observers and texts involved in the writing of Boswell's biography—the notes, the journals, the letters, the correspondents, Malone's revisions, until at long last, the two quarto volumes were published on 16 May 1791—makes apparent the complexity of the social process by which what Carlyle was to call the hero as Man-of-Letters was made. The gaps between Johnson the man and Boswell's biography force us to realize that the Johnson of the *Life* who defined the role of the writer in the age of print, though based on Johnson the man, is largely the work of James Boswell. In the face of this fact, it is important to recognize the equally obvious fact that that figure was created in part to satisfy Boswell's own interests, and his needs as a man and a writer. In this way his motives for writing, and his ways of doing so, become a critical aspect of what was made, the new image of the writer.

Boswell produced during his life a gigantic cache of personal letters, notes, journals, and other written materials that has in our century appeared with comic regularity and numerosity from the cabinets, attics, croquet boxes and outbuildings of Scotland and Ireland. It seems at times that Boswell must have written more, and certainly more about himself, than any other person who ever lived. There is no question that he wrote more about himself in the sense that he recorded, more than Rousseau, perhaps more even than Casanova, both of whom were his contemporaries, the seamier and more unattractive details of his life: his coarse sexual adventures, his vanity and self-deceptions, his meanness, pettiness, even cruelty to others, particularly his remarkable wife, Margaret Montgomerie. Yet through it all come the saving mixtures of vitality with self-pity, of insatiable curiosity with strutting pomposity.

Boswell was not unique in his intense interest in writing nor in his compulsive, almost pathological, attempts to construct and maintain a full written record of the self. Memoirs, journals, files of correspondence, biographies, confessional writings—some printed, others not—were becoming a major literary genre in his time. Walpole's vast collection of letters—only recently printed in one of the most extraordinary scholarly works of this century—Cowper's and Gibbon's memoirs, Rousseau's *Confessions*, eventually Wordsworth's *Prelude*, all, along with the Boswell papers, testify to a vast eighteenth-century attempt to stabilize the self in writing. There seems to have been at this time an increasing breakdown of the older view (excepting Montaigne and a few others) that identity is established by a set of social relationships, a situation in life, and participation in historical events. As identity based on social existence waned, it was replaced with a belief—probably encouraged by reading books in privacy—that authentic being could be realized only in intense self-awareness and consciousness. John Morris points out, for example, that "Boswell is . . . one of the first to set down how it feels to live in the belief that, in point of reality, nothing exceeds the data of consciousness." The data of consciousness are evanescent, hard to realize, localize, and grasp, and autobiographical writing—like the parallel emphasis on epistemology so characteristic of post-Cartesian philosophy—became one of the primary literary modes by which uneasy people like Boswell tried to fix and retain past consciousness, and thereby objectify an elusive sense of self. As Morris says, "Basically, Boswell wishes to be always all of Boswell, the sum of his moments of consciousness, whatever that may be. He is never certain of his own nature for long [but always] insecure in the tenure of his identity. . . ."

In the definitive history of the Boswell papers, *Pride and Negligence*, F. A. Pottle suggests that the motives that account for most in the extraordinary frankness and quantity of Boswell's writing were, "a passion for being known, a hunger for self-analysis and good advice, a sheer disinterested love of the varieties of human nature, and a compulsion to extend life by a written record." In the first volume of the authoritative biography of Boswell, Pottle offers a further explanation for the compulsive writing of the journals: "The workings of his own mind fascinated him, and he relished every other variety of human nature. But the experience was not complete, not lived through, not wholly *realized*, until he had explored it verbally and had written it down. 'I should live no more than I can record,' he once wrote, 'as one should not have more corn growing than one can get in.' "

Given the power of print to fix and objectify, Boswell could have realized both his experiences and himself more concretely by printing his journals. But except for the Corsican and the Hebridean journals, which he published in modified forms, and the portions of these and other journals used in the *Life of Johnson*, the journals remained unread and unknown until the 1950s when publication began with the sensational *London Journal* covering the period of the initial meeting with Johnson. When the selected trade edition of Boswell's journals is finally completed, Boswell at last will rival Johnson, if not obscure him, as the image of *the author* of late eighteenth-century England. But, like Johnson, though for different reasons, Boswell was unable to make himself real in print, despite all his brashness, vanity, and raw desire for literary reputation. He published whenever he could—mainly some anonymous satires and the travel books, as well as the *Life*—and he swaggered about for a time as Corsica Boswell, arranging publicity for and even writing reviews of his own printed work; but he couldn't or wouldn't clean up and print his other journals. Later mem-

The Octagon in the King's Library, built 1762–1766 by Sir William Chambers in the private royal residence, the Queen's House, later transformed by Nash into Buckingham Palace. The situation in the picture conforms to the scene in which Johnson met the king, including even the fire mentioned specifically by Boswell, but the regency dress of the single figure indicates a later period. The picture reproduced here is from a colored plate in W. H. Pyne, The History of the Royal Residences, *published by A. Dry, London, 1819. The illustrators are given by Pyne as J. P. Stephanoff and J. Baily. H. Clifford Smith reproduces this view facing p. 82 of his* Buckingham Palace, *where he says flatly that this is the room in which Johnson and the king met. Harris refers to a drawing of the Octagon Library being built in a 1768 publication, which could mean that the room was unfinished in 1767; but the drawing probably represents the state of the library at an earlier date.*

The King's Great Library, the first of the galleries built to accommodate the king's collection.

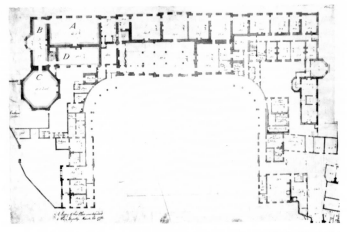

Plan of the ground floor, 1776, of Buckingham Palace, with the King's Library shown in upper left, the southeast corner. "C" indicates the Octagon, "A" the original area of the Great Library. Harris, note 23, p. 99, says only: "the illustration is from a set of wall plans in the Royal Library, Windsor Castle." Reproduced by permission of the Westminster Public Library.

Johnson reading, portrayed by Sir Joshua Reynolds, c. 1775. One of five Reynolds' portraits of Johnson. The original is in the possession of Courage Limited, London. The portrait establishes the exact way in which Johnson read, with the book close up to the right eye. He did not like this portrait and said to Mrs. Piozzi, "I will not be blinking Sam" (Anecdotes, *I, 313). The portrait is described by Kai Kin Yung, Registrar of the National Portrait Gallery, in his catalogue for the exhibition of Johnson portraits in 1984, pp. 110–12.*

An Oxford Book Auction, 1747, signed "Wm. Green Jun." The picture is the property and copyright of the Bodleian Library, Oxford, which describes it as "Canvas, cm. 33.7 x 91.5," and suggests that it may portray the shop of James Fletcher, who started bookselling in 1731 in Turl Street, Oxford.

bers of his ill-fated family found his writings so vulgar and dis-
tasteful that they continued the secrecy, mutilating, censoring,
burning, dispersing and hiding his papers for over a century.
It has taken a group of dedicated twentieth-century collectors
and scholars to at last make Boswell the British Rousseau that
he so desperately wanted to be.

A few years after Boswell's death, Keats was to speak of the
"egotistical sublime" in a poet, Wordsworth, so intensely real to
himself that he had to reach out and touch stones and trees to
remind himself of the existence of anything outside his consciousness; and many other poets, from Dante and Petrarch to
Whitman and Mailer, have been able openly and loudly to sing
songs of themselves and say with Genêt's role-making hero in
The Balcony, "I shall be not the hundred-thousandth-reflection-
within-a-reflection in a mirror, but the One and Only, into
whom a hundred thousand want to merge." But Johnson rising
from his deathbed to burn his private papers, and Boswell endlessly writing journals to be carefully secreted away, voracious
though their appetites for being in writing were, lacked the full
confidence in self felt by writers who have been able to transform their identities directly into public literary roles.

The "Boswell" of the *Life* is a literary character, not conform-
ing so much to that very odd man, the James Boswell of the
journals, as serving the structural need of the biography for a
contrasting foil to Johnson. As the naïve narrator, conventional, worshipful, uncertain, foolish, he is always willing to ask
the booby question—"Why is a cow's tail long? Why is a fox's
tail bushy?"—to draw out his hero and make him shine. So
skillful was Boswell in depicting himself in this way in the *Life*
that a long line of commentators like Macaulay have expressed
wonder that so clownish, sycophantic, and even despicable a
person could have written such a great biography. But as the
naïf, Boswell enacts not only his own folly and confusion, but

the social circumstances that explained and required a great author of the kind he made Samuel Johnson.

In making Johnson the great cham of literature, Boswell satisfied, in at least an indirect fashion, his own wish to be a great writer, as well as honoring his distinguished friend. The writer's image he made in the *Life* goes far beyond crude fantasy, however, even as it exceeds the reality of its original. The Samuel Johnson of the *Life* not only fills the literary world with his writing and his being, but he does so in ways that satisfy Boswell's particular needs. In times of great and disturbing change in all areas of society, Johnson was in the *Life* the father figure that Boswell sought all *his* life, the authority in writing and in all other things, wise, hard-headed, courageous, humane, sure of himself, the guarantor of certain reality and sure meaning against a tide of despair, disorder, melancholy, and even madness. In Boswell's hands biography became a narrative genre in which in the face of the confusing swirl of actual existence, he constructed a story with all the marks of solid truth: dates, letters, family, conversation, finances, friends, topography, writing, household details, altogether a very full social setting. It was also a story of the breakdown of an old aristocratic world and its system of polite letters at a time when troubling new orders of things were appearing in men and their books: John Wilkes and General Paoli in politics, Rousseau and Voltaire in social theory, John Wesley and William Law in religion, Adam Smith in political economy, Berkeley and Hume in philosophy, Gray and Macpherson in letters. Johnson's most interesting conversations with Boswell in the *Life* are frequently somewhat nervous discussions of the works of these and similar writers, and the ways they and their ideas were shaking the foundations of the old society: the set principles of subordination, the relationship of the sexes, the sanctity of property, the authority of Scripture, the traditional methods of education, the duties of magistrates, the value of the literary classics in a time of commercial printing. The *Life* portrays the uneasiness of a historical moment, which reverberated in both men as a deep existential uneasiness that was both manifested in and defended against by "symptoms" such as Boswell's melancholy, mercurial activity, extraordinary appetite for sex, rebellion against his father, insatiable need for love and recognition, profound boredom with normal life, and, later in life, his alcoholism. The enormous amounts of writing that both men did was, by their own admission, another and a primary defense against anomie, and in the character of Johnson that Boswell constructed in the *Life*, the life of writing became an integral part of a continuing psychological as well as social struggle against chaos, meaninglessness, even nothingness. It seems likely that this psychomachia reflects at least something of Boswell's own existential uneasiness, probably something of Johnson's as well. But the image transcended these personal concerns to become a culture hero, a generally accepted definition of the writer in the age of print, a struggler with words against emptiness, a maker of meaning in language in the face of a threatening meaninglessness. It worked because Johnson, and even more Boswell, were close to and felt intensely the central concerns of their place and time, and because a wonderful biography realized a powerful response to the situation. In making writing and the literary life the center of that response, they constructed for letters and writers a new and a centrally important role in modern print culture. In his own writings, as we shall see, Johnson enacted this Promethean role again and again, so frequently that the movement from surety, to a confusion verging on chaos, and then a heroic return through writing to a useable meaning became his standard plot for describing the way in which he wrote his books. But before looking at the various ways in which he used this plot to give meaning to letters, and to organize his writing life, let us look more closely at the way in which Boswell gave to his image of John-

son the writer the power and vitality needed to make it live in
the social world and to be accepted in the culture as the role of
the poet in the age of print.

Boswell's Johnson

From the moment of birth, things began to go wrong for Johnson, to go wrong in ways that forced him out to the margins of
life where the seemingly self-evident "realities" with which society surrounds and protects most of its members barely exist
or disappear altogether. He himself thought that the root trouble was genetic, as sufferers from existential fear and despair
so often do. The constitutional melancholy, which "made him
mad all his life, at least not sober," was inherited, Johnson told
Boswell, from his father, the Lichfield bookseller, Michael
Johnson. But other evidence suggests that Michael was, though
uneasy in his home, a cheerful enough person, and Johnson's
problems can be understood as beginning in a series of mal-
functions in biological development and the socializing process
without reference to genetics. His mother was forty, his father
fifty-two, when he was born 18 September 1709, a blue baby
who did not cry and breathe for some time after birth. Oxygen
lack in the brain during this critical time could account for his
shambling walk, general lack of muscular coordination, and
some of his various tics, such as rolling his head and torso while
talking, which marked him as peculiar all his life. His bad luck
continued when shortly after birth he was given to a wet-nurse
from whom he contracted scrofula, tuberculosis of the skin. As
a result, he became partially deaf and almost blind, being able
to read only by holding a book up close to the one eye in which
sight remained, the right, as portrayed in the 1775 portrait
by Reynolds. He also had to endure for a long time an incision
for drainage in his arm, kept open by a thread. One of the last
people to be touched by the monarch for the cure of what was

still known as the king's evil, he was taken by his mother to London to be touched by Queen Anne, who had restored the old practice.

Many generations of scholars have worked out these biographical details with great care, and I wish to establish here only that a number of unfortunate physiological accidents combined early in life to isolate Johnson by physical peculiarities, by continued sickness, and, most importantly, by sensory deprivation, near blindness and partial deafness, from his fellows and from the natural and social world that other men saw, heard, participated in, and therefore fully believed. We can get some sense of the limited world he inhabited from Boswell's memorable and touching picture of the small, nearly blind boy on his way to school, down on his knees peering closely at the curbstone he is determined to negotiate by himself. The ensuing social isolation is described well by his stepdaughter, Lucy Porter, in a picture of him at a party at age twenty-five when his strangeness and its consequences were complete: "his appearance was very forbidding: he was then lean and lank, so that his immense structure of bones was hideously striking to the eye, and the scars of the scrophula were deeply visible. He also wore his hair, which was straight and stiff, and separated behind; and he often had, seemingly, convulsive starts and odd gesticulations, which tended to excite at once surprize and ridicule." How Johnson himself felt in society is expressed in his own sad commentary on his usual place at the great feast of the world: "broken off from mankind; a kind of solitary wanderer in the wild of life, without any direction, or fixed point of view: a gloomy gazer on a world to which I have little relation." Although intended only as insult, a contemporary description of Johnson as "the Caliban of literature" defines Johnson's position in the social as well as the literary world with more precision than its author could have known or Johnson would later admit when he became famous and revealingly boasted of his social ease, "I'm never in a strange place."

Lucy Porter's description of the reaction of "surprize and ridicule" to Johnson's strange appearance at the party figures a recurrent pattern in Johnson's life in which the standard rituals or ceremonies designed to incorporate individuals into society only further confirmed his marginality. The crucial event probably came at Oxford. A little money having been found to send the promising scholar to Pembroke College, he entered with high hopes on one of the few careers which would take his oddness for granted. But he was a very strange and, though very widely read, not a particularly effective student, and when after a year the money ran out and no further support was available, he simply left Oxford and returned to Lichfield with a sense of total failure. It is difficult for us now to understand just how catastrophic this failure was for an ambitious but poor young man, without, as the social formula so tellingly puts it, "connections." A university degree offered the only possible entry for him into the upper levels of the social world through the church, the law, government service or teaching at a respectable level. Without the degree, the choice for a bookish person like himself could only be apprenticeship in some trade, a clerk's position, a job as a teaching assistant beating Latin grammar into unwilling boys, or Grub Street.

His marriage was even more disorienting. No one can say for sure—Boswell, as usual, offers conventional and sentimental explanations while hinting at something darker—why Johnson, without money or prospects, in 1735 married the widow of a Birmingham merchant, Elizabeth Porter, a woman nearly twice his age. It may have been simple loneliness, the only way in which an odd and ugly man with strong sexual desires could satisfy his need for companionship. It may have been an attempt to deal with an unresolved Oedipal conflict, for Johnson's relationship with his mother was both intense and difficult. It may be, though the true Johnsonians seem reluctant to consider it, that the several hundred pounds left to Mrs. Porter by her husband offered the only source of the capital Johnson needed to make a place for himself in the world. Certainly he used the money immediately to open a school, which soon failed, and later, presumably, to finance his first attempts in the late 1730s to set up as a writer in London.

We can only guess about motives, but the effects are definite, for the marriage instead of confirming the rightful place of these two odd lovers among the couples of the social world, like the multiple marriages ending a Shakespearean comedy, only highlighted their grotesque differences from the norm. Johnson's appearance at the time of the marriage has already been described in Lucy Porter's words, but the full effect of the wedding scene can only be felt when he is placed alongside his bride, cruelly described by Garrick for Boswell: "very fat, with a bosom of more than ordinary protuberance, with swelled cheeks, of a florid red, produced by thick painting, and increased by the liberal use of cordials; flaring and fantastick in her dress, and affected both in her speech and her general behaviour." On the wedding journey on horseback, the bride, as Johnson recounted, having read too many romances "had got into her head the fantastical notion that a woman of spirit should use her lover like a dog" and tried to treat him accordingly, with farcical results not unlike what occurs in the travels of Kate and Petruchio to his country house in *The Taming of the Shrew*.

Johnson insisted to Topham Beauclerk that "it was a love-marriage upon both sides" and perhaps in its strange way it was, but the lovers soon agreed to live apart, and they remained separated during the latter years of Tetty's life. Johnson's prayers frequently record a deep sense of failure in his relations with her, and refer to promises of reformation made to her and strong resolutions voiced "when she lay dead before me." Whatever tangled emotions the marriage involved for husband and wife, and whatever they may themselves have been like—Tetty may not have been the *absolute* fright Garrick described—the union appeared very odd to others. How the world viewed the marriage may be understood from the fact that the actor David Garrick frequently amused company by exhibiting Tetty with "his exquisite talent for mimickry, so as to excite the heartiest bursts of laughter. . . ." But it was even worse than this, for Garrick had been one of the only three students in the small school Johnson tried to keep after the wedding and had spent some time peeking through the keyhole of the newlyweds' bedroom. The scene was apparently awesome, and in later life Garrick amused his friends with what Bate calls one of "his set parlor pieces," in which he would play the part of Johnson in the bedroom sitting at a table writing *Irene*, absent-mindedly stuffing the bedclothes into his trousers like shirttails, while a shivering Tetty pleaded with him to come to bed.

Johnson's luck was often bad, but it would seem to have been the work of some malevolent joking god that one of the only three schoolboy observers of his bizarre attempt to "press in . . . amongst the rest of the country copulatives" as Touchstone describes his own efforts in this area of social life, would become the greatest mime of the English stage. But the grimmest and most conclusive evidence of the failure of the marriage to incorporate Johnson and his wife into society comes from the reaction of Tetty's sons by her earlier marriage to it. The older son was so upset by this remarkable marriage that he never again saw his mother, and it took the younger son years to overcome his "disgust."

Johnson records in his *Life of Mr. Richard Savage* (1744) nights spent walking the London streets talking with this strange companion—who was in many ways, some feared and some desired, his "secret sharer"—when they had neither lodgings nor money to go to a tavern. These scenes of dark city wandering, shut out from the houses of men, fairly represent Johnson's lack of a place in society at this time. Even within a house he could still feel the exclusion he enacted on one occasion by retiring behind a screen at Cave's home to eat his dinner in solitude while Cave ate with a late-arriving guest, Walter Harte, and talked about Johnson's writing. Harte never knew of Johnson's presence until Cave told him later that the "plate of victuals . . . sent behind a screen . . . was to Johnson, dressed so shabbily, that he did not choose to appear; but on hearing the conversation, [he] was highly delighted with the encomiums on his book."

Johnson's marginality, the lack of certainty and secure place in the world given by society to most of its members, either led to or was paralleled and intensified by a psychological marginality which we would nowadays call alienation and anomie. His sensed condition of being an outsider was mentally experienced as the hopelessness and helplessness which Johnson identified frequently and poignantly in his *Prayers and Meditations* as "perturbations of mind," "vain terrours," "disturbances and distractions." His prayer for Easter Day, 1777, gives a more extended sense of what this condition felt like: "When I survey my past life, I discover nothing but a barren waste of time, with some disorders of body, and some disturbances of the mind very near to madness, which I hope He that made me, will suffer to extenuate many faults, and excuse many deficiencies." Johnson's own time knew this state of mind generally as melancholy, and while the causes of it were unknown, then as now eluding "the most minute enquiry," as Boswell says, the effects or symptoms were "well known to be a weariness of life, an unconcern about those things which agitate the greater part of mankind, and a general sensation of gloomy wretchedness." In other words, deep depression, a profound sense of what Johnson in his most famous poem more dramatically called "The Vanity of Human Wishes." During at least two lengthy periods in Johnson's life, the depression, which was ordinarily experienced as an immense lassitude, became so intense as to immobilize him. Both attacks followed events that further undermined his always precarious sense of social order. The first occurred after Johnson at the age of twenty left Oxford in December 1729, without a degree, and returned to Lichfield and his father's failing business. A first attempt to teach school quickly ended in disaster and humiliation. The marginal position in which Johnson had always lived biologically was now socially confirmed as well, and his place in the world became even more uncertain when the ordering reality of his father was removed by death in 1731, with the consequent breakup of the familiar family and business structure. Since Johnson destroyed most of his private papers, and was always reluctant to speak of this period, we know little of his life between 1730 and 1735, but we do know that his desperate situation led to a deep depression which was close to madness. His passivity during this time, the long, aimless, rambling walks, the wretched appearance (as if ugliness were being cultivated as well as endured), the unwillingness to undertake any work in the bookstore or elsewhere except for the one brief term of schoolmastering, the tics and compulsions that became increasingly noticeable, and the near paralysis of will that kept him in bed for long periods of time, all enact a sense of hopelessness, a life lived with no sense of meaning or value in existence. Toward the end of this period, his friend Edmund Hector in an attempt to save him, got Johnson a contract from a bookseller to translate from the French a book about travels in Abyssinia by the Jesuit, Father Lobo. This was not the first, nor by any means the last time that writing and books provided the stable reality Johnson needed so desperately. So deep was the depression, however, that the book very nearly failed to provide the solid printed world where there was a place called

Abyssinia, with a river named Nile, with waterfalls and with crocodiles real enough, Johnson notes gratefully in his Preface, to "devour their prey without tears." For a long time he was unable to work, but in the end, lying on his bed, he dictated his translation to Hector, who eventually saw the book through the press. Johnson himself thought that he was mad during this period and submitted a description of his symptoms to a medical friend, who was most alarmed by what he read; but the publication of the book, his subsequent marriage, and the school at Edial marked a renewed attempt to live in the social world. Even when the school failed he found the energy to go to London, walking with David Garrick, where he took up the life of a Grub Street hack.

Johnson often told Boswell that he considered himself on the edge of madness all his life, and in the early to mid-1760s he became extremely depressed once again. Boswell, who first met Johnson a year earlier, records that in 1764 "he was afflicted with a very severe return of the hypochondriack disorder, which was ever lurking about him," and describes Johnson's intensified feeling at this time of uselessness and guilt for what he considered his indolence and sensuality. He avoided society, and one of his friends who sought him out eloquently described for Boswell the "deplorable state" in which he found him, "sighing, groaning, talking to himself, and restlessly walking from room to room. He [Johnson] then used this emphatical expression of the misery which he felt: 'I would consent to have a limb amputated to recover my spirits.' " Johnson himself phrased his bleak feelings at this time in his prayer of 21 April 1764 in the following way: "A kind of strange oblivion has overspread me, so that I know not what has become of the last year, and perceive that incidents and intelligence pass over me without leaving any impression." It was during this period that he purchased the famous lock and fetters to control himself if he felt his sanity going. In a curious and complex gesture, the lock and fetters were later given to Mrs. Thrale, whose friendship and care of Johnson had much to do with his gradual recovery from this intense and lengthy depression.

The social circumstances of this second major breakdown are not as obvious as those of the first. During the 1760s, Johnson, far from having no place in the society of men, was firmly established as the author of the English dictionary, completed in 1755, the distinguished series of essays, *The Idler* and *The Rambler*, and the moral tale *Rasselas*; his reputation as a writer was publicly recognized by the crown with a pension of £300 annually; he met and was praised by the king; and he was the literary lion of London whom ambitious young men like Boswell wanted to meet. His mother had, however, died in 1759, and the combination of release and guilt connected with this event must have been intense and intricate. George Irwin in his careful psychological study of Johnson has shown us that although he frequently, publicly, and piously proclaimed the highest reverence for his mother, and all mothers except that of his alter ego Savage, he did not return to Lichfield to visit her for nineteen years before her death, avoided returning during her final sickness by writing *Rasselas* in order to pay, he said, for her funeral, and did not attend the funeral. But he then visited Lichfield twelve times between Sarah's death and his own.

The most sensitive investigator of this period in Johnson's life, as well as of so many other Johnsonian matters, Walter Jackson Bate, has concluded that the crisis of the 1760s had been building for a very long period of time and that, whatever triggered it, it was an inevitable disintegration resulting from Johnson's "most deeply ingrained habit of self-defense." He had built up, according to Bate, a method of protecting himself against the "radical unhappiness of human life" by anticipating in detail every possible disaster in advance, by, in short, denying himself all hope. The result was a "massive attitude of dis-

trust toward life" that "extended . . . to the universe at large."
This sense of alienated hopelessness was complicated and
made intensely more painful by Johnson's habit of turning his
helpless anger at the bleakness of life inward on himself, rather
than outward on God or on the world and other men. Gradually, Bate's argument continues, this painful combination of
calculated despair and guilt, though a useful, even a necessary,
spur to writing and work in the hard years when Johnson was
making a place for himself in the literary world, opened a
psychic wound of unredeemable hopelessness and endless
meaninglessness, for which he bore responsibility and which
he experienced most intensely in madness.

We still lack an agreed-upon and therefore convincing psychology which permits us confidently to diagnose the causes of
madness, or even to define it, and Bate's informed, sympathetic, and subtle explanations come as close as we are likely to
get to understanding the mechanism of Johnson's alienation.
But we can say with some confidence that his experience of
madness was a part, an intense form, of a more extensive, massive distrust of life, probably originating in and certainly an extension of his biological and social marginality. Madness, that is
to say, was the acting out, in symbolic form, of his continuing
fear that society had no place for him, and of his even greater
fear, always present because of sensory deprivation, that the
world itself was not so real as it was said by most to be. Ordinarily these fears were only the confirmed outsider's wary
uneasiness about the reality of the social world that had rejected him, a highly sensitized awareness that its language, its
political system, its religions, its philosophies and sciences, all
the social orders which seem so sure and firm-set to those who
have a secure place within them, are carefully constructed and
maintained illusions, always precarious because of some usually ignored but obvious ontological deficiencies.

Johnson's situation in relationship to the culture as a whole is uncannily like that which Diderot set up in his "Letter on the Blind" (1749) in which he describes the situation of the blind and their inability to understand many cultural ideas and values because as he says: "The state of our organs and of our senses has a great influence on our metaphysics and our ethics, and our most purely intellectual ideas, if I may express it thus, are very much dependent on the structure of our body. . . ." The skeptical philosopher's blind man is, however, only his stalking horse for the blindness of philosophers, scientists, and other men in possession of all of their senses who believe firmly that they see and understand all that there is, when they are themselves in fact no more than blind people who from their limited points of time and space are completely ignorant of the realities of a world which is ultimately no more than "a composite entity subject to revolutions, all of which display a continuous tendency toward destruction, a rapid succession of beings that follow one another, thrust one another aside, then disappear; a passing symmetry; a momentary order." Johnson, of course, combines in his consciousness all these points of view simultaneously, for if his skepticism began in his own blindness and deafness, he ultimately achieved the overview of the philosopher as well.

Boswell often comments on what he calls Johnson's "dexterity in retort" and "wonderful fertility of mind," and the free movement of his thought in conversation and writing, his ability to move ideas about and think outside any fixed habit or system of thought, his openness to the actual evidence and frankness about things as they are, all qualities for which he is famous, and which show the most positive and attractive side of a mind which well understands that what most people think, say, and do are finally only conventions. The truths of this world were for him, as has often been observed, socially and historically established. As he says in his "Preface to Shakespeare," "The reverence due to writings that have long sub-

sisted arises . . . not from any credulous confidence in the superior wisdom of past ages, or gloomy persuasion of the
degeneracy of mankind, but is the consequence of acknowledged and indubitable positions, that what has been longest
known has been most considered, and what is most considered
is best understood."

The darker side of this kind of skepticism begins to appear
in his frequent observations of how things really work in this
world. Johnson, Boswell tells us, "had penetration enough to
see, and seeing would not disguise the general misery of man
in this state of being. . . ." What he saw is expressed in a series
of hard, unblinking remarks, such as, "Pity is not natural to
man. Children are always cruel." To Boswell's hopeful question of whether it is not sometimes possible for man to be
happy in the present moment, the reply is direct and flat:
"Never, but when he is drunk." Johnson lived with the knowledge that there can be no settled satisfaction in a life that is always "a progress from want to want," that "people in distress
never think that you feel enough," that it is only "opinion by
which we have a respect for authority," and that "most schemes
of political improvement are very laughable things" because
there is always a lack of sufficient wisdom and virtue to carry
them out. As for the basic social values, they become true, he
believed, only in a tragic historical process in which their reality
is established by blood: "the only method by which religious
truth can be established is by martyrdom. The magistrate has a
right to enforce what he thinks; and he who is conscious of the
truth has a right to suffer. I am afraid there is no other way of
ascertaining the truth, but by persecution on the one hand and
enduring it on the other." Like most of Johnson's remarks, this
last can be read as assuming some absolute truth underlying social life but discoverable only in the process of history; but like
most of Johnson's remarks, it also suggests, and rather more

powerfully, a relativist viewpoint in which truth is only what is most familiar and "best understood."

This is all stoutly put, but Boswell brings us closer to the near despair implicit in this knowledge in his famous image of Johnson's mind as a "vast amphitheatre, the Colisæum at Rome. In the centre stood his judgement, which, like a mighty gladiator, combated those apprehensions that, like the wild beasts of the *Arena*, were all around in cells, ready to be let out upon him. After a conflict, he drove them back into their dens; but not killing them, they were still assailing him." Here the fears still have at least substantial shapes, but behind and below these metaphors of beasts there seem to have been further reaches of meaninglessness that Krutch describes as a "sense of the ultimate emptiness of life which he had rationalized into something like a philosophic system." Mrs. Piozzi speaks in her *Anecdotes* of an "incredulity" in him that "amounted almost to disease." "The vacuity of life had at some early period of his life struck so forcibly on the mind of Mr. Johnson, that it became by repeated impression his favorite hypothesis, and the general tenor of his reasonings commonly ended there, wherever they might begin." He would, she goes on, accept almost any kind of odd or seemingly meaningless activity as a way of "filling up the time," a telling metaphor for the emptiness of life and the defense against it.

When he failed to fill up the time in some way, Johnson fell back into the vacuity of his vast lassitudes, indolences so great that work, always difficult, became impossible, and his rising from bed delayed until it could be avoided no longer. Or he might fall even deeper into his extraordinary fear of death, so terrifying to him that he could say that "the whole of life is but keeping away the thoughts of it." He feared the Christian hell, in which his mother had carefully and devastatingly instructed him as a child, but he feared annihilation even more: "Now mere existence is so much better than nothing, that one would rather exist even in pain, than not exist." Johnson always carefully surrounds his discussions of death with expressions of conventional piety, but that God was a defense against a more immediately felt sense of emptiness in death is established in a conversation with Boswell, Mrs. Knowles, and others who take the orthodox Christian view that death is only the beginning of true and eternal life and therefore not to be feared. Johnson, with his usual delight in opposing any unexamined, generally accepted view, but also with a grim, authentic knowledge of what he speaks, responds that not only can no one be sure of salvation when he dies, but that he himself as a living man has in fact "made no approaches to a state which can look on [death] as not terrible." After some more empty chatter and a fatuous remark by Miss Seward that the fear of death is "absurd" since annihilation "is only a pleasing sleep without a dream," Johnson responds in terms that open up his existential consciousness of some vast emptiness beneath the surface of all life: "The lady confounds annihilation, which is nothing, with the apprehension of it, which is dreadful. It is in the apprehension of it that the horrour of annihilation consists."

Johnson was not, however, a Pascal, Kierkegaard, Nietzsche, or Sartre, those great skeptics who profess to enjoy facing the void directly and trying to build a life in terms of full and paradoxical acceptance of the absurdity of the human condition. He resisted his own knowledge of emptiness, and he shrank from discussing it openly. Except for acting it out in his torpors and depression, we get only oblique glimpses of what he feared most, such as the discussion of annihilation in death, or his criticism of Shakespeare's description of Dover Cliff in *King Lear*. Someone suggested to him that this passage was an excellent piece of pure poetic description. But Johnson objected in terms that reveal an awareness of some vastness that Shakespeare had not made as empty as Johnson himself had found it to be: "No, Sir; it should be all precipice,—all vacuum. The crows impede your fall. The diminished appearance of the boats, and other circumstances, are all very good description; but do not impress the mind at once with the horrible idea of immense height. The impression is divided; you pass on by computation, from one stage of the tremendous space to another." Johnson may have found an image of what he feared during his journey to the western islands of Scotland where he encountered "a wide sweep of sand-dunes in Coll" that the more romantic Boswell greatly admired, but Johnson found "horrible, if barrenness and danger could be so," as if, Frank Brady remarks, "the vacuity of mind he feared became mirrored in the landscape."

Johnson tells us that he could never bear to re-read the final act of *King Lear* with its minimal restoration of sanity and meaning to the world, perhaps because his own life was itself a constant and never completed attempt to return from Dover Cliff and Lear's heath, those primary images of nothingness in our culture. Unlike Hume with his genial skepticism and confident assertion that, as Boswell maliciously reported, "he was no more uneasy to think he should *not be* after this life, than that he *had not been* before," Johnson could not live easily with such knowledge. He was, seemingly paradoxically, what Boswell called him, "truly social," and his awareness of and response to the vacuity of human life were those of society as a whole, which always seeks to create in the face of chaos a liveable human world, a culture with the order, value, solidity, and purpose that people require and collectively construct by making objectively and subjectively believable social worlds. The great majority of individuals are born into and live their lives within one of these societies, taking their given worlds for granted as real, even as facts of nature. They are only momentarily disturbed by marginal personal experiences such as dream or death, or marginal historical events such as the great Lisbon earthquake, the official test case for theodicy in Johnson's time, or the Holocaust in our own. But Johnson's position in his world as an individual, as we have seen, was marginal from the beginning, and he lived always within near sight of the alien emptiness on the perpetual edge of which society constructs, in Prospero's words, its "cloud-capped towers, . . . gorgeous palaces, . . . solemn temples."

If at times this emptiness paralyzed him, there was also in him the enormous biological determination of life itself to survive, simply to be, that appears nakedly in the single-minded intensity, gluttony really, with which he ate—head down in plate, veins standing out in his head, sweating, giving off a distinct and unpleasant odor. At the end of life, disabled by strokes, scarcely able to breathe because of asthma, tortured by an ulcerous leg, dropsy, a bad heart, and arthritis, he still refused to yield: "I will be conquered; I will not capitulate." His energy extended into social life where he talked for victory and would knock his conversational opponent down with the butt of his rhetorical pistol if it misfired, and into his intellectual life where he gutted books for their meaning, read more voraciously than any man of his age, and wrote and spoke with overwhelming power. This vitality, at the intermittent times he could generate it, was inversely proportionate to his indolence at other times, and its aggressive force gave his life and writings their authority. He could, when he was up, do nothing in moderation, not even close a door without emphasis.

Johnson's vitality had its demonic outlets, such as tics like rocking his head and torso while talking, but its direction was mainly social, which is to say, utilized to construct in the midst of fear of nothingness and meaninglessness a liveable world for himself, acting out, as it were, in individual ways the primary activity of society as a whole in making and maintaining culture. There were, of course, homely and familiar remedies for the darkness—a candle and book by the bedside in case of night waking, endless cups of tea, sleeping as late as possible, constant conversation to escape the fatal aloneness—but there were also more elaborate efforts to construct an orderly and meaningful world, beginning with some of his more idiosyncratic and bizarre activities, such as turning around before going through a door, measuring his steps to place his foot on a crack in the floor or sidewalk, touching every post between the tavern and his house. These and his many other habitual games are often described as compulsion neuroses, forms of mental sickness themselves, but their function in Johnson's life was pretty clearly defense against anomie; more precisely, they were attempts to construct at a very rudimentary level an arbitrary but meaningful order in the midst of what was felt as chaos or empty space. These games provide the key to more complicated constructs such as his extensively elaborated sense of guilt, which also filled up the emptiness and gave life some meaning, though perhaps not always of the most helpful kind, even as scraping raw the knuckles of his writing hand, working out elaborate mathematical problems, and falling to his knees to pray behind his chair at dinner parties played out numerical and moral orders in which what one is and does means something. Seen from this angle, even Johnson's madness and his more-or-less constant anxiety are not what was wrong, but last-resort attempts, in not unfamiliar human ways, to deal with what was really wrong, fear of annihilation, by objectively acting out some structured, meaningful reality. To be odd or even mad is still to be something, a standard though very risky role in the social repertory, with a well-defined and very interesting place in the scheme of things.

These quirky, even pathological, games of order give us some insight into the intensity and constancy of Johnson's need for a structured reality, and help to explain the vigor and absoluteness, often the belligerence, with which he publicly maintained established social values. When Dr. Johnson, the great Tory, pronounces that what Scripture tells us is certain, that the will is free and there's an end on it, that the teacher has a duty to beat his students so long as he does not permanently maim them, that any woman who has sexual relations outside marriage is a whore, and that conformity to the practices, though not necessarily the beliefs, of the established church must be maintained with blood if necessary by the magistrate, he is not speaking out of some narrow-minded certainty, for his mind was neither narrow nor certain, but willfully closing his mind to shut off the spaces that frighten him, and to restrain his own doubts, the intensity of which can be measured by the force of his expression. His is the familiar stance of the great conservatives, like his friend Burke, who always work with an understanding of how arbitrary, precarious, *and* necessary is any given social order.

Johnson's constant drive to construct order and to maintain already-established social structures and meanings against the encroachment of vacuity provides the appropriate context in which to understand the elective affinity of Johnson and print. He himself, as we have seen, thought of his involvement in the life of writing for the press as a matter of chance. If things had gone differently, he always said, he might have been a lawyer or a schoolmaster. He was right to the extent that either would have served his need for order, but there was a perfect match between a man with a precarious grip on reality and a technology that could, with unusual potency, make authors and ideas real in books by assembling only a few pieces of movable type carrying a limited set of arbitrary phonetic and logical signs. Working, like Johnson, against emptiness, print fixes ideas solidly in the world in individual printed books and library collections, and it organizes all the parts of the print world—types, books, printers, or writers—in an efficient, systematic way. We normally say, of course, that Johnson was simply a bookish person, but that term covers over the real attraction of the printed word and the printed world for a boy with loose ties to the sensible and social world who held on to reality by reading all the books in his father's shop and became famous for having read and written more books than any other Englishman of his time. Books and the larger world of letters of which they were a part were Johnson's principal means for making reality, not so sacred, perhaps, but serving the same purpose as religion, sermons, and prayers, to shield him from nothingness.

He not only took his needed reality from the firm, structured printed reality of books, he also made reality in the same place. Working as a professional author for pay, enjoying the independence and the ownership of his literary property that print encouraged, meeting copy deadlines, seeing printed and bound works with his name on the title page, and hearing them praised by the world, all established an area of social reality for him and oriented him within it. But the activity of writing itself was also a psychological realization of the kind of ordered reality he sought so consistently, so urgently, and in so many different ways in his life. Something of what was involved at this deep psychological level is suggested by his remarkable letter of 30 December 1755 to Hill Boothby, the beautiful young lady of fashion whom the sad ugly man loved with deepest hopelessness: "You know Des Carte's argument, 'I think therefore I am.' It is as good a consequence 'I write therefore I am alive.' "

But if the printed book and the life of writing that print structured for Johnson gave him the foundations of the ordered and meaningful reality he needed to exist, he, particularly as Boswell painted him in the *Life*, in return supplied letters with an author who gave the entire literary enterprise in the age of print a vital, humane motive and purpose. No longer able to base literary legitimacy on a court, a hierarchical view of the world, and a few venerated classics, as the old order of polite letters and its gentlemen-poets had, a print-based system of letters, if it were to be anything more than a mere business, had to find a new source of authority for itself. It was this that Johnson supplied as an author writing to meet existential needs, and that Boswell later intensified and formalized in a biography that further satisfied his own closely related needs as a person and a writer.

As an extremely interesting and powerful personality who wrote books, Johnson provided the kind of legitimation for letters that would increasingly in the future validate literary activity and its primary product, books. The romantic cult of authorial personality, which really begins with him, and still continues, can and usually does involve nothing more or less than the idea that interesting people, particularly oddly, quirkily interesting people, write interesting books. But Boswell's Johnson is an interesting writer in ways that particularly fit the realities of print and the needs of letters in eighteenth-century England, and he therefore became in Boswell's hands not just an important writer, but the type of the modern writer. The writer's aptness is established in Johnson's knowledge of print ways and the skill with which he explains and uses technology for human ends. The writer's authority is made dramatically real in Johnson's force and the conclusiveness with which he "puts things right," not only in the world of letters but in all moral, political, and social areas where confusion and disorder threaten. The writer's authenticity in all these areas where Boswell shows him controlling and making sense of things ultimately derives, however, not from some absolute certainty but rather from its opposite, from an experience of vacuity and from a marginal existence that drive him to create order and meaning, particularly in books, which thus become defenses against alienation and meaninglessness. Johnson dramatizes this power in a standardized plot of writing which he regularly enacted in his writing projects and frequently describes in the prefaces he attaches to his works. He begins in this story by undertaking with confidence and eager anticipation some huge project such as a dictionary of the English language or an accurate edition of the plays of Shakespeare. The work turns out in practice to be very difficult and quickly becomes impossible as the supposed object of inquiry, *the* language or the ideal Platonic text of Shakespeare, begins to break up under scrutiny, leaving only "the boundless chaos of a living speech" or, in the case of the Shakespearean texts, "fragments . . . minutely broken, and . . . fortuitously reunited; . . ." After a period of despair, however, heroic efforts and the establishment of reasonable but arbitrarily chosen standards allow order to be imposed on chaos and meaning realized in the face of emptiness. In its purest form, this is the story of the *Debates in the Senate of Lilliput.* Johnson, using shorthand notes, supplied by another, of oral debates in Parliament, of which reports were prohibited, composed speeches which were printed in *The Gentleman's Magazine* as verbatim copies of the originals. These were sometimes later accepted as authentic by the supposed speakers. This was a bit too much even for Johnson, who later repudiated the *Debates.*

It is possible to hypothesize that Johnson became the type of the print writer because his role as a truth-making author matched exactly the needs created by print technology and by a medium that provided an increasingly baffling surplus of information, much of it contradictory, all of it confusing and unsettling in its multiplicity and novelty. But, whether we trace the problem directly back to print or not, his public authorial role provided a solution to the increasing difficulty his society felt, in an age close to political and economic revolution— partly as a result of the many books the press had made available—of putting the world together, as we say, in a meaningful way. The recurrent rhythm of Johnson's life in Boswell's biography is successful struggle with meaninglessness; and this was the felt reality of his age as well. His portrayal in his personality and in his writing of the intensity of this problem, his realization of its dangers and his heroic and successful responses to it, gave letters a new kind of authenticity by giving it an author deeply, centrally, personally involved with the most pressing technological, psychological, and social questions. By projection, this type of author helped to create for individual books, and for letters in general, a place and function of importance in society as primary defenses against meaninglessness and nothingness.

Writers and their writing were, after Johnson and Boswell, what they have, with many variants, remained: an enactment of the difficulty—and the necessity—of making, out of the self and the multitudinous contradictory things the world knows and feels, a believable structure of meaning. The history of romantic literature is a chronicle of the numerous ways that this can be done, but Johnson's activities in this regard remain paradigmatic in that in him we see the radical problem and its radical solution. Having looked at the new type of author that the print era required, we must in subsequent chapters, to round out our view of the new print-based literary system being constructed, look at the printed literary text, the expanded audience of readers who bought printed books, and the place of letters in modern culture. In each of these areas, Johnson's activities provide specific instances of the author making meaning by writing in the face of emptiness, the man of letters being legitimated anew in the age of print.

CHAPTER V

CREATING AN AURA FOR LITERARY
TEXTS IN PRINT CULTURE

Literary Aura

In his noted essay, "The Work of Art in the Age of Mechanical Reproduction," Walter Benjamin reasons that so long as an art work remains unique, or is limited to only a few copies, it maintains an "aura," a special value or authenticity derived from such qualities as rarity, a single specific location in space and time, and a particular history recorded in its patina and provenance. By virtue of its aura, the unique art work has cult value in a sacred system of authority, where, as a magical object, it absorbs its viewers through their contemplation of it into the work, suppresses criticism, and transfers its mana to its owner. Once, however, an art object is copied in large numbers, as, to use Benjamin's examples, photography in combination with printing has reproduced paintings, and the film has made many duplicates of theatrical performances, the aura of the original is lost, cult value disappears in mass art, and everyone, because of the familiarity of the art object, feels free first to criticize and then eventually to become artists and make their own art.

Benjamin focuses his attention in this essay on the visual arts of painting and theater, and on photography as the primary means of mechanical reproduction; but in another essay, "The Storyteller," he makes the novel, the product of print, the mechanically reproduced form of the older oral story and tale. This essay concentrates on the qualities of the oral story and therefore does not go into much detail about the effects of print, but Benjamin's general theory of the demystification of art through numerous reproductions explains precisely what happened when in the eighteenth century, the printing press with its logic of multiplicity stripped the classical texts of the old literary order of their aura.

A scribe, we have been told by the historians of the book, Febvre and Martin, could turn out on an average only two complete manuscripts a year, but the printers of Europe in the first fifty years of printing, 1450 to 1500, produced between 10,000 and 15,000 different titles, which, figured conservatively at an average print run of 500, means that during this time they produced up to 7.5 million individual volumes. In England, from Caxton's time until 1640, the printers produced approximately 26,000 different editions, and, again at runs of 500, about 13 million individual books. Using the conservative *ESTC* numbers from Chapter II, we get an average of about 1,100 titles a year during the eighteenth century, and still using the low-side figure of runs of 500, about 55 million English books during that period. These numbers are, of course, very rough approximations, but they show a distinct trend and at least suggest the magnitude of the increase.

By the eighteenth century this flood of books, in its accumulation both of different texts and identical copies of the same texts, threatened to obscure the few idealized classics, both ancient and modern, of polite letters, and to weaken their aura by making printed copies of them, and of books in general, familiar, even commonplace objects. Books became ordinary, frequently seen and handled. Printing further cheapened books by making them commodities to be bought and sold in the marketplace, available to all who could read, owned by all who could afford them (though they remained comparatively expensive until the nineteenth century), and found in increasingly numerous public and private libraries. Since printed books were for the most part in the vernacular, they further desacralized letters by expanding its canon from a group of venerable texts written in ancient languages known only to an elite to include a body of contemporary writing in the native language understood by all who could read. The Greek and Latin classics maintained a privileged position in education and continued to occupy an honored place in the world of letters, but the printing press insured the victory of the moderns over the ancients, eventually literally "translating" all the ancients into moderns by rendering them in the vernacular, and creating the larger scene of reading and writing that Johnson, as always on the side of print, described in the following optimistic fashion: "It has been maintained that this superfoetation, this teeming of the press in modern times, is prejudicial to good literature, because it obliges us to read so much of what is of inferiour value, in order to be in the fashion; so that better works are neglected for want of time, because a man will have more gratification of his vanity in conversation, from having read modern books, than from having read the best works of antiquity. But it must be considered, that we have now more knowledge generally diffused; all our ladies read now, which is a great extension."

With the loss of aura consequent on the existence of numerous identical copies of the art work, Benjamin posits a release of the critical, judging spirit that appeared in letters in the late seventeenth and early eighteenth centuries when writers like Addison and Steele, and later Johnson, first undertook to instruct the public taste in literary matters, and popular journals like *The Monthly Review* (1749) and the rival *Critical Review* (1756) discussed and judged new books. Systematic theoretical criticism at this time became, in the works of Boileau, Dryden, and Pope, a standard literary genre. Literary criticism, of course, always presents itself as if it were eternal, or at least as if it had a continuous history from Plato and Aristotle to the present, but Johnson perceived correctly that "Dryden may be properly considered as the father of English criticism, as the writer who first taught us to determine upon principles the merit of composition." Elsewhere in his "Life of Dryden," he comments on both the disenchanting effect that criticism had on the text and the close connection between criticism and the practicalities of printing and marketing books: "To increase the value of his copies," Johnson says of Dryden, "he often accompanied his work with a preface of criticism; a kind of learning then almost new in the English language, and which he, who had considered with great accuracy the principles of writing, was able to distribute copiously as occasions arose. By these dissertations the publick judgement must have been much improved; and Swift, who conversed with Dryden, relates that he regretted the success of his own instructions, and found his readers made suddenly too skillful to be easily satisfied." The other consequence of mechanical multiplication predicted by Benjamin's theory, that as copies of art works become familiar everyone feels free and able not only to criticize but to become an artist, was also realized in letters, in ways we have already seen in detail in Chapters II and III, by the mob of gentlemen-writers, publishing pedants, writing women, Grub Street hacks, and other members of the multitudinous scribbling race who appeared during the eighteenth century after it was discovered how easy it was to write and print once the press had removed the taboo from books.

The theory that the multiplication of art works by mechanical means begins a desacralization of the objects, the appearance of criticism, and a democratization of authorship is anticipated by Swift's little mock-epic, *The Battle of the Books*, written in 1697, but published in 1704 as part of his *Tale of a Tub*. Here Swift does not so much object to print as such—printed versions of classical texts are accepted—but to print's effects, particularly the large number of vulgar modern books that the printing press had put on the shelves of another royal library, located this time in St. James's palace. Insolent and crudely confident in their numerical superiority, the moderns attack the classics, transforming the library from a place of peace and orderly learning to a noisy mock-epic battle between old and new ways of writing. In Swift's allegory, the modern printed books' physical attack on the classics represents a more fundamental attack on the calm epistemology of the old order—a few truths in a few texts—by a great variety of conflicting styles and many loud opinions. Many books say many things in many ways, Swift understands, and they thereby strip the aura from the older works by encouraging skepticism about the truth and criticism of the styles of the classics, leaving them epistemologically as well as ontologically only a few among many. The fundamental issue and, ironically, its outcome were present in the actual occasion for the writing of *The Battle of the Books*. Sir William Temple, Swift's employer and patron, had written a defense of the ancients against the moderns, citing Aesop's *Fables* and Phalaris' *Epistles*, but he was then attacked by the critic William Wotton, and by the great scholar and keeper of the king's libraries, Richard Bentley, who by using the kind of comparative philological skills made possible and encouraged by the existence of many printed texts demonstrated that Aesop and Phalaris were not the authentic classical texts Temple had assumed. Criticism in this case literally destroyed two of the ancient texts by showing them to be spurious in various ways.

From their very difficult historical points of view, the rationalistic classicist Swift and the romantic Marxist Benjamin with their shared dislike of machines and their products concur in their analyses of how mechanical means of reproduction weakened and ultimately destroyed an older literary world, which they, of course, understand in very different ways—Swift identifying with neoclassical polite letters and Benjamin with the folk tradition that neoclassicism warred against throughout the Renaissance. They are also similar in their mistaken belief that the press produced only some kind of printed sludge in which one book, good or bad, is indistinguishable from another and all are totally lacking in aura. The world of letters would never again after print be as small as it once had been, nor its central texts quite as sacred, but the history of romantic literature since that time has been largely a continuing series of successful attempts to, as we would now say, remystify or privilege the literary text, or in Benjamin's terms to provide these printed literary works with an aura. This text-intensifying and sacralizing activity has succeeded so well that—though it is under attack at the present time—the integrity of the literary text, figured as a well-wrought urn or a verbal icon, has become one of the accepted "facts" of literature, the verbal form of beauty fixed in time, and the manifest reality of the essential poetic faculty, the creative imagination. The literary work of art with its "wholeness, harmony and radiance," in Joyce's, and Dedalus', definitive terms, its perfect structure, spatial form, and concrete universals, had become the primary fact of a text-centered institution by 1917, when, looking back along the history of literature, T. S. Eliot could see only a long line of idealized texts that embodied the mind of Europe and the reality of civilization: "The existing monuments form an ideal order among themselves," while "the mind of the poet," in his famous analogy, had become only "the shred of platinum" that catalyzes the poem. "Honest criticism and sensitive appreciation," he goes on to pronounce in "Tradition and the Individual Talent," are directed "not upon the poet but upon the poetry." The actual experience of Gutenberg aura as it is felt and smelled is more powerfully and immediately rendered by George Gissing in *The Private Papers of Henry Ryecroft* (1903):

> I know every book of mine by its *scent*, and I have but to put my nose between the pages to be reminded of all sorts of things. My Gibbon, for example, my well-bound eight-volume Milman edition, which I have read and read and read again for more than

thirty years—never do I open it but the scent of the noble page restores to me all the exultant happiness of that moment when I received it as a prize. Or my Shakespeare, the great Cambridge Shakespeare—it has an odour which carries me yet further back in life; for these volumes belonged to my father, and before I was old enough to read them with understanding, it was often permitted me, as a treat, to take down one of them from the bookcase, and reverently to turn the leaves.

Efforts to pretend that printed books are only a form of manuscript and to give them an aura by continuing to exploit manuscript, not print, logic lasted on for a long time, and have never entirely disappeared. Rare book libraries with their cathedral atmosphere represent an essentially old-order attempt to maintain an aura for printed books by means of a manuscript strategy of rarity and scarcity: collecting unique or rare books, first editions, sumptuous printings, hand-colored illustrations, fine bindings. But the attempt to preserve the old aristocratic cult of polite letters and a manuscript aura for its texts was, like the parallel attempts of authors to avoid print or remain anonymous, doomed to failure, or at least to something less than full success, in a print culture where books became increasingly numerous, widespread, and familiar. An aura for the printed literary text had to be and was constructed in accordance with print logic and in terms of the possibilities offered by print situation. In this respect, Johnson again offers us a paradigm of the ways that letters in general, and literature in particular, created over time an aura for its printed texts, rescuing them thereby from the imminent danger of being no more than ephemeral print commodities for sale in the marketplace.

Canon-Making

Canon-making may be considered the central activity of letters, the principal way that a text-centered institution formally objectifies its reality, defines itself, and gives an aura to its primary writings. In the eighteenth century, the first, most radical tendency of print and its logic of multiplicity was to destroy the canon of courtly letters centered on the classics and in a revolutionary, democratic manner to level all books in a continuous surge of new, ever-accumulating print products. But the systematizing logic or *esprit de système* of print imposed inbuilt restraints on this literary Maoism by offering new kinds of literary order and new sources of literary authority. It is possible to see Johnson actually realizing these possibilities to construct a new print-based literary canon in his criticism, in his biographies of the important English poets, and in his dogmatic social pronouncements about literature.

His vigorous canon-making shows an activity proceeding by exclusion as well as inclusion: Pope is a true poet but the metaphysicals, being obscure, are not; Percy's border ballads are acceptable but Ossian is spurious; Richardson is superior to Fielding because he knew the human heart; Sterne is transitory because novelty pleases only briefly, but Shakespeare will endure because he depicts the eternal truth of human nature. The Literary Club, including such notable writers as Goldsmith, Burke, Gibbon, Reynolds, Garrick, Hawkins, Percy, Boswell, and, presiding, the great cham of literature, gathered in an informal literary synod the men who helped to determine the canon. Collectively and individually they sorted out true literature from the literary apocrypha of ephemeral mass-cult trash the printing press spewed out daily; established in criticism such key principles as Burke's sublime or Johnson's "just representations of general nature" that were to become the new orthodoxies on which canonicity was based; and edited authoritative scholarly editions, Percy's border ballads or Johnson's Shakespeare.

The activities of the Literary Club reveal the human basis of canon-making, the personal prejudices, the chance interests of the individuals involved, the power struggles outside and inside the group, the mistakes such as Johnson's declaration that *Tristram Shandy* "did not last." But for a definitive model of the dynamics of canon-making we can look at the determinations of the sacred books of Judaism and Christianity by synods of experts convoked to define orthodoxy by this means in times of challenge and great social change, when Judaism was threatened by Christianity, and when Christianity became the official religion of the Roman state. A set of canonical books was chosen as authentic, these examples tell us, in the midst of severe controversy, to defend and reinforce a fundamental set of religious and social values. According to some historians of religion, books were included in the Old Testament canon if the rabbis judged that they were written before the true age of prophecy had ended, thus defending the law and the older books against new writings. The New Testament canon was, by some arguments, selected in order to stress continuity with the Old Testament (typology), the actual human existence of Jesus, and his mission to all of mankind, not to a single sect or people. We might say that the canonical books of the Christian bible were chosen with an eye to making Christianity historical and actual in a way that included and appealed to all conditions of life, and all peoples. The biblical canons also reveal that the making of a canon generates not only the sacred canonical texts—"texts that defile the hands" in Hebrew—but several types of supporting texts as well, such as an apocrypha of non-canonical texts that defines the canonical by contrast, and a collection of commentary, midrash and church fathers, which interprets the essence of the canonical, explains contradictions in the original, and adjusts its meanings to changing historical circumstances. Supporting specialties, such as textual editing and bibliography appear in time to establish and guard the true form of the texts that have been canonized as sacred.

The literary canon, having no specific location and no official form, such as a bible, remains always more open and more elusive, both in the history of its development and its substance at any given point in time, than the biblical canons; which is one reason why letters is always a less coherent and definite social institution than religion. But the making of a new literary canon in the eighteenth century follows the pattern of the making of the biblical canons. The official synod may be lacking, or appear only as a loose, informal group like the Club, but the distinctive marks of canon-making—such as the apocrypha of Grub Street hackwriting, the increase of legitimating criticism, the enormous growth in the activity of editing literary texts— all appear at this time. And they emerge in a time of crisis when the old courtly literary order was falling apart in a flood of printed books and an increasing rational skepticism about the value of letters.

The history of biblical canons reveals that the essence of canon-making is an effort to legitimate some central value or quality, by this means, in the face of a real threat to the existence of the institution. The deepest threat to letters, the root of its crisis in Johnson's time and since, has been nothing less than a question of its truth and its social value. No longer legitimated by its association with the old aristocratic social order, no longer justified by correspondence with prior and well-established moral, political, religious, and philosophical systems, letters in a commercial age had to find and validate new ways of associating itself with truth in some form. Most of the literary activity, including canon-making, in Johnson's time and later can be understood as, at root, attempts to establish and make believable a particular kind of literary truth. The new role of the writer as a struggler with meaninglessness that Johnson and Boswell constructed was one approach to the problem; Burke offered another in his conception of the sublime as the true poetic subject, and later romantic writers would attack the issue even more aggressively, as Keats did, for example, when he declared in a letter to Benjamin Bailey, "What the imagination seizes as beauty must be truth—whether it existed before or not" (22 November 1817), and as Blake did in declaring the truths of rational science—"the atoms of Democritus and Newton's particles of light"—to be no more than "sands upon the Red Sea shore Where Israel's tents do shine so bright."

Johnson's canon-making activities are efforts to establish letters as the source of particular kinds of truth, but, for reasons his remarkable experience with the *Debates in the Senate of Lilliput* makes clear, he was unable and unwilling to use the eventual romantic solution of the problem: that fiction is a superior kind of imaginative truth. Working very freely from reporters' handwritten notes of oral performances, Johnson wrote, early in his career, a series of articles for *The Gentleman's Magazine, Debates in the Senate of Lilliput*, which declared themselves to be fictional while actually offering themselves with a knowing wink as true renderings of contemporary parliamentary debates. In Johnson's opinion the *Debates* bore little resemblance to what was actually said in Parliament. They were mainly fictions brought into being by the parliamentary politics of the time, which still concealed its workings from the public by prohibiting any publication of its proceedings. A reasonable desire on the part of the public to know what the legislators said, offered the editor Cave a chance to capitalize on this interest, and Johnson a way to meet his need at this early stage in his career to make a living by any work which came to hand. The result of these casually linked motives was a new printed reality, considerably firmer than the mysterious parliamentary actuality, for Johnson's fictions were "thought genuine," and so well did he write that Voltaire used the *Debates* to compare British and Roman oratory. Later, various members of Parliament were to claim as their own the speeches Johnson had created and assigned to his characters. Johnson laughed when he discovered in an edition of Lord Chesterfield's miscellaneous works "two speeches ascribed to him, both of which were written by me:

and the best of it is, [the editors] have found out that one is like Demosthenes, and the other like Cicero." In a letter to Boswell, printed by Waingrow, Bowles reported that Johnson also said of these speeches that "they came both from the Garret where I thought neither of Demosthenes nor Cicero, but only of my dinner." The power of print to make fiction of fact and fact of fiction went even further than Johnson thought, for he could not, according to G. B. Hill in a note to the passage quoted above, have written one of the speeches he claims since it appeared in *The Gentleman's Magazine* before he began writing for that journal.

Johnson was, though he laughed at Lord Chesterfield, deeply troubled when he first discovered that his *Debates* were taken for truth and "determined that he would write no more of them; for 'he would not be accessary to the propagation of falsehood.' " This remark, along with his deathbed repentance—"the Parliamentary Debates were the only part of his writings which then gave him any compunction"—voice his often reiterated concern of the necessity for distinguishing fiction from fact. What the *Debates* really show, however, with their pattern of actual speeches transformed to notes changed to stories taken for fact by the original speakers and the author who thought he knew they were fictions, is how very tangled the whole question of fact and fiction was becoming in print culture. The nature of truth was, of course, an increasingly difficult question in the culture at large, as the mere names of Locke, Berkeley, and Hume make clear, but it was a particularly pressing and difficult problem for letters, and one on which the construction of the new literary canon centered. Unable and unwilling to declare boldly the superior truth of fiction to fact, Johnson sought and made new kinds of truth, and new sources of aura, for letters in a variety of ways that anticipate some of the principal ways later used to legitimate letters.

Print Fixity and the Edition of Shakespeare

Johnson, standing as he did at the point of change from a manuscript to a print culture, was very sensitive to the reality conferred on a text by print fixity, and explained it very fully and accurately in *Rambler* 23:

> I have had occasion to observe, sometimes with vexation, and sometimes with merriment, the different temper with which the same man reads a printed and manuscript performance. When a book is once in the hands of the public, it is considered as permanent and unalterable; and the reader, if he be free from personal prejudices, takes it up with no other intention than of pleasing or instructing himself; he accommodates his mind to the author's design; and, having no interest in refusing the amusement that is offered him, never interrupts his own tranquillity by studied cavils, or destroys his satisfaction in that which is already well, by an anxious enquiry how it might be better; but is often contented without pleasure, and pleased without perfection.
>
> But if the same man be called to consider the merit of a production yet unpublished, he brings an imagination heated with objections to passages, which he has yet never heard; he invokes all the powers of criticism, and stores his memory with Taste and Grace, Purity and Delicacy, Manners and Unities, sounds which, having been once uttered by those that understood them, have been since re-echoed without meaning, and kept up to the disturbance of the world, by a constant repercussion from one coxcomb to another. He considers himself as obliged to shew, by some proof of his abilities, that he is not consulted to no purpose, and, therefore, watches every opening for objection, and looks round for every opportunity to propose some specious alteration. Such opportunities a very small degree of sagacity will enable him to find; for, in every work of imagination, the disposition of parts, the insertion of incidents, and use of decorations, may be varied a thousand ways with equal propriety; . . .

Johnson recognizes that while there is no absolute rightness, "propriety" as he puts it, in any particular text—it could equally well be put together in any number of other ways—once printed it becomes "permanent and unalterable," and a reader accepts it as fact in a way he will never accept a manuscript.

What Johnson describes so well here is print's remarkable ability to confer authoritative being and firm truth on its texts in a wide variety of particular ways, such as, by way of obvious example, a scholarly edition that idealizes the text. This type of edition is both the historical and conceptual product of print, for not only could there be no authoritative texts before print—every manuscript inevitably being different—but print greatly strengthened a belief that there can be an absolute text of any work. A printed text—written in manuscript and edited, set in type, printed, proofed, corrected, addenda and variants attached—is capable of being "accurate," if not absolutely, then still to a degree that a manuscript can never be, and it achieves further accuracy in successive corrected editions. What it corresponds to in its accuracy is not so obvious; it is usually said to be the author's intention, but in fact it turns out to be some form of itself generated and fixed in the process of writing, editing, and printing. Furthermore, the availability, side by side, of several different editions of a printed book, often including printed versions of earlier manuscripts, points to the possibility of establishing an ideal though nonexistent text underlying and reconciling all versions. Print logic, we can say, encourages in many different ways the concept of a single accurate text, offers the means to assemble such a text, and realizes its idealizing potential in an actual printed text, solidly fixed in permanent form on the printed page, always exactly the same in copy after copy. This platonizing power of print has been in the Gutenberg age one of the major sources of literary aura, in the form of pure and permanent textual being, and literary people have capitalized on this potentiality in many ways, such as establishing a science of bibliography and publishing elaborately edited authoritative editions. These then become the true texts, the essential canon, ideal and perfect in form, objectifying that idealization in the elaborate and carefully printed authoritative editions that look so distinguished and solid on our library shelves.

Johnson, in many ways our first Ph.D., well understood the importance of the scholarly and editorial role in letters. He spoke frequently of the necessity for every generation to edit and annotate old works such as Walton's *Lives*; he loved languages and collected specimens of ancient tongues; he was probably the most widely read man in England. An excellent bibliographer, he also had a firm historical knowledge of the ways past and present differed in language and beliefs. The learned compiler of the *Dictionary*, editor of Shakespeare, and critical authority, as well as the biographer of the English poets and the historian of English poetry, he was the ideal scholar-editor he so feelingly defended in the "Preface to Shakespeare" against Pope's contempt: "In perusing a corrupted piece, [the editor] must have before him all possibilities of meaning, with all possibilities of expression. Such must be his comprehension of thought, and such his copiousness of language. Out of many readings possible, he must be able to select that which best suits with the state, opinions, and modes of language prevailing in every age, and with his authour's particular cast of thought, and turn of expression. Such must be his knowledge, and such his taste. . . . Let us now be told no more of the dull duty of an editor."

Johnson was an honest scholar who searched out and reported actual historical facts. He was also a man who in his deepest being was disposed to view human and social life, and all of their products, as a murky, confused, and often meaningless jumble of accidents in which solid facts and definite patterns are very difficult to find. When in 1756 in preparation for his edition of Shakespeare's plays he surveyed in his "Proposals for printing . . . Shakespeare" the history of the Shakespearean texts, he found not a single ideal text representing the "true" intention of the author but a complex historical tangle of human accidents:

> [Shakespeare] . . . sold [his plays], not to be printed, but to be played. They were immediately copied for the actors, and multiplied by transcript after transcript, vitiated by the blunders of the penman, or changed by the affectation of the player; perhaps enlarged to introduce a jest, or mutilated to shorten the representation; and printed at last without the concurrence of the authour, without the consent of the proprietor, from compilations made by chance or by stealth out of the separate parts written for the theatre: and thus thrust into the world surreptitiously and hastily, they suffered another depravation from the ignorance and negligence of the printers, as every man who knows the state of the press in that age will readily conceive.
>
> It is not easy for invention to bring together so many causes concurring to vitiate a text. No other authour ever gave up his works to fortune and time with so little care: no books could be left in hands so likely to injure them, as plays frequently acted, yet continued in manuscript: no other transcribers were likely to be so little qualified for their task as those who copied for the stage, at a time when the lower ranks of the people were universally illiterate: no other editions were made from fragments so minutely broken, and so fortuitously reunited; and in no other age was the art of printing in such unskilful hands.

Robert Scholes, in a summary discussion of Johnson's edition of Shakespeare, says that he might have been aware that an "ideal manuscript may never have existed, even in the poet's mind," and while there may be some ambiguity in the passage just quoted about the existence, somewhere, somehow, of a "true" text, the full weight of Johnson's argument surely falls on the side of showing that there never was an absolute, freestanding, text that embodies the final will of the author and is, therefore, *the* fact of the play. The *facts* are a long line of human accidents, carelessness in the printing house, pirated compilations, blundering scribes, illiteracy, changes made by actors fattening their parts, and an author who wrote for performance in the theater and took no care to see his plays printed. The reality of Shakespeare's plays is a complex *history*, not an absolute *text*, a history to which Johnson was about to add another chapter by producing still another text, compounded of earlier editions, elaborated with a biography, critical opinions, and explanatory notes.

This view of things, according as it does with Johnson's skepticism about any absolutes, is but one instance of the abyss of meaninglessness that his big writing projects always encounter, only to be ultimately bridged by heroic effort and assertion of common-sense principles. And here as elsewhere the certainty of a true text was largely supplied by print itself. Johnson's edition of a Shakespeare edition free of "corruptions" was a print-based activity from planning to editing to publication. Underwritten by a conger of booksellers in 1756, sold by subscription in an attempt to reduce the amount of capital that had to be risked and to guarantee sales, advertised by a printed "Proposal," the edition was printed by Strahan and proofread by Johnson play by play over nine years. It was at last published, after Johnson had been publicly shamed for his long delay, in one thousand sets of eight octavo volumes for the price of 2 guineas in 1765, immediately reprinted with corrections and then reissued with changes several times in following years. Print's power to constitute the ideal text extended below these surface events to the construction of the actual text as well. Johnson proposed two main editorial tasks for himself: notes that would clarify the meaning of obscure passages by interpreting them from passages in the printed books of Shakespeare's time, and a text free of accumulated corruptions. He was far more successful in the first project, which was what really interested him, than in the second, which required more

scholarly patience and detailed knowledge of the Shakespearean texts than he or any other scholar of his day possessed. The
first Shakespearean editor with something like a full understanding of the textual issue was Edmond Malone, who helped
Boswell so greatly in writing the *Life*.

Earlier editors of Shakespeare, from Rowe through Warburton, had assumed that all the earlier printed texts were corrupt
in various ways, and substituted their own versions of what
they thought Shakespeare should have written for any passage
they found difficult or not to their taste. Sometimes these conjectural emendations succeeded brilliantly, as Theobald's famous transformation of Falstaff's dying words in the 1623 Folio, "a Table of greene fields," to "a babbl'd of green fields," but
more often the substitutions were less satisfactory. In the
"Preface" to his edition, Johnson rejected this emendatory criticism—"that intuition by which the poet's intention is immediately discovered, and that dexterity of intellect which des-
patches its work by the easiest means"—in favor of a collation
of the earliest texts, to exhibit, he goes on, "all the observable
varieties of all the copies that can be found." In execution his
edition fell far short of this goal, but his Gutenberg trust in the
authority of the printed book, even though a number of them
had to be collated to produce the true text, remained the central pillar of his project: "It has been my settled principle, that
the reading of the ancient books is probably true, and therefore is not to be disturbed for the sake of elegance, perspicuity,
or mere improvement of the sense. For though much credit is
not due to the fidelity, nor any to the judgement of the first
publishers, yet they who had the copy before their eyes were
more likely to read it right, than we who read it only by imagination."

He recognized that the history of the Shakespearean texts
gave no grounds for confidence in the possibility of disentangling a true text, but this he insisted in the "Proposal" was an

exception to the general rule that print makes true texts: "To have a text corrupt in many places, and in many doubtful, is, among the authours that have written since the use of types, almost peculiar to Shakespeare. Most writers, by publishing their own works, prevent all various readings, and preclude all conjectural criticism. Books indeed are sometimes published after the death of him who produced them, but they are better secured from corruptions than these unfortunate compositions. They subsist in a single copy, written or revised by the authour; and the faults of the printed volume can be only faults of one descent." How surprised would Johnson be could he see the huge bibliographic industry that has grown up since his time to edit many texts, including his own, that the authors themselves took the care to publish. In the end, Johnson's belief in the printed book overcame his awareness of the historical problems of the actual Shakespearean texts, and he in practice settled most often for the readings of the First Folio (1623) that had been published by two of the playwright's fellow actors to provide, they said, "true and perfect copies" of plays that the author had taken no care to print and which had previously existed only in various "maimed" quarto versions. Modern scholarship has shown that Heminges and Condell must have known that their claims to accuracy were at least partly false, and Johnson surely knew that the Folio was imperfect in many very obvious places, but such was the authority of the printed book that Johnson still "resolved to insert none of my own readings in the text. Upon this caution I now congratulate myself, for every day encreases my doubt of my emendations." The result was not really a modern scholarly edition, for Johnson, despite his stated intention to do so, did not compare many of the printed versions. He did, however, change punctuation freely, believing, with cause, that the original pointing was often a printing-house accident; he also suggested emended readings in his notes, and printed a number of lines as emended by previous editors. But Johnson's *Shakespeare* can fairly be called the first modern edition of the plays, printed and edited with a firm Gutenberg belief that, despite contrary evidence, there is behind all the historical accidents a true uncorrupted text, which represents the authoritative intention of the author and which can be most nearly approached in the early printed versions of the plays, no matter how complex their relationship. The circularity of this kind of textual idealization is normally concealed but runs something like this: print encourages the conception of a single authentic text, identified with the author's unchanging intent, which is then assembled by the editor collating the previously printed texts and printing the result in an authoritative edition that in turn objectifies the original hypothesis of a true text. In this way the literary text is taken out of history and acquires an aura of idealized perfection, authorized by the author's mind and realized as hard bibliographical fact, solidly out there, typographically fixed, in eight octavo volumes costing two gold guineas.

Both the value of the text and its reality were further enhanced by the notes of the printed edition. In the "Preface" to his Shakespeare edition, Johnson refers to himself as a scholiast, and although the footnotes in a printed book do not usually surround the text like manuscript *scholia*, they too set off the text visually as a distinct object on the page and increase its firmness of being by making it a subject which the notes engage in dialogue in order to discover its nature and meanings. "Where any passage appeared inextricably perplexed," says Johnson, using a metaphor which makes clear both how substantial the text was for him and the way in which meaning was inscribed in it, "my first labour is, always to turn the old text on every side, and try if there be any interstice, through which light can find its way. . . ." Notes keyed to the text are characteristic products of print, made possible by its technology and encouraged by its general *esprit de système*, and Johnson took full advantage of what was offered by writing copious notes, correcting and adding to them in proof, printing additional notes as addenda to the final volume, and making changes in them in subsequent editions. They are usually praised as acute interpretations of Shakespearean language, which they are, but they also quietly intensify the aura of the literary text they explain by attributing to it an inherent, unchanging, and mysterious meaning of its own.

Style and the Printed Text

It became the custom in the eighteenth century for editors of Shakespeare, and of other writers, to call attention to what Johnson in his "Preface" refers to as "poetical beauties or defects," the more prominent features of verbal style. The word "style" is derived from the stylus, the instrument for writing; but style, as an aspect of rhetoric, was an important feature of oratory, and writers from Aristotle in his *Rhetoric* to Pope in his translation of *The Iliad* distinguished between an oral and a written style. The oral style was generally thought to be concerned with large-scale effects, for example, the uses of the plain, the middle, and the high styles in persuading listeners at a public performance; the written style was believed properly to emphasize the smaller, more precise effects that determine meaning for readers. The tendency of writing to emphasize a detailed style was intensified by print and by new interests in psychological processes such as associationism, the sublime, and the behavior of genius, all qualities that found expression in style and increasingly made it an important element of the literary text in the course of the eighteenth century. In *From Classic to Romantic*, W. J. Bate speaks of a "transition to empirical aesthetic criticism" in the latter half of the eighteenth century, and describes a new print-based emphasis on style in the following way: "Before this period . . . neo-classic discussions of rhetoric had been rather general: now, however, problems of diction, metaphor, sentence-structure, and prose-rhythm were investigated in great detail, with continual reference to concrete illustrations. This half-century also witnessed the flowering of the study of English versification. Few problems in English prosody have since been discussed which were not explored or at least recognized then." It is ironic that printed texts designed to be read in silence provided the basis for a thorough analysis of the sounds of poetry, but only when the texts were fixed by print could the metrics be thoroughly analyzed.

The way in which print foregrounded style appears in a little scene in which, appropriately enough in the presence of a printer, Mr. Allen, Boswell brags to Johnson about the accuracy of the stenographic method he had developed for recording scenes and conversations. Johnson challenges Boswell's accuracy and tests it by means of a simple device: "he made the experiment by reading slowly and distinctly a part of Robertson's 'History of America', while I endeavoured to write it in my way of taking notes. It was found that I had it very imperfectly; the conclusion from which was, that *its excellence was principally owing to a studied arrangement of words, which could not be varied or abridged without an essential injury*" (my italics). All the media contending for dominance at the time, voice, writing, print, are present in this little scene, but print is used as the source of the text and the standard of accuracy, and its "excellence" is found to lie in its ability to fix and hold precisely in place for extended perusal a carefully structured verbal pattern which is conceived of in its exact details as "essential" to the being of the text. Print foregrounds style in the way this scene shows by locking the exact arrangement of words permanently into place, down to the smallest detail, thus encouraging the writer to shape his sentences with extraordinary care and the reader to consider and reconsider the finer points in a way that a listener never can. Print fixity, and print's tendency toward system, make style an obvious fact, we might say, of any printed text, where it becomes the source of the stylistic aura that Sainte-Beuve memorializes in his famous remark that "There is nothing immortal in literature except style." In the age of print, style has increasingly become a crucial element of the true literary work, not only, as it was in rhetoric, the tool of persuasion or the ornament that makes content more attractive, but true meaning and content in itself, the signature of imaginative genius, and even the language of unconscious or transcendental knowledge. For the great stylist and theorist of style, Paul Valéry, the power of style is such that it can achieve its own organic being and become itself a new Adamic language rising above the dialects of Babel: "Style, so pure is the word in sound and aspect, it would be a delightful name for some choice being, a rare bird, a character in a fairy tale. It is one of those names whose musical quality suggests a language whose words sound out their meaning."

Samuel Johnson was not the first writer with a pronounced and distinctive style—in our modern view, all great writers of any age have a powerful style—nor was he by any means the first critic to analyze style in a cogent way. The importance of style for Johnson is, however, impossible to overestimate, for not only was the style the man, as the familiar saying, with which Johnson agreed, has it, but in his case the man was the style. In a way earlier unknown, this prototypical man of print was real to his contemporaries by a distinctive style, which from the outset of his career made both his person and his writing stand out from the other hacks and their work. It was as a style—"Sir, the truth of the matter is"—that the man himself had his being in social life, and imitating and parodying the Johnsonian style in manners, writing, and conversation, chiefly his use of gargantuan words, ultimately became one of the fashionable parlor games of the time.

Johnson was himself intensely self-conscious about his style and said that he had formed it on Chambers' "Proposal for his *Dictionary*," and the writings of Swift's patron, Sir William Temple; but Boswell perceived that their "styles differ as plain cloth and brocade," and rightly added that "the style of Johnson was, undoubtedly, much formed upon that of the great writers in the last century, Hooker, Bacon, Sanderson, Hakewell, and others." What Johnson primarily took from these writers and made his own was, Boswell remarks at various times, a rhythmic sentence structure, referred to in its different aspects as cadenced, balanced, melodic, periodic, and rounded. Boswell also calls attention to Johnson's fondness for big words and his abstract latinate diction, as well as to his precise metaphors and the vigor or drive of the Johnsonian sentence. Later criticism, and here I mainly follow W. K. Wimsatt in his analysis of Johnson's style, has been somewhat more precise, though no more effective in catching the feel of Johnson's prose. The sentences are long, an average of 51.4 words, but they are kept clear and harmonious by constant parallelism: the exact balancing of grammatical elements, words, phrases, and clauses; and by equally constant antithesis, the matching of each unit with an opposite. The Johnsonian sentence is not periodic in the exact classical sense in which meaning remains suspended until the absolute grammatical conclusion, though the individual clauses are often structured in this way; but the sentences get much of their strength from an overall periodic architectural pattern in which a series of parallelisms and antitheses is fully completed only when the final element locks solidly into place. At the level of individual words, grand and abstract terms are frequently paired with a more solid common word. Nouns derived from Latin, for example, are often modified by adjectives of Germanic origin. The effect of the style in its sun-

nier moments can be heard in Imlac's famous description of
the style of the true poet at the end of Chapter X of *Rasselas*:
"he must know many languages and many sciences; and that
his stile may be worthy of his thoughts, must, by incessant practice, familiarize to himself every delicacy of speech and grace
of harmony."

   Johnson's style was another device, among many, with which
he made the solid reality he needed, taking what is vague and
uncertain, the abstract conceptions represented by the polysyl-
labic latinate words in this case, and locking them firmly into
a structure of similarity and difference, always pairing or opposing one element to another in a way that forced reciprocal
illumination and precision, building up the elements of composition until the whole is as stable as a line of print, as fully
self-verifying in little as a language or a philosophic system on
a larger scale. In the very suggestive terms used by Paul Frankl
to define architectural styles, the Johnsonian style is a "Style of
Being" rather than a "Style of Becoming," fixing a certain
meaning solidly in place, making it absolutely real, rather than
enacting a process of becoming or following an elusive, indeterminate meaning. Valéry, not thinking, of course, of Johnson, nevertheless described his style perfectly when he praised
the style that has the "magnificent balance" of the tiger rather
than the "instability, futile gambols, aimless leaps" of the mon-
key. The tiger's style, Valéry continues in a way that fits Johnson perfectly, suggests "a very perceptible but indefinable law,
which tempers the individual character of acts or works and
lends them the dignity of a type or model . . . [and] becomes a
kind of deviation towards the ideal." Boswell describes the
same authoritative effect of this style in a more literal way:
"Johnson writes like a teacher. He dictates to his readers as if
from an academical chair. They attend with awe and admiration; and his precepts are impressed upon them by his commanding eloquence."

A style, Johnson believed with his age, bears the mark of the individual who writes it: "Why, Sir, I think every man whatever has a peculiar style, which may be discovered by nice examination and comparison with others: but a man must write a great deal to make his style obviously discernible." Johnson did write a great deal and what that writing makes obvious is that the Johnsonian style expressed and satisfied his own existential need for authority and substantial reality. He made in his style what he sought everywhere, structure, solidity of being; and his verbal style enacted linguistically his primary activity of constructing satisfactory and believable realities in all areas of human life. But if the style was the man, a satisfaction of his needs and an expression of his being, it was also a print style, carrying into his arrangement of words such essential print characteristics as clarity, accuracy, linear order, and substantiality or factualization of its contents.

The close relationship of the Johnsonian style to print logic appears most obviously and convincingly in the ways it was developed and used by him as a writer to deal with the realities of working in the print world. Boswell, as we have seen, could not understand how Johnson while never appearing to write always managed to produce so much printable copy. He managed apparently, by consciously developing and making habitual a style which enabled him, literally while the printer's boy was waiting at the door for copy, to produce first drafts with great speed and such accuracy that they could be printed without revision: "he had early laid it down as a fixed rule to do his best on every occasion, and in every company; to impart whatever he knew in the most forcible language he could put it in; and that by constant practice, and never suffering any careless expressions to escape him, or attempting to deliver his thoughts without arranging them in the clearest manner, it became habitual to him." So habitual was this print style that it became Johnson's way of speaking as well as his way of writing.

He was, Boswell says of his talk, "always most perfectly clear and perspicuous; and his language was so accurate, and his sentences so neatly constructed, that his conversation might have been all printed without any correction." Even if we discount Boswell's characteristic exaggeration of the achievements of his hero, this is still a most remarkable statement, suggesting that print was becoming in Johnson's time sufficiently powerful to impose its standards—clarity, accuracy, orderly construction—on the oral world of conversation, where the quality of speech could now be measured by its ability to be "printed without any correction." In the world of letters at large, the close relationship of print and style was forcefully demonstrated by Johnson's continuing success and rise from drudgery to the dictatorship of the literary world primarily by the development, perhaps to the point of hypertrophy, of his distinctive style. To be a great writer in a print culture meant, his success shows, to be a great stylist, which meant in turn the deliberate cultivation of pronounced and exaggerated ways of writing and saying things. Johnson's good sense, learning, honesty, and wit are always admirable, but would any of his writings have had more than modest success in his time or ours had they not been so highly and distinctively styled?

Given the importance of style in Johnson's life and writing, it was inevitable that his literary criticism should focus on style in a manner which extended to letters in general his personal emphasis on style, making it a central fact of poetry and the literary text. There had, of course, been many discussions of poetic style before Johnson and most of the technical terms he used for analyzing style came from the ancient vocabulary of rhetoric. But Johnson, principally in his various essays and in *The Lives of the Poets*, established style as one of the principal facts of the literary text by making it an inextricable part of any discussion of poets and poetry, and by examining it with the kind of careful detail that print both allowed and encouraged. *The*

Lives are more spacious than most modern literary criticism, including as they do biographies, incidents illustrating character, publishing history, and literary quarrels, along with specimens of the poetry and plot summaries of major works. Then, at the end of each life, Johnson provides a formal discussion of the style of each poet, thus making it an important part of the total literary reality and a source of the excellence, or aura, of true literary texts.

At many places his reflections on style are grand and general in the old-fashioned oral kind of way: the superiority of rhymed to unrhymed verse in English, the importance of diction neither too familiar nor too remote, the positive effects of smooth numbers, the attractions of sublimity, and the pleasure provided by "vigorous sallies and sententious elegances." But if he says magisterially in his "Life of Dryden" of some of the poet's lines that they are "lofty, elegant, and musical," the critic's eye, closely focused on the printed text—that "microscope of *wit*," as Pope accurately if disparagingly called it—also peers intensely and long enough to perceive that Dryden's prose, in contrast to his own, has "not the formality of a settled style, in which the first half of the sentence betrays the other. The clauses are never balanced, nor the periods modelled; every word seems to drop by chance, though it falls into its proper place. Nothing is cold or languid; the whole is airy, animated and vigorous: what is little is gay; what is great is splendid." "He that reads many books," Johnson says in his "Life of Pope," "must compare one opinion or one style with another; and when he compares, must necessarily distinguish, reject, and prefer," and his own distinctions are most often those of a careful reader working with and comparing the printed texts before him. Indeed, he frequently puts the texts before his reader as well, printing specimens of the poetry he is examining, making his history of English poetry, *The Lives*, an anthology of style as well as a set of biographies, over which he labored diligently, dissecting the elaborate conceits of those poets whom he named "metaphysical," pausing to examine whether triplets or alexandrines are worth the metrical variety they provide, noting and disparaging the alliteration of "ruin" and "ruthless," "helm" and "hauberk" in Gray. He found his hero of style in Pope, who, he says in his life of that poet, "sent nothing to the press till it had lain two years under his inspection" and thereby achieved a style worthy to be praised without qualification by a careful reader: "He examined lines and words with minute and punctilious observation, and retouched every part with indefatigable diligence till he had left nothing to be forgiven." Turning to a poet whose style he did not like, he dismembers his writing with a detailed *explication de texte*: "Gray seems in his rapture to confound the images of 'spreading sound' and 'running water.' A 'stream of musick' may be allowed; but where does Musick, however 'smooth and strong,' after having visited the 'verdant vales,' 'rowl down the steep amain,' so as that 'rocks and nodding groves rebellow to the roar?' If this be said of Musick, it is nonsense; if it be said of Water, it is nothing to the purpose."

When Johnson considered the works of the poets he, of course, looked at printed texts, not oral performance or a few manuscripts. But to take the printed texts for granted would be to miss the crucial point that print inscribes style in the text in ways and to a degree that other media do not. The point can be made by a story Johnson tells in his "Life of Pope." When Pope was translating the *Iliad*, he read several sections of his work aloud to Lord Halifax, a noble poetaster and patron of letters. The performance was oral, though there was a manuscript behind it. Several times during the reading, Pope was, according to his own account, interrupted by Halifax who stopped him and said, rather vaguely, "there is something in that passage that does not quite please me.—Be so good as to mark the place, and consider it a little [more] at your leisure.—I'm sure you can give it a little [better] turn." After puzzling for some time over these vague criticisms, Pope, on the advice of Garth, waited on Halifax again, saying that "I hoped he would find his objections to those passages removed; read them to him exactly as they were at first: and his Lordship was extremely pleased with them, and cried out, 'Ay, now [Mr. Pope] they are perfectly right: nothing can be better.' " The first point of the poet's story is, of course, only the pretension to fine and exact taste in style by a foolish lord, but it also reveals strikingly how in an oral situation, style, not fixed by print, remains vague and general, somehow not quite fully there, even during the moment of saying and hearing.

Language and the Literary Text:
Johnson's DICTIONARY

Knowledge of the leading principles of print logic, such as fixity, multiplicity, and systematization, makes it possible to predict the tendencies but not the *exact* ways in which they were to manifest themselves in the history of writing and in the world of letters. The idealization of the literary text and the attribution to it of a stylistic essence are both developments of latent print possibilities, but there was, I believe, no precise necessity beforehand that letters would be valorized in *these* particular ways. Something at least of the intricate social activity and interplay of many factors that lead to the realization, from among the many possibilities, and the subsequent establishment of some particular kind of literary aura can be glimpsed in the long and intricate story of the commissioning, the assembling, and the publication of Johnson's *Dictionary.*

The *Dictionary* started, like most of Johnson's books, with the publishers. While Johnson later told Boswell that he had himself long thought of a dictionary, James Dodsley remembered his brother suggesting such a work to Johnson sometime in the early 1740s. Johnson declined to undertake the project at this time but then reached an agreement in the spring of 1746 with Robert Dodsley, wrote an outline, the "Short Scheme," in April, and signed a contract on June 18 with a conger of booksellers and printers formed to underwrite the considerable costs of a dictionary of the English language that would improve upon earlier English dictionaries such as those of Bailey and Chambers, and rival the great French and Italian dictionaries recently produced in those countries by the efforts of entire academies. Johnson later described in the "Preface" to his *Dictionary* his own feelings on this occasion as pleasure "with a prospect of the hours which I should revel away in feasts of literature, with the obscure recesses of northern learning which I should enter and ransack . . . and the triumph with which I should display my acquisitions to mankind." The publishers agreed to a total fee of £1,575, to be paid at intervals, and Johnson estimated that three years would be sufficient for the project. He proceeded to set up a little dictionary factory in the garret of the house at 17 Gough Square and settled down to work with several assistants, five of whom were Scots, paid 10 shillings a week, half a printer's wage. In August 1747, the famous *Plan* for the *Dictionary* was printed to advertise the *Dictionary*, and at Dodsley's urgings Johnson reluctantly but fulsomely addressed it to Lord Chesterfield, who thus became the nominal patron of the project.

The book was not printed all at one time when the manuscript was completed, but in batches of pages at different times, beginning in October 1750. Printing could proceed only when sufficient copy had accumulated, and Strahan could conveniently fit the work into his schedule. A fairly steady flow of copy was therefore needed. Johnson, in order to meet the printer's requirements for copy developed a production method in which he would read books, underline the words to be used in the *Dictionary*, mark off a context to be used to define a meaning, and put the first letter of the entry in the margin. His assistants would then copy out the marked passages, which were later sorted and pasted up in the proper order after Johnson wrote the main entry. He proceeded slowly, and the publishers had to exert constant pressure on him, urging speed because of the steadily increasing amount of capital absorbed by the venture, and demanding a steady flow of copy and speedy correction of the proofsheets because, as Strahan forcefully demonstrated to Johnson, the press stood idle and the type locked up until author's corrections of proof were made. Interestingly enough, many of the changes Johnson made in proof, some sheets of which still exist, were not, according to Sledd and Kolb in their detailed history of the *Dictionary*, made in the type. The printer also dictated that a number of manuscript sheets written on both sides in an attempt to save costly paper had to be laboriously and expensively redone because the compositor, for reasons neither entirely clear nor ever specified, would set only from copy written on one side of the paper. The publishers cut the number of entries and illustrative quotations in order to save space and money, and to keep the final cost of the book down to a price at which it could be sold. Given Johnson's irregular work habits and the unexpected Sisyphean difficulty of the task, the work inevitably dragged, the first volume not being completed until 1753 and the second until 1755, at which time the bookseller Andrew Millar, who coordinated the work for the conger, could say on receiving the final sheets of copy, "thank GOD I have done with him." To which Johnson, somewhat deflated, but amused, could only reply, "I am glad . . . that he thanks GOD for anything."

But it was done finally: about 40,000 entries, 114,000 illustrative quotations, over 2,500 double-column pages, a preface, a history of the language and a description of English grammar, all sumptuously printed in two thousand copies of two folio volumes, price £4.10s. Of its greatness and its success, which made the "humble drudge" into "Dictionary Johnson," little remains to be said, but of its relationship to print and letters something perhaps remains to be observed. The brief history of Johnson's *Dictionary* just sketched tells us that the printing business originated the project and shaped it in various practical ways, but these influences are only the signs, surface manifestations, of a still deeper involvement. The *Dictionary* was in the first place a practical handbook needed by the printing business to establish the authoritative spellings and, to only a slightly lesser degree, the fixed meanings which print, with its inbuilt tendency toward systematic regularity, required for its day-to-day operations of editing manuscripts and setting type with some consistency. It was also a book whose conception owed much to print and its characteristic *esprit de système* which made it possible to think of and then produce a systematic arrangement of all the words in the English language. Johnson was simply being practical when he used printed books, including earlier dictionaries, as a source for the words he included in his *Dictionary*, and then established their meanings by copying out passages that contained the same words from other books; but this way of working reveals the close dependence on print culture and its books of the dictionary idea that a language has a limited number of words, each with a few correct meanings. Johnson observed in his "Preface" that the varieties of pronunciation "will always be observed to grow fewer and less different, as books are multiplied," and this tendency is equally at work in the lexicon and its spellings and meanings, for his, or any, dictionary objectifies print's pressure toward normalization by limiting, ordering, and fixing language in its various aspects in an authoritative way. A dictionary, we might say, is not just another book but the essential book of print, Gutenberg's secular bible, at once a supremely practical manual for author, compositor, and proofreader, and a revelation of the metaphysics of print, its ability to abstract, order, and idealize language. Roy Harris in *The Language Myth* points out that "The distinction between a language and its use, like the distinction between a language and its acquisition, is a theoretical artifact," and that theoretical artifact objectively realized is, of course, the printed dictionary.

Once the work was done and the *Dictionary* printed and bound in two folio volumes, it became *The English Language*, and so great is the power of type to create a positivist linguistic reality that to subsequent generations it has seemed apparent that language is what a dictionary makes it, a limited number of "real" words ordered alphabetically, with correct pronunciations, orthography, derivations, and a limited range of meanings.

In writing his *Dictionary*, however, Johnson came to understand that the order conferred on language by a dictionary is a print-derived rationalistic system imposed amid and upon a chaotic scene of actual living speech and writing, of which the circumstances in which he had to work on the *Dictionary* were a fair image: "the English Dictionary was written with little assistance of the learned, and without any patronage of the great; not in the soft obscurities of retirement, or under the shelter of academick bowers, but amidst inconvenience and distraction, in sickness and in sorrow." Written, that is, by a living man whose wife, with whom he had a deep and complicated relationship, died while he was working on the *Dictionary*, by a man always pressed for money who was forced to beg two-pound advances from the publishers and who undertook the writing of a series of essays, *The Rambler*, partly to support himself and partly to relieve the boredom of the endless search for words and their meanings. He worked sitting on a chair with only three legs. He struggled with and helped his assistants like the Scot Macbean, improvident and needy, learned in quirky ways and fond of gambling and drink; he borrowed the books he needed to work with but

could not afford to buy, and marked them up to the annoyance
of their owners; and always he was depressed, worried about
his health, and uncertain of his place in a social world in which
he had no absolute confidence anyway. And in the midst of all
these gut-wrenching disturbances and glum confusions he had
constantly to make a series of precise linguistic decisions of a
kind which W. K. Wimsatt, who had a real sense of Johnson,
describes very feelingly: "Imagine yourself half-way through
Johnson's program of reading for the *Dictionary*, arriving at [a]
page of Bacon's *Natural History*. . . . Which of the words and
passages on the page would you mark in black lead pencil for
your amanuenses to copy? Which would you pass over? By
what norms would you make your selection? How many min-
utes would you need to reach your decisions on one page?" In
his "Preface" to the *Dictionary*, Johnson himself describes with
great exactitude his own feelings in these same circumstances,
the actual turns and twists of thought, the feelings of hopelessness at the task, and at the passage of time, the sudden blank-
ness of a mind struggling to order a swirling world of words:

> consider that no dictionary of a living tongue ever can be perfect,
> since, while it is hastening to publication, some words are bud-
> ding, and some falling away; that a whole life cannot be spent
> upon syntax and etymology, and that even a whole life would not
> be sufficient; that he, whose design includes whatever language
> can express, must often speak of what he does not understand;
> that a writer will sometimes be hurried by eagerness to the end,
> and sometimes faint with weariness under a task, which Scaliger
> compares to the labours of the anvil and the mine; that what is ob-
> vious is not always known, and what is known is not always pres-
> ent; that sudden fits of inadvertency will surprise vigilance, slight
> avocations will seduce attention, and casual eclipses of the mind
> will darken learning; and that the writer shall often in vain trace
> his memory, at the moment of need, for that which yesterday he

knew with intuitive readiness, and which will come uncalled into his thoughts to-morrow.

Print with its constant demand for copy, with its steadily increasing stacks of printed pages in the warehouse, moved inexorably toward realizing its own logic of system and fixity in language stabilized by a dictionary. But Johnson's actual experience of writing the book, though these events are not usually considered part of the book, shows what a desperate and uncertain enterprise fixing and systematizing language was from a human point of view. His experienced life as he worked was the whirl of things, feelings, people, and events that he knew so well, a life which for him was always likely to open on an emptiness where understanding fails completely. Language is the culture's and the individual's primary defense against meaninglessness, and Johnson, the great language man, began his dictionary work with at least a stated belief that language is an ideal, absolute order underlying the particularities and confusions of actual usage. He speaks, for example, in his "Preface," of English as if it had an essence that during the course of history had been "neglected; suffered to spread, under the direction of chance, into wild exuberance; resigned to the tyranny of time and fashion; and exposed to the corruptions of ignorance, and caprices of innovation." He never entirely gave up this idealizing belief that behind historical change and randomness there is still a true language, "the fabrick of the tongue," as he called it, which it is the work of the lexicographer to find and restore.

Though Johnson never entirely abandoned his view of an essential language, as he worked on the *Dictionary* and became more deeply involved with the linguistic actualities he had so happily and hopefully undertaken to order, "resolved to leave neither words nor things unexamined," he records in his "Preface" that he found neither the Adamic language of earlier lin-

guists—"*words*," he discovered, "*are the daughters of earth, and . . .
things are the sons of heaven*"—nor any regular laws of historical
change such as those developed by nineteenth-century Indo-
European philology; nor did he find the *langue* below the *parole*
of twentieth-century structural linguistics. Instead, he came
face to face with "the boundless chaos of a living speech" that
was "copious without order, and energetick without rules:
wherever I turned my view, there was perplexity to be disen-
tangled, and confusion to be regulated; choice was to be made
out of boundless variety, *without any established principle of selection*; adulterations were to be detected, *without a settled test of pu-
rity*; . . ." (italics mine). Not only was there no existing linguistic
order, there were not even (as the italicized words indicate) any
known or discoverable rules for ascertaining a pre-existent order or for creating one. For example, fixing the orthography,
one of Johnson's first tasks, seemed relatively straightforward
at first, but he soon discovered that the written language rests
on speech, and a word which is pronounced differently in various dialects inevitably has different spellings, none authoritative. Furthermore, the vowel sounds of English are so uncertain, no two mouths ever quite pronouncing them in the same
way, that pronunciation cannot determine spelling: "some
combinations of letters, having the same power, are used indif-
ferently without any discoverable reason of choice, as in *choak,
choke; soap, sope*." It is also, he found, impossible to ascertain
spelling by means of derivation since it is almost never certain
whether a word entered English directly from French or Latin.
Finally, he remarks, the written language is itself filled with
anomalies and irregularities of spelling, such as *length* from
long and *darling* from *dear*, which have become so deeply fixed
by custom that no lexicographer can change them.

   Johnson did not like these linguistic irregularities and uncer-
tainties, which he, still reluctant to give up the idea of a "true"
language, called "spots of barbarity impressed so deep in the

English language, that criticism can never wash them away."
But he discovered them in every area where his dictionary
work forced him to look carefully at linguistic actualities. Pronunciation, where he sought only to mark the primary accent,
is in practice, he found, various and arbitrary. Etymologies, an
area in which he was weak, particularly in the Teutonic languages, are uncertain and "words which are represented as . . .
related by descent or cognation, do not always agree in sense."
Even the basic question of trying to decide which words were
to be included in the dictionary as "true" English words
brought an infinity of actually used words into view: proper
names, technical terms, foreign words, compounds, partici-
ples, and other derivatives, archaisms, and even signs from a
strange linguistic limbo where Johnson found "words of which
I have reason to doubt the existence."

However, it was when he came to the matter of definitions,
or as he called them "explanations," that the major difficulties
of the dictionary project appeared. Meaning begins to crumble
when he tries to define particles and expletives "of which the
sense is too subtle and evanescent to be fixed in a paraphrase,"
and it disappears altogether when he finds words "which I cannot explain, because I do not understand them." And often in
the case of even more apparently solid words "the signification
is so loose and general, the use so vague and indeterminate,
and the senses detorted so widely from the first idea, that it is
hard to trace them through the maze of variation, to catch
them on the brink of utter inanity, to circumscribe them by any
limitations, or interpret them by any words of distinct and settled meaning; such are *bear, break, come, cast, fall, get*. . . ." In the
end he inevitably comes to and describes the tautology that
structuralists have identified as the principle by which language—being "non-referential" or not connected to some ex-
tra—linguistic, prior reality—makes meaning. Johnson describes the semantic circle as the necessity "that *the explanation,*

and *the word explained, should be always reciprocal.*" "Explanations," he continues, "are unavoidably reciprocal or circular, as *hind, the female of the stag; stag, the male of the hind*: sometimes easier words are changed into harder, as *burial* into *sepulture*, or *interment, drier* into *desiccative, dryness* into *siccity* or *aridity, fit* into *paroxysm*; for the easiest word, whatever it be, can never be translated into one more easy."

After describing how much Johnson borrowed from earlier English and continental dictionaries and linguistic theories, the most scrupulous historians of his *Dictionary*, James Sledd and Gwin Kolb, conclude that "Johnson was not an original thinker about language," and pronounce that there is very little real lexicographic innovation in his work. Both the truth, and the necessary qualifications, of this position, are to be found, by way of example, in Johnson's doubts about Adamic language, doubts which fit into his Lockean century's rejection of innate ideas in general and of all the older idealizing linguistic theories that are described by Murray Cohen as "characterized by assumptions of the divine origin or divine guidance of language, prospects of a renewed universal language, and faith in the correspondence between words and the order of things (or, later, between syntax and the ways of the mind). [The] earlier writers integrated philosophical, pedagogic, and descriptive linguistics in a synchronous system." Like most educated men in the eighteenth century, Johnson probably knew Locke better than any other philosopher, and nowhere is he more the follower of Locke than in linguistic matters, where he quotes him more than any other author, no less than 1,674 times in the first volume of the *Dictionary*. Both the working principles of the *Dictionary* and its "Preface" are closely related in some ways, practical applications really, at least at the outset, of the theoretical views that Locke sets down in the third book, "Words," in his *Essay Concerning Human Understanding* (1690). Locke's argument here is notoriously inconsistent, or at least *very* difficult, but the general interpretation, which Johnson seems to have shared, of the nature of language was straightforward. Language, for Locke, is not innate, as the different languages of mankind prove, nor is it Adamic in the sense that there is some mystical connection between words and the things they name. Instead, language is a system of conventional signs, socially agreed upon, which, as Locke puts it, are "the voluntary signs of our own ideas." Ideas are, in turn, the mental forms of knowledge derived from sensible observations of "things as they do really exist." Complex ideas are built up in the mind by combining or extrapolating simple ideas in several ways. Locke rationally proposes that words representing complex ideas are to be determined by reference to their constituent simple ideas, while these simple ideas, which, lacking constituents, cannot be defined in the same way, can be referred to the things, however imperfectly known, from which they derive. Pictures and diagrams might be useful for this purpose, Locke thought, and these devices are a feature of many later dictionaries, though not of Johnson's early editions. Words, Locke says very plainly in III, ii, 8, "*signify* only men's peculiar *ideas*, and that *by a perfectly arbitrary imposition.*"

These and other Lockean proposals for clarifying the meaning of words—like using no word which does not signify a distinct idea, or avoiding ambiguity by always using the same word for the same idea—provide a logical philosophy for thinking clearly and using language accurately. Locke himself admitted, however, that "it was not so easy to be done," and recognized that in language as used, many words—prepositions, for example—do not refer to any distinct ideas at all, that words shift their meaning from person to person and time to time, and that the ideas to which a word refers, and the things to which ideas refer, are not the same in every mind. Hans Aarsleff, the historian of the philosophy of language, has demonstrated that Locke's theories of language share in his general skepticism about the possibility of any absolute knowledge or of any total system of understanding, but in practice he proceeds straightforwardly and appears to offer an analytic view that clear thinking and clear language can be achieved by giving "settled and fixed names" to all ideas and referring these in turn to distinct and precisely observed things. These views of Locke, according to Cohen, determined the boundaries of the language world for most eighteenth-century linguists, for whom "the ostensible categories and capacities of language seem settled even if they were not completely inarguable."

Samuel Johnson obviously belonged to this group of admirers and followers of Locke and his clear world of words, ideas, and things. He draws heavily on Locke for ideas about language and the relation of words to the world and to human thought in the "Preface" to the *Dictionary*. Even his ultimate doubts about any absolute linguistic system are basically very Lockean. But when it came to the actual work of putting together a dictionary of the English language, Johnson was unable to follow the Lockean precepts of breaking complex ideas down to simple ones and making certain that the words annexed to them refer to things "clear and distinct," that they must be "conformable to things as they exist," and that verbal signs must consistently stand for "such ideas as common use has annexed them to. . . ." Instead, Johnson found himself as an actual dictionary maker unable to escape from the historical world that Locke was proposing a way out of, a scene of speaking and writing where people make and change language from moment to moment to suit their particular purposes, where Vanity affects peculiar pronunciations and meanings, where the diction of laborers and merchants is "casual and mutable . . . formed for some temporary or local convenience." In advanced societies which have the leisure to increase knowledge and to produce new words, fashion and convenience, he found, create terms which flourish briefly and die easily, sci-

ence amplifies language "with words deflected from their original sense," translation from other languages changes grammar itself, altering "not the single stones of the building, but
the order of the columns." As Johnson warms to describing the
practical problems he discovered while working on the *Dictionary*, the catalogue of linguistic mutability grows epic:

> The tropes of poetry will make hourly encroachments, and the
> metaphorical will become the current sense: pronunciation will be
> varied by levity or ignorance, and the pen must at length comply
> with the tongue; illiterate writers will, at one time or other, by
> publick infatuation, rise into renown, who, not knowing the orig-
> inal import of words, will use them with colloquial licentiousness,
> confound distinction, and forget propriety. As politeness in-
> creases, some expressions will be considered as too gross and vul-
> gar for the delicate, others as too formal and ceremonious for the
> gay and airy; new phrases are, therefore, adopted, which must,
> for the same reasons, be in time dismissed.

Though his prose always retained traces of an Adamic view
of language—e.g., "the *original* import of words"—language in
the Johnsonian view ultimately is unable to escape from its en-
tanglement in human history and is therefore tied to constant
mutation and chance, to mere accident and casual interests. If
it has any overall direction, it is downward, insofar as a linguistic down and up can be distinguished: "tongues, like governments, have a natural tendency to degeneration." The radical
difficulty is deep in human nature itself, far below Locke's optimistic rationality: "Most men think indistinctly, and, therefore, cannot speak with exactness." But even if language were
used as logically and precisely as Locke proposes, it would still
be flawed, for experience is larger than language and there are
many ideas, feelings, and perceptions "which words are insuf-
ficient to explain."

The study of language brought Johnson to the point that his

thought always came to: the edge of nothingness. Johnson's marginal position in the social world and the vacuity which haunted his thought in so many ways prepared him perfectly for this discovery of language as the baseless and unsystematic babbling of imperfect people moving through the confusion of history. We get an unobstructed view of this perception of linguistic chaos in his remark that "to enchain syllables, and to lash the wind, are equally the undertakings of pride, unwilling to measure its desires by its strength." But this was not where he ended, for in the standard plot he used so often to dramatize his experiences as a man and a writer, the view of chaos and the first reaction of paralysis are followed by a refusal to accept the emptiness on which his mind opened or, as Boswell said, to "acquiesce with silence . . . in the . . . insurmountable distresses of humanity." And, so, supported as well as coerced by print's insistence that the language could and would be schematized and fixed, he went on to provide another heroic image of the author in the age of print by constructing the *Dictionary*, compromising, improvising, admitting ignorance, simultaneously aware of the arbitrariness and the necessity of his belief that in language, as elsewhere, "there is in constancy and stability a general and lasting advantage. . . ."

He laughs in his "Preface" at the Borgesian etymologies of Francis Junius (1589–1677) who in his *Etymologicum Anglicanum* derives "*dream* from *drama*, because *life is a drama, and a drama is a dream*; and who declares with a tone of defiance, that no man can fail to derive *moan* from . . . *monos* . . . who considers that grief naturally loves to be alone." But his own method for establishing the existence and meaning of words in the linguistic void is only more familiar, not less imaginative, than the etymologies of sympathetic magic Junius constructed. The *Dictionary* was generated by typographical fixity in the first place, originated and driven by a group of booksellers, structured in the systematic ABC style of print, and ultimately locked into reality by the printing of the completed book. The words it contained and the meanings they were given were also derived from printed books. Johnson frequently refers in the "Preface" to the oral basis of language, but a word was real enough for inclusion in the *Dictionary*, or a sound became a true word, only when it appeared in print, and he omitted many, he says un-self-consciously, that he had heard or found printed only in earlier dictionaries, "because I had never read them." He admitted some other words appearing only in dictionaries "because they may, perhaps, exist, though they have escaped my notice." He had never read them, but there is a possibility that they may exist, may, that is, have been printed in some book other than a dictionary. Only printed books, but not earlier dictionaries, in Johnson's thinking, conferred true and full existence on a word. Print established meaning, or meanings, as well. Johnson, perfecting a method borrowed from earlier lexicographers, considered a particular meaning legitimate only if it could reasonably be derived from a passage in a printed book. Recognizing that meanings change over time, he collected passages containing the word to be glossed from different books and printed excerpts from them in the *Dictionary* to authorize his definitions and to hold at bay at least for a time his fundamental awareness that "words are hourly shifting their relations," that is, that meanings are ultimately as indeterminate as spelling or pronunciation.

But not all books would do as authorities for the existence of words and the sources of their meanings. Some were excluded because Johnson disapproved of the morality of their authors, and practical considerations of the amount of reading he could do forced him to narrow the range still further. In the end he decided to concentrate on books printed between 1580 and 1660, between Sidney's works and those of the Restoration. The choice was justified in various ways: the writings of this period were said to be, adapting Spenser's description of Chau-

cer, "*the well of English undefiled*," in which could be found a vocabulary and range of meanings spacious enough that "few
ideas would be lost to mankind, for want of English words, in
which they might be expressed."

Works printed before 1580, it was argued, contained too
many obsolescent words and meanings, works printed afterward were too much influenced by the French and were too recent for their language to have been approved by the test of
time. Actual practice, Wimsatt points out in *Philosophic Words*,
departed considerably from this focus on the Golden Age of
English, and in the first volume alone, as Freed shows, the most
frequently quoted authors were Locke, 1,674; Hooker, 1,212;
South, 1,092; Arbuthnot, 1,029; Boyle, 592; Watts, 509.

Roy Harris has aptly described, in "The History Men," this
kind of lingusitic authority as a "black-and-white lexicography"
that "takes the language of the literate strata of society as having priority, and treats literary, educated usage preserved for
posterity in the published works of major writers as providing
the permanent standard against which to judge any other
forms of English." To make the works of major writers the linguistic standard seems very logical when argued in Johnson's
superb prose in the "Preface," and it becomes a self-evident
fact when it is objectified in the pages of the printed *Dictionary*,
ordered word by word alphabetically, and numerically page by
page, each entry printed in a regular format—spelling, pronunciation, etymology, order of historical definitions, illustrated and backed up by quotes from the best English authors.
This surely is *the* language, complete with all the attributes of
reality—form, authority, repeating order, history, fixity—and
yet, as Johnson well knew, and says in his "Preface" to the *Dictionary*, it is not the record of a pre-existent linguistic order, but
a man-made inscription of order on "the boundless chaos of a
living speech," admittedly arbitrary, imperfect, temporary,
and made with the dark understanding "that for the law to be

known, is of more importance than to be *right*," when there is finally nothing to be absolutely right about.

The *Dictionary* was a typical achievement of print, a language book made out of still other books that would determine the language of books still to be written. It was at the same time a characteristic achievement of the man Samuel Johnson, and a paradigmatic work of the writer in print culture, the construction of meaning and order out of words in the face of chaos. Johnson speaks in his "Preface" of his earlier plans to record the language in all its fullness and perfection as "the dreams of a poet, doomed at last to wake a lexicographer," but in the *Dictionary* he becomes one of the quintessential poets Shelley praises in his *Defense of Poetry* as those "who imagine and express . . . indestructible order." There are a few, Robert Browning is the most famous, who have read through the *Dictionary* as a great poem, or at least as an anthology of great writing, and there are many others who have seen the *Dictionary* as having pronounced poetic qualities such as metaphor, wit, and style. The book has even become, after it and its author were supplanted as lexicographically authoritative by James Murray and the *OED*, a minor literary classic, and some of its funnier definitions such as "Oats: A grain which in England is generally given to horses, but in Scotland supports the people," or "Pastern: The knee of an horse" ("Ignorance, Madam, pure ignorance") are frequently collected as instances of the wit and wisdom of Dr. Johnson. But the real poetic power of the *Dictionary* is its print-based ability, like literature itself, to order and fix the language, to abstract it from the linguistic flux of Babel and give it boundaries, stability, and meaning. And by treating the printed works of certain famous writers as definitive of what language is and means, it not only solved the problem of how to crystallize language but at the same time established that the English language belongs to and is shaped by its great authors and their texts, by "literature" in its broad eighteenth-century sense of all categories of excellent writing, Hooker and Bacon as well as Sidney and Shakespeare. The *Dictionary* established as fact the primary source of the aura of the literary text over the last two centuries, its special proprietary relationship to language. This is accepted as so obvious by now that it seems almost pointless to remark that the literary artist officially rules language, maintains its strength, expands its range of possibilities, creates new words and meanings, reworks the tropes, and in the end is the ultimate authority on wordcraft. Poetry has always been a verbal art, but the axiom that the literary text is the source of and the authority for linguistic meaning is not an eternal fact of either culture or nature. It is a print-society concept that has existed between, on the one hand, an older oral poetry where singers of tales worked with invariable linguistic metrical units fixed by social tradition, and, on the other hand, increasingly influential modern linguistic views that language is prior to and generates texts—"language writes, not the author"—and that therefore no particular writer or set of texts is empowered to define language. In objecting in "The History Men" to the standards used for establishing words and definitions in a recent supplementary volume to the *OED*, that greatest of monuments to literary authority in linguistic matters, the linguistic philosopher, Roy Harris, makes it clear both how concretely Johnson fixed the linguistic authority of the writer in our culture and how arbitrary it is now beginning to appear:

> Under Murray's broadminded successors . . . literary snobbery continued to pervade the OED, and by 1972 had hardened into official policy as regards new admissions. If you happened to be a famous author, you could take the liberty of inventing a word, or cribbing one from a foreign language, and your boldness was likely to be held to "enrich" the English language (however absurd, unnecessary or trivial the innovation). But if you were just a reporter writing for the local paper, or a civil servant drafting a document, you apparently had no business introducing new

words at all, however useful. This is an editorial policy which will admit almost anything into a dictionary, provided it comes from the prestigious pen of some literary lion—a Samuel Beckett (*athambia*) or a Virginia Woolf (*scrolloping*). No protest against including fun-words in a dictionary is here intended. The point is that the OED's "fun" has to be sanctioned by literary respectability. And the obligatory route to literary respectability is via the printed word.

The popular success and extraordinary usefulness of the *Dictionary* guaranteed the general acceptance in the long run of its central idea that the great writers and their books determine the language. This belief was immediately established socially by a dramatic power struggle for control of the language. In many ways Lord Chesterfield was a perfect image, perhaps the last, of the old polite letters and of the old oral culture. A brilliant conversationalist, he was also a notable public speaker—which Johnson, for all his fluency in *conversation*, was not—famous for his eloquent, though seldom persuasive, orations in the House of Lords. Said to be a man without a single friend, he was in his day considered the arbiter, and sometimes styled Petronius, of correctness in both manners and language. His literary eminence was supported not only by his wealth, family, and remarkable *hauteur*—he never after childhood laughed aloud—but also by a few elegantly phrased essays printed in journals, and the famed letters, that most enduring form of manuscript culture, to his natural son, and later to his godson, which were known though not, of course, published in the earl's lifetime. He was also a patron of letters, taking up the most noted writers of the day, Pope in the '20s, Fielding in the '30s, Smollett in the '40s, and attempting Johnson, when he began to look like a winner, in the '50s. In the end he disappointed the writers he patronized, but he conversed with them for a time on terms of easy familiarity, inquiring, for example, of Pope when he found a copy of the Bible on his table: "Are you going to write an answer to it?"

Lord Chesterfield stood to language in the public world very much as his sovereign, King George, did to letters in his kingdom, and his claims that he and the aristocratic order he represented controlled language and were the authority for correctness, were equally gracious, and equally insistent, as his king's commands to Johnson to write. Though Johnson grumbled at first, he submitted to Dodsley's practical urgings that Chesterfield be addressed as patron, and the 1747 *Plan* for the *Dictionary* was fulsomely addressed to the noble peer by a writer who submits himself as only an artless drudge laying his work before his linguistic liege lord: "And I may hope, my Lord, that since you, whose authority in our language is so generally acknowledged, have commissioned me to declare my own opinion, I shall be considered as exercising a kind of vicarious jurisdiction, and that the power which might have been denied to my own claim, will be readily allowed me as the delegate of your Lordship." Chesterfield played his part in this old-style literary ritual by acknowledging the role of patron offered to him with a gift to the author of £10. But beneath the surface there remained a fundamental antagonism between the two men, which Scott Elledge has described as two conflicting theories of language, "Johnson's desire to explore . . . at odds with Chesterfield's desire to civilize." While Johnson at first submitted and Chesterfield acquiesced, in the nine long years in which the *Dictionary* was awriting, things changed. At the deepest level, we can see from the 1755 "Preface" that Johnson discovered some things about "a living speech" that he did not know when he wrote the 1747 *Plan*, and these discoveries inevitably changed his sense of the relationship of the language to the highest social class. A language, he found, has a democratic basis, existing finally only in the mouths and hands of the many who in their variety and endless change of interests make of it a "boundless chaos." Johnson, while always quick to perceive chaos, also understood the social necessity of imposing some firm and orderly scheme upon it in the name of some authority. In linguistic matters, as in so much else, that authority had traditionally resided with the aristocracy and "The King's English." The 1747 *Plan* suggests that Johnson was as willing to accept kings, lords, and the hierarchical social order in language as he was in politics and religion. But as his work on the *Dictionary* proceeded, increasing awareness that there is no absolute language, no ideal meanings for words, no set of eternal rules governing form and development of languages, inevitably undermined the linguistic authority of a social class which claimed its privilege in all areas of life, including language, from its connection with an immutable divine and natural order. Johnson's understanding of the actualities of language unlinked any linguistic great chain of being as surely as Locke's theory of contract destroyed the absolute authority of kings, and Hume's skeptical philosophy uncoupled any sure sense of the cause-and-effect relationship of things.

Between them, Johnson and Chesterfield proceeded to act out a linguistic revolution that paralleled what was going on in the philosophical world and dramatized the central changes in the world of letters. Chesterfield, unconsciously, played out a part that could not have been written better to show how irrelevant he and his class were becoming in the realms of language and letters. He had ignored Johnson during the time that he was struggling with the *Dictionary*, but at the end of 1754 when publication was near and the book was rumored to be a great success, Chesterfield attempted to re-establish himself as patron and reassert aristocratic authority over language in two clever articles in Dodsley's periodical, *The World*. In these he snobbishly recommended the forthcoming dictionary to all who could afford it, praised Johnson graciously, and suggested inclusion of a few words that by their nature tell us why he and his class were losing a language struggle where the victor would be the person who could define "to be," "to have," and "to make," not the man who could, as Chesterfield did, trace the origin of the word "flirtation" to "the most beautiful mouth in the world," define the obscure verb "to fuzz" as "dealing twice together with the same pack of cards, for luck," or recommend restriction of the overworked word "vastly" as in the description of a snuffbox as "*vastly* pretty, because it was *vastly* little."

Boswell saw these two articles for what they were, a "courtly device." Chesterfield may have had, as recent biographers of Johnson seem to want to agree, only the best intentions of helping to launch a new and worthy book, but, under his pretense of democratic spirit and Lockean terminology of contract—"a total surrender of all my rights and privileges in the English language, as a free-born British subject, to the said Mr. Johnson, during the term of his dictatorship"—Chesterfield was still attempting to preserve "The King's English." But Johnson was about to make it "The Authors' English," his own and his great predecessors', Spenser's, Shakespeare's, Milton's, Pope's. He now made the point in action that his *Dictionary* had made in print by writing the famous letter to Lord Chesterfield in which he proclaimed his sole ownership of the *Dictionary*, and the professional writer's ownership of the language: "I . . . have brought [the *Dictionary*], at last, to the verge of publication, without one act of assistance, one word of encouragement, or one smile of favour." He went on to clinch the matter by publishing the *Dictionary* without a dedication and without a reference to the man he now openly declared to be not "a Lord among wits; but . . . only a wit among Lords." The English language that the *Dictionary* now realized was authorized by the writer Samuel Johnson, whose name alone appeared on the title page, and by 114,000 quotations from other authors whose writing established English words and their meaning, and whose texts in turn shone with the bright aura of being the golden sources of English undefiled.

By the twentieth century, the true literary text had fully recovered the aura that letters seemed to have lost forever in the print revolution of the eighteenth century. Created by genius, filled with mysterious presence, imaginative works like *Hamlet*, *Paradise Lost*, and *The Waste Land* now rise far above the normal range of writing. Few of Johnson's writings—perhaps by the strictest tests none finally—belong to these masterworks of the imagination. An imperfect edition of Shakespeare, a dictionary, a set of uneven poetic biographies, a number of occasional essays, a few imitative poems, an oriental moral tale, and various prefaces and critical writings—this is not, for all the skill, honesty, and intelligence with which it was done, a great romantic literary *oeuvre*. It is the work of a professional writer who sought reputation and earned his living by turning out what the publishing business would pay for because it could be sold to the broad reading public. But in this kind of plain publishing activity, Johnson realized the kinds of truth printed literary texts could provide, and his writings established as fact the sources of literary aura in a print society in an idealized and perfect Platonic text, in the pure meaning of style, and as the source of an authentic language.

CHAPTER VI

READING AND READERS:
THE LITERACY CRISIS OF THE
EIGHTEENTH CENTURY

Johnson as Speaker, Talker, and Reader

In earlier chapters we have observed the appearance of a new kind of author and a new kind of literary text in such social events as the meeting of a writer with his king, the assembling of a dictionary, passage of a copyright law, and in other places where we do not ordinarily look for literary history. To these radical print-based literary changes we must now add the crucial transformation of the audience from a few well-bred listeners with shared tastes—like Eugenius, Lisideius, Crites, and Neander, talking together about letters, while being rowed on the Thames, in Dryden's *Essay*—to a reading public of the kind Johnson addressed in his writings. So long as poetry has been written down, that is, at least since the sixth century B.C., in the West, readers have been a component of the basic literary triad of author-text-audience, but readers remained largely in the shadows in older literary traditions that featured great poets and monumental texts. Even when literary works were written down in manuscript, the audience was still conceived of, when they were taken into account at all, as listeners in an oral and public situation, where they were to be amused or persuaded to some course of action by the arts of rhetoric. Only in the eighteenth century when the old oral arrangements finally and conclusively changed did readers emerge as important figures in letters. Then they became, in fact, the crucial figures, though their dominance was not openly acknowledged until recently, because their position as buyers of books in the marketplace gave them the power to determine what was written, and to judge what would be read and preserved.

During the eighteenth century, print altered the relationship of the reading to the talking world in significant ways. These general changes were immediately and sharply felt in the world of letters, and as a leading man of letters, Johnson was always and in many ways involved with the shift from orality to literacy. This professional involvement, as usual with him, was shaped by a personal involvement in the change and an experienced awareness of its meaning in actual social and psychic life. The pattern of Johnson's speaking, talking, and reading offers a lived-out model of the ways that increased reading was affecting the society and its individual members, and an insight into how an individual experienced the change and its psychological dynamics. The argument is not that Johnson was your normative eighteenth-century talker-reader, but rather that he was in this, as in so many of his other literary activities, a culture hero whose outscale activities emphatically show the pattern and meaning of what was happening.

There were still among Johnson's acquaintances a few great orators in public places—Burke and Chesterfield in Parliament, Wesley and Whitefield in the churches and countryside, and John Wilkes in the streets of London—but the public world of speech was steadily being narrowed, and Johnson the great talker was not himself a great orator. Quite the reverse. Though Boswell demurred, Johnson himself confessed that on several occasions when he had tried to speak in the Society of Arts and Sciences, he "had found he could not get on . . . all my flowers of oratory forsook me." He makes it sound as if nervousness and insecurity were the sources of the difficulty, and perhaps they were, but the style of his speech, which was, as we have seen, based on print norms, was also involved. The matter was occasion for public discussion, and one analyst of the question, Flood, proposed that Johnson "having been long used to sententious brevity and the short flights of conversation, might have failed in that continued and expanded kind of argument, which is requisite in stating complicated matters in publick speaking," and Flood instanced the *Debates in the Senate of Lilliput* which though brilliantly written were, he said, not "at all like real debates." He could not have chosen a more telling, or a more ironic, example than a group of fictional printed debates which though they might not have been effective if actually delivered, were later able to replace or even to *become* the delivered speeches. Boswell's informant's description of the printed quality of Johnson's speech specifies what Flood meant about the limitations of Johnson's style for public oratory: "He was always most perfectly clear and perspicuous; and his language was so accurate, and his sentences so neatly constructed, that his conversation might have been all printed without any correction."

Boswell intends his remarks on the similarity of print style and Johnson's conversational style as praise, not blame, and Johnson's reputation as a talker supports Boswell's claims for the effectiveness of this style in that semiprivate world of talk which is located between the fully public scene of oratory and the totally private scene of reading. If on one hand print discouraged public oratory by fostering an ineffective oratorical style and by providing a more authentic source of information, on the other hand as Walter J. Ong argues, in "Reading, Technology and the Nature of Man," it actually encouraged conversation and generated an effective style of talking in small groups: "The use of writing does not suppress talking, but encourages it more, if only because there is more to talk about. But writing changes the way people talk. Once the mind has become familiar with extensive analytic thinking through the use of writing, it becomes possible to proceed orally to some degree in analytic fashion." Ong's theory of the relationship of print and conversation is substantiated by Glenn J. Broadhead's descriptions of the vast increase of conversation and talk "in a century enthusiastic for the buzzing fellowship of coffeehouses, bookstores and printshops, for clubs and societies, for 'conversation pieces' in painting, for 'conversation groups' in interior decoration, and for salons and *conversaziones* ('at homes') as fashionable modes of social and intellectual life, particularly for women."

It was in this conversational world that Boswell shone so brightly that, while many personally disliked or morally disapproved of him, no one seems ever to have been bored with his company. Even Rousseau in seclusion found himself babbling away to Boswell, though he does not mention his visit to Motier, while recording others, in his *Confessions*. Boswell's Johnson was even more famous as a talker, and in the *Life* we see him almost always in company, engaged in talk with Savage or the strange George Psalmanazar in the tavern, at dinner parties with Boswell and others, in the back rooms of booksellers' shops, in the Thrales' household, at the meetings of the Literary Club, having tea late at night with Anna Williams. He sought company always to escape his own melancholy thoughts: "Whenever he was not engaged in conversation, such thoughts were sure to rush into his mind; and, for this reason, any company, any employment whatever, he preferred to being alone. The great business of his life (he said) was to escape from himself; this disposition he considered as the disease of his mind, which nothing cured but company." From our earlier discussions of Johnson's psychic fears, we can guess what he sought to escape, and a brief look at one of his more famous conversations will show what he sought and found in talk.

On Sunday, 12 April 1778, Johnson went with Boswell and Mrs. Williams to dine with Bishop Percy, and they fell to talking about a travel writer named Pennant who in his book had not, the Bishop felt, done justice to the garden of Alnwick Cas-

tle, his ancestral seat. Johnson, with his usual perverse delight
in opposing any self-satisfied position, argued with vigor, using
a series of heavy disabling metaphors, that Pennant had described the garden "very well," and that he knew this for a fact
because he too had seen the gardens. Percy began to be
aroused, and having tried the "quip modest" he now gave
Johnson the "reply churlish." "But, my good friend, you are
short-sighted, and do not see so well as I do." Johnson was very
sensitive about his near-blindness, and there was a moment of
angry silence. Then Percy, unable to let it go, attacked Pennant
again, and Johnson exploded: "This is the resentment of a narrow mind, because he did not find every thing in Northumber-
land." That did it, and the black flag of no conversational
quarter was instantly run up: "PERCY. (Feeling the stroke) 'Sir,
you may be as rude as you please.' JOHNSON. 'Hold, Sir! Don't
talk of rudeness; remember, Sir, you told me (puffing hard
with passion struggling for a vent) I was short-sighted. We have
done with civility. We are to be as rude as we please.' " Taken
aback by the anger he had provoked, and already relieved by
the expression of his own anger, Percy at once gave in, "Upon
my honour, Sir, I did not mean to be uncivil." But Johnson was
not yet appeased. "I cannot say so, Sir; for I *did* mean to be uncivil, thinking *you* had been uncivil." At this, Percy rose, went to
Johnson, took him by the hand and made reassurances of
friendship, and Johnson, at once in a good humor again, told
Percy that he could "hang" Pennant if he wished. The name excited Percy all over again, and the word "hang" reminded him
that the wretched Pennant had said rather cryptically "that the
helmet is not hung out to invite to the hall of hospitality." He
remarks with all the authority of the great antiquarian he was,
"I never heard that it was a custom to hang out a *helmet*." But
Johnson refuses to be baited again and ends the discussion with
a laugh, both genial and triumphant, "Hang him up, hang
him up."

It is a delightful exchange between these two distinguished old bears, but it is also a picture of complex and adroit face-to-face conversation in which each cues and plays to the other and to the audience at the table. Pennant's book cannot defend or explain itself, but here in the room emotions and tones are felt and responded to immediately. Submission is made and reinforced with actions when the situation becomes dangerous. And humor finally establishes and maintains a draw in which both antagonists give in, yet don't surrender. Scenes like these give some sense of how warm and emotionally satisfying, discharging aggression and releasing humor, the talking world still was for a man like Johnson, how socially reassuring and sensorily fulfilling, almost an animal contact with other bodies of your own kind, such exchanges could be. Many writers were unable to cross the bridge from writing to speaking, and Johnson, proud of his own talk, never ceased to comment, or the jealous Boswell to report, on how well his friend Goldsmith wrote and how ineptly he talked. There was, he perceived in the conclusion of *Rambler* 14, something in writing that threatened not only public oratory but talk in general: "A transition from an author's books to his conversation, is too often like an entrance into a large city, after a distant prospect. Remotely, we see nothing but spires of temples, and turrets of palaces, and imagine it the residence of splendor, grandeur, and magnificence; but, when we have passed the gates, we find it perplexed with narrow passages, disgraced with despicable cottages, embarrassed with obstructions, and clouded with smoke."

While the world of talk was not only important but emotionally necessary for Johnson, he was at the same time the master reader, as well as writer, of his time, a man who spent enormous amounts of time alone reading and writing books. For obvious reasons, a biographer cannot dwell too much or too long on these quiet scenes, and Boswell necessarily makes a mystery of when and where Johnson found the time to write his huge *oeuvre* and to read more books than any other contemporary Englishman. But he did find the time, and as a result Boswell's Johnson is the great reader who seldom reads, the prolific writer who avoids writing as long as he can, the man who established his reputation in books and still seeks his reality in the public world of conversation, an authoritarian who gets most of the information he uses in conversation from books and yet distrusts their neat schemes and constantly measures them against the facts of lived experience. This was the way Boswell knew Johnson and wrote about him, and in doing so he partly made, partly caught a tension between Johnson's life as a private reader-writer and as a public conversationalist, which reflects at the level of the self the stresses and strains of the more general change from an oral to a print society.

As a reader, Johnson dramatizes what it is and means to be a reader of printed books just as forcefully as he enacts what it is and means to be a professional author in an age of print. By way of obvious instance of this observation, we can begin with the number of books he read. Boswell remarks again and again on his reputation as the best-read man in England, saying, for example, that "Dr. Adam Smith, than whom few were better judges on this subject, once observed . . . that 'Johnson knew more books than any man alive.' " The full potential of literacy, his example tells us, is realized not just in being able to read but in reading many books.

Reading began early in a home located above a bookseller's shop, and Johnson who may have been self-taught, for he could read "as a child in petticoats," worked his way through his father's stock after opening a folio copy of Petrarch while searching for apples he believed his deeply resented younger brother had hidden behind the books. The apples, the hidden knowledge, and a hostile brother make it sound like an Eden myth, but this is what Boswell reports. By the time he arrived at Oxford, he could be told that he was in terms of reading the best-prepared student who had ever arrived there, and though he frequently remarked on a decrease in the desire to read books as he grew older, it is clear that throughout his life he read, as Boswell says, "a great deal in a desultory manner, without any scheme of study, as chance threw books in his way, and inclination directed him through them."

The variety of his early writings for Cave and *The Gentleman's Magazine*—a life of Drake, a description of China, thoughts on agriculture, a history of the Amazons, information for which could only have been derived from books—indicates a wide-ranging appetite for reading which would later carry him through many thousands of volumes in search of words and definitions for the *Dictionary*, and which at the end of life was still, despite some bibliographic ennui, getting him through the study of so many lines a day of Virgil and the Greek Testament. Books, he knew, provided the furniture of a writer's mind and his working materials, and in his interview with the king, Johnson had parried questions about what he was writing by saying that "he had pretty well told the world what he knew, and must now read to acquire more knowledge." To Boswell he stated the dependence of the writer on the books he reads even more forcefully: "The greatest part of a writer's time is spent in reading, in order to write: a man will turn over half a library to make one book."

The great reader was also a collector of books, who wrote a proposal and a number of learned bibliographical entries for a catalogue of the Earl of Oxford's library, and, as we have seen, offered the king's librarian professional advice on how to assemble a royal collection. E. L. McAdam, working from the incomplete catalogue of the sale of Johnson's library, has been able to show that he was an excellent bibliographer who "owned many Aldine editions . . . the Plantin Aeschylus, 1580, and many works issued by Foulis in Glasgow. . . . He loved old books—he particularly mentions books in black letters." When Johnson's library was sold by the founder of the Christie firm at auction two months after his death, it contained about 3,000 volumes, plus a large number of pamphlets, papers, prints, and portraits. By way of comparison, Mack's informed estimate of Pope's library is that it consisted of about 600–700 volumes, and that this was approximately the size of the collections of other learned men (Swift, 657; Congreve, 659) of the earlier part of the eighteenth century. The total sale of Johnson's books realized £292.9s. The *Catalogue of the Valuable Library of Books of the Late Samuel Johnson, Esq; LL.D.* can, in the words of Donald Greene, in his guide to Samuel Johnson's library, "claim the distinction of being the worst book catalogue ever produced"; but Greene has, with his usual ability to make closely studied detail reveal meaning, ordered and analyzed its contents—religion, philosophy, history, language, literature, natural history and science, medicine, law, geography, politics and economics, biography, and encyclopedias in many languages and from many ages—to establish, as he says, "Johnson's very real and impressive intellectual attainments."

Books were not sacred objects, reverentially treated by Johnson. They were, instead, what print had made them, articles for use, and he seems to have had few favorite books. Mrs. Thrale tells us that there were three books of which he never tired, *Robinson Crusoe, Pilgrim's Progress,* and *Don Quixote,* the last a cautionary tale for an age of reading. Burton's *Anatomy of Melancholy* was, he said, the only book he would rise early to read. Perhaps something of his complex attitude toward books is caught in what Boswell saw when he visited what he considered the *sanctum sanctorum* of reading, Johnson's library: "a number of good books, but very dusty and in great confusion. The floor was strewed with manuscript leaves, in Johnson's own handwriting. . . ." The same attitude appears in Johnson's often noted carelessness with books, such as the borrowed volumes he marked up heavily in preparing the *Dictionary*. As a reader in a print culture, he apparently took books for granted, and Boswell's description, quoted earlier, of Johnson reading "in a variety of books: suddenly throwing down one and taking up another," is an image of a true Gutenberg reader, accustomed to many books, using them quickly and casually rather than treasuring every word of sacred texts. Gutenberg too is his awareness, again born of familiarity with many books, that the essential argument of a book can be discovered very quickly by an intent reader and that the entire book required neither to be read through nor to be treated with reverence in all its details. McAdam regards the standard view that Johnson seldom read books through as "a dreadful canard," and offers evidence, not exactly to the point, that he was a scrupulous bibliographer and historian of print. The weight of the evidence is, I believe, against a view of Johnson as, at least ordinarily, a careful, thorough reader. When he read a book through, as he did Fielding's *Amelia*, it was worthy of remark, for ordinarily he skimmed books, reading a few pages until he could tell, as he quickly could, what the argument was. He defended himself against the charge, to which he was sensitive, not with a denial that he never read a book in its entirety but with some rude reply such as, "No, Sir; do *you* read books through?" When the Reverend Herbert Croft advised a young gentleman "to read to the end of whatever books he should begin to read," Johnson found the idea fantastic, "This is surely strange advice," and went on: "A book may be good for nothing; or there may be only one thing in it worth knowing; are we to read it all through? These Voyages, (pointing to the three large volumes of 'Voyages to the South Sea' which were just come out) *who* will read them through? A man had better work his way before the mast, than read them through; they will be eaten by rats and mice, before they are read

through. There can be little entertainment in such books; one
set of Savages is like another."

In his reading, Johnson was learned and literate in the style
of the Gutenberg era. In a world of many books he read many,
easily and quickly; he was familiar with and not unduly impressed by printed materials; and he knew how to get at once
to the essential argument of a book without wasting time on the
details. He also had the professional bookman's understanding
of how to make use of catalogues, indexes, and libraries:
"Knowledge is of two kinds. We know a subject ourselves, or we
know where we can find information upon it. When we enquire into any subject, the first thing we have to do is to know
what books have treated of it. This leads us to look at catalogues, and at the backs of books in libraries."

This all seems rational and sensible enough. Perhaps the casual way Johnson treated books as the writer's raw material of
information conflicts somewhat with the bibliographic reverence we expect in our great literary figures; but, on reflection,
this attitude fits a professional man of letters and seems even to
be fairly inevitable in a world of so many books. But Johnson's
reading appears in a stranger light in some of his other deal-
ings with books. On entering a room, for example, Johnson's
first movement was often to the bookshelves, where he would
stand looking at the titles on the spines, and, ignoring his host
and the assembled company, pull down and examine briefly
and intently one book after another. All readers know what this
means, as did Boswell, for we have seen it, perhaps done it,
many times. The familiar gesture reveals in one more way the
feelings of social marginality Johnson suffered so acutely, and
at the same time suggests the way in which books were used to
defend against the feared exclusion. The rawness of his need
in this regard and the crudeness with which he satisfied it with
books appears more overtly in a little social gathering, brilliantly sketched by Boswell: "Before dinner Dr. Johnson seized

upon Mr. Charles Sheridan's 'Account of the late Revolution in Sweden,' and seemed to read it ravenously, as if he devoured it, which was to all appearance his method of studying. 'He knows how to read better than any one (said Mrs. Knowles;) he gets at the substance of a book directly, he tears out the heart of it.' He kept it wrapt up in the tablecloth in his lap during the time of dinner, from an avidity to have one entertainment in readiness when he should have finished another; resembling (if I may use so coarse a simile) a dog who holds a bone in his paws in reserve, while he eats something else which has been thrown to him."

He tore the heart out of books even more violently than "the ingenious Quaker lady," Mrs. Knowles, thought. She probably meant only that he got to the central issues of books very quickly, which as an expert reader he did, but he engorged books with the voracity suggested by Boswell's metaphor equating his reading with his usual animalistic manner of eating. Not only did he rapidly read vast numbers of books, but he devoured books in the way depicted in the 1775 Reynolds portrait, which Keith Walker describes as showing Johnson in concentration before the contents of a book which he holds "scrumpled before his eyes in a moment of terrible intensity." His vision was limited in fact to a single eye and Reynolds seems to show him reading with his left eye, but what he saw was imprinted on his mind as accurately and durably as it was on the page itself, as if his mind were a Lockean *tabula rasa* printed on not by things but by books. His memory was not confined only to what he read, for Boswell tells us "that he never forgot any thing that he either heard or read," which makes him, at once, the ideal of oral society, the person with the prodigious and accurate memory of what has been said, and of print culture, the person who knows *exactly* what is in books and can find information at once. What he read he recorded in his head with something close to what we would now call photographic accuracy. In the numerous examples that Boswell gives of this retentive power, such as dictating a copy of his letter to Lord Chesterfield from memory, Johnson sometimes makes small changes in the original, as he did when he substituted "confines" for "precincts" in reciting a stanza of Gray's *Elegy*. He added that he had forgotten another stanza entirely, but that was a joking way of saying that he disliked Gray. That he had at least something very like a "photographic memory" is illustrated by a childhood story Boswell tells: "Mrs. Johnson one morning put the common prayer-book into his hands, pointed to the collect for the day, and said, 'Sam, you must get this by heart.' She went up stairs, leaving him to study it: But by the time she had reached the second floor, she heard him following her. 'What's the matter?' said she. 'I can say it,' he replied; and repeated it distinctly, though he could not have read it over more than twice."

The remarkable memory lasted to the end, but the desire for reading waned as time passed, and on his deathbed Johnson "lamented much his inability to read during his hours of restlessness." "I used formerly, (he added,) when sleepless in bed, *to read like a Turk.*" The image of the Turk suggests both the ferocity of Johnson's reading and the sense of being an alien, both socially and psychologically, against which vast reading, and the violent possession of books defended. Books served his needs more directly, and once in a discussion with Boswell of his lifelong disease of melancholy, he told him that to attempt to *think* down his black thoughts was "madness," and that one "should have a lamp constantly burning in his bed-chamber during the night, and if wakefully disturbed, take a book, and read, and compose himself to rest." This is only a humble instance of what he used reading for throughout his life, reading books as a small boy shut out from the ordinary society of children to create his own fictional reality, reading books to locate the English language amid "the boundless chaos of a living speech," clutching books to him at dinners and other gatherings where he felt like a Turk in civilized society. The intense concentration with which he read, and the omnivorous quality of his reading, tell us how great was his psychological need for reading. His rapid gutting of books for their ideas, his skill in using a library or an index to locate the precise information he wanted, and his constant ranging over a wide variety of books to gather material for his own writing tell us that what he sought and made from reading was what he was everywhere and always seeking in his life, some kind of solid and coherent structure of meaning.

That print made readers is a truism, and stated in this flat way perhaps not even a very interesting one, but it becomes much more interesting in the highly charged human context of Johnson's talking and reading.

His experience reveals both the historical pattern and the social and human meaning of the change in the primary mode of discourse in his time. His obvious and painful difficulty in speaking in public before large groups defines the trend of his time when power and reliable information, as well as a sense of community, were less and less to be made in the public arena and more and more to be found in conversation and smaller private gatherings, where he spent so much of his time, and in the private, silent reading of books. We can follow in him, too, the transition of the old powers of memory, so crucial to an oral society, which, though they remain in full force in him (being simply extended to the exact memory of the printed page) were being supplanted by indexes, catalogues, bibliographies, and libraries, the mechanical forms of memory in an age of print, which he understood and used well. In his careless handling of books, his eagerness to strip whatever meaning they may have from them as quickly and efficiently as possible, and in his general utilitarian views of the printed word, we also get a sense of a more general loosening up and depreciation of information in a print society, of there being much that can be known and many ways of understanding and organizing it. The change might be thought of as a movement from "wisdom" to "knowledge" or even "information."

So much seems reasonably obvious, but to see the change from an oral to a print society not as an operation of some piece of machinery, but as the experience of an intense and existentially uneasy man like Johnson is to become aware not only of the human cost of radical social change of this kind but of the changes in consciousness and the psychic stakes that go along with it. First of all, he sensitizes us to the fact that there was—contrary to the usual Whig views of history as a smooth movement of progress—a considerable tension between the talking and the reading worlds, which is enacted in his own nervous movements from the solitude of reading and writing to the scene of busy talk, only to weary of this and fall back on the privacy of reading and writing. The talking world and the print world are not so much complementary, his example seems to say, as at odds in some fashion that was difficult but important to reconcile. Johnson's difficulty in achieving this end points to a much more general public division at the time between two ways of knowing, the public and the private, which in many ways was dividing the social world, as well as phenomenology, in his time. That tension inevitably was felt in letters, where it was enacted most dramatically in the form of a separation of the author from his audience. Many of the prime characteristics of modern literature can be traced to various attempts to deal with what was felt to be this unacceptable situation, and by looking at Johnson's way of bridging the gap between author and reader, we can get some immediate insight into the ways that print affected letters in the eighteenth century, and at the same time explore further the complexity of technology's pressures on culture, and the human response to situations generated in this manner.

The Writer's Audience in a Print Culture

On a memorable occasion when he and Boswell were being sculled down the river to Greenwich, Johnson remarked that the boy who rowed them could do so just as well without being able to read "the song of Orpheus to the Argonauts, who were the first sailors." But when he amused himself by asking the boy, "What would you give, my lad, to know about the Argonauts?" the answer, "Sir, . . . I would give what I have," pleased him so much that he gave the boy a double fare and declared what he always really believed, that "a desire of knowledge is the natural feeling of mankind." And knowledge for him came from reading, for he often remarked that without printing the "mass of every people must be barbarous," and that "you can never be wise unless you love reading." He even argued once that selling books rather than giving them away would encourage reading since people value more and therefore read more of what they have paid for than what they have received free. To the frequently heard elitist argument "that a general diffusion of knowledge among a people was a disadvantage; for it made the vulgar rise above their humble sphere," Johnson responded plainly and forcefully:

> Sir, while knowledge is a distinction, those who are possessed of it will naturally rise above those who are not. Merely to read and write was a distinction at first; but we see when reading and writing have become general, the common people keep their stations. And so, were higher attainments to become general, the effect would be the same.

Nor should it be forgotten that reading was for Johnson so important that he could champion the harsh view that the use of main force was acceptable to teach reading, among other subjects, so long as the scholar does not go from the master "either blind or lame, or with any of his limbs or powers injured or impaired."

Despite Johnson's, and many others', optimism about literacy, and his professional commitment to it in all he wrote and said, many people in eighteenth-century England were profoundly uneasy about the consequences of the new readership and its increasingly tyrannical power. What was feared socially appears openly in a book like Thomas Paine's *Rights of Man* with its startling sales in the hundred thousands and, only slightly more obliquely, in James Lackington's Temple of the Muses, the famous remainder bookstore which first put bookselling on a large-scale basis with a turnover of about 100,000 volumes in 1791. CHEAPEST BOOKSELLERS IN THE WORLD, read the large banner on the store's façade. Below these visible disturbances caused by literacy, radical changes were taking place also in the literary world where talkers were becoming writers and listeners readers; where knowledge was becoming what was read privately rather than what was seen, heard, and shared with others; and where meaning was losing some of its substantiality and certainty, becoming more abstract and ambiguous.

We usually think of different kinds of audiences—those who look and hear in public, for example, and those who read in private—as being sufficiently interchangeable that the single word, "audience," which specifically refers to hearing, can cover all cases. But books like Eric Havelock's *Preface to Plato*, McLuhan's *Gutenberg Galaxy*, Walter J. Ong's numerous writings on the subject summed up in his *Orality and Literacy*, and various types of "reception aesthetics" and other reader-response theories, have recently begun to focus on the reader sharply enough to reveal how radically different readers are from listeners. The reader sits alone in silence holding a book, interpreting the abstract and relatively toneless typographical signs on the printed page and storing the decoded information in the mind. Knowledge comes to readers not through the ear but through the eye alone, not from exchange of views with others *viva voce* but by scanning and interpreting fixed rows of silent signs, not in a noisy community of other persons but in the silence of the library and the isolated consciousness. In a concentrated summary of what we know about reading— "Reading, Technology, and the Nature of Man"—Walter J. Ong explains that "reading is a special activity and cannot be understood as simply an activity parallel to listening." "Faced with a text," Ong goes on, "the reader finds that both the author and original context are absent," and reading thus becomes "always a preterite activity" in which texts that "come out of past time . . . are things, not events." In this situation the text is always "marked by absences, gaps, silences and opacity." What is missing from the reading situation is the kind of explanatory context that a face-to-face conversation like that of Johnson and Bishop Percy supplied. The author is no longer *there* to explain his meaning—nor, conversely, is the reader *there* to reassure that author that his intended meaning has been understood. Gesture, tone, the responses of others who are present disappear, leaving only the incomplete fact of the printed text fronting the isolated mind of the individual reader.

This new, and during the eighteenth century increasingly normal, condition in which author and reader were isolated from one another was the primary form the first literacy crisis took in the world of letters. Bertrand Bronson, in a seminal article, "Strange Relations: The Author and His Audience," declares this separation of author and audience to be the central issue in modern writing. "If this seem a trivial point," he begins, "it is important to correct the impression. For the relation of author and public, actual or imagined, expressed or implied, is of profound significance to literary causes and effects, a universally pervasive concern of the subtlest psychological complexity and abiding perplexity. The gradual detachment, through print, of the writer from a present and familiar audience is one of the most far-reaching influences of modern times in our Western civilization; and its special problems emerge with crucial insistence for the first time in the eighteenth century. Not that the question was simple, even before the invention of printing: but it was different."

As a writer, as well as a reader, Johnson was very sensitive to these solipsistic dangers for authors and readers. Many of his *Ramblers* explicitly picture authors writing alone in the study, facing only themselves and seeing only their own intentions in the mirror of the text: "We are blinded in examining our own labours by innumerable prejudices. Our juvenile compositions please us, because they bring to our minds the remembrance of youth; our later performances we are ready to esteem, because we are unwilling to think that we have made no improvement; what flows easily from the pen charms us, because we read with pleasure that which flatters our opinion of our own powers; what was composed with great struggles of the mind we do not easily reject, because we cannot bear that so much labour should be fruitless." The reader, removed to a distance and reading in privacy, he goes on, "has none of these prepossessions, and wonders that the author is so unlike himself, without considering that the same soil will, with different culture, afford different products." In time, the remote individual reader becomes for the writer even more impersonalized and collectivized as an unpredictable, often hostile, general public that, as Johnson describes it, forgets some writers and remembers others for no very obvious reasons, desires constant novelty, and capriciously demands a steady stream of new writings, while fretfully censuring the new for not measuring up to the old.

Jane Tompkins approaches the isolation of author and reader from another direction, pointing out that a "separation between literature and political life begins to occur in the second half of the eighteenth century when the breakdown of the patronage system, the increase in commercial printing, and the growth of a large reading public change the relation of authors to their audiences." The result of this change was a new and problematic emphasis on the *meaning* of printed texts. Before this time and these changes, she continues, language had been "a form of power and the purpose of studying texts from the past [had been] to acquire the skills [i.e., rhetoric] that enable one to wield that power." But once reading became the norm, language ceased to be "a force acting on the world" and became instead "a series of signs to be deciphered." Since "the text [was] no longer in a situation that immediately clarifies its intent," decipherment became increasingly difficult, and, Tompkins argues reasonably, criticism, focused on the issue of hermeneutics, appeared at this time, and continued to increase in volume and complexity in an attempt to supply the meanings of texts which had in their printed state become increasingly problematical.

Johnson's numerous and notorious doubts about what Cyril H. Knoblauch calls "the integrity of the book as a cultural artifact" perfectly exemplify the kinds of difficulty with the meaning of printed texts that Tompkins identifies with the enormous increase of criticism in the late seventeenth and eighteenth centuries. Johnson understood, for example, that many books on many subjects darken knowledge as well as inform, and he frequently remarked on the inability of books to fulfill the contracts to supply information as set forth in their prefaces. His penetrating and explicitly skeptical remarks about the imperfections of books, both internally and in relation to other books and to the world they pretend to describe, which are the observations of a careful reader, not a listener, have been fully and expertly assembled and analyzed by Knoblauch:

> Johnson knows well enough what the trouble [with books] is: as products of imperfect human imagination, books are inevitably flawed from their conception, as is the writing process which

yields them and the very reasoning capacity which energizes and controls the writing. Any book's limited, always diminishing impact reflects, not merely the intellectual laziness or changing tastes of readers, but something intrinsic as well, the unstable nature of its own composition, as a tissue of unavoidably partial insights, incomplete lines of reasoning, overdrawn conclusions, mistaken emphases, arbitrary connections and patterns of development. Writing is always contrived and never complete: a different choice could always have been made, another sentence, paragraph, or chapter written, another direction taken. Books engender other books, as sentences engender other sentences, each responding to inadequacies in what has come before, each condemned to some inadequacy of its own. For this reason, the writer's natural condition is disappointment. A finished work [Johnson said] "seldom gratifies the author, when he comes coolly and deliberately to review it, with the hopes which had been excited in the fury of the performance."

Total solipsism may not have settled in on writer and reader until Vladimir Nabokov's *Pale Fire*, but *Tristram Shandy* is a handbook of the problems for both built into their separation in the Gutenberg situation, and "literary loneliness," John Sitter's evocative term, became after the 1740s, in such settings as country churchyards or castaways on an empty ocean, the scene of a new romantic poetry that had as its primary subject "a lonely poet surrounded by 'nature.' " But writers were not merely content to dramatize their isolation. Tompkins treats the growth of criticism as an attempt to deal positively with the problem, and Bronson in "Strange Relations" treats the development of the eighteenth-century English novel—Defoe, Richardson, Fielding, and Sterne—as a series of attempts to close the gap between author and reader. Ong in "Reading, Technology, and the Nature of Man" considers the form of the novel itself, particularly the characteristically "massive and dense" texture of the loose, baggy monsters that preceded the art novel of Flaubert and James, as an attempt to supply the context needed to make printed books fully meaningful to a reader. And the novel is, still in Ong's words, only one of "the noetic structures encouraged by print . . . to apotheosize closed systems" and to fix the printed "world in the consciousness of the reader." Many other distinctive features of modern letters can, according to Ong, also be traced back to the desire to construct on the printed page something that will substitute for the full context of the talking world. He agrees with Tompkins that the growth of criticism has been a continued effort to double the already dense and lengthy texts—Tolstoy or Joyce, for example—typical of modern literature by constructing for each work a context of other texts, "intertextuality" and literary history, and then redoubling these contexts with further critical interpretation that connects the text "to what the reader knows of actuality" to elaborate "potential meanings (implicit, unconscious, etc.) submerged in the text, making the text more fecund than oral utterance can normally be. . . ."

In one way or another, sometimes directly, sometimes more obliquely, many of the features that we take to be characteristic of letters in the eighteenth century can be traced to the "literacy crisis" of that time. The characteristic self-consciousness of much of modern and romantic literature first appeared or at least became standard practice then. It is then, too, for example, that author figures and readers, or models of readers, appearing as characters in the work become literary commonplaces in an attempt to bridge the separation of author and reader in the actual world. Johnson's criticism with its central image of "the common reader" provides a good instance of the use of this device and an excellent and remarkably clear example of the link between the problem and the response. It also shows the way, once again, that Johnson in dealing with a practical problem managed at the same time to come up with a more general literary value, in this case a roundabout justification of the place of letters in individual life and in print culture.

Johnson's Criticism and "the Common Reader"

In his criticism Johnson frequently addressed himself to "the common reader," a term he may have coined and certainly made his own by frequent use. The common reader, as the name suggests, corresponds in many ways with his potential customers, the actual reading public, more common now than aristocratic, to whom Johnson, as usual accepting the reality of the print situation, bowed his neck in authorial submission. When his heroic tragedy *Irene*, peculiarly dear to him as one of his first writings and one of his few works in a traditional and prestigious literary genre, failed in the performance given it out of friendship by Garrick in 1749, he accepted the judgment of the town without audible murmur: "A man . . . who writes a book, thinks himself wiser or wittier than the rest of mankind; he supposes that he can instruct or amuse them, and the publick to whom he appeals, must, after all, be the judges of his pretensions." This is only the most perfectly phrased and, because of the context of deep personal disappointment, the most convincing of many Johnsonian insistences that "that book is good in vain which the reader throws away."

This acceptance of the authority of the reader was not just an attitude he struck at times but was woven into the fabric of his criticism, where literary questions are consistently examined, and determined from the point of view of "the publick, which . . . never corrupted, nor often deceived, [will] pass the last sentence on literary claims." Fame and a place in the canon are said in *Rambler* 23 to be determined finally by no other "test . . . than the length of duration and continuance of esteem. What mankind have long possessed they have often examined and compared, and if they persist to value the possession, it is because frequent comparisons have confirmed opinion in its favour." A century of reading and esteem was, Johnson finally decided, about the right length of time to establish canonicity. The true subject of poetry, Johnson reiterates, is not the particulars of the world but "just representations of general nature," for the reason that only these universal truths "can please many, and please long." Judgment of a style is determined by the reader's likes and dislikes—"one loves a plain coat, another loves a laced coat"—and the ornaments of poetry "are useful because they obtain an easier reception for truth." Rhyme is said in the "Life of Milton" to be preferable in English verse not for any theoretical reason but because "The musick of the English heroick line strikes the ear so faintly that it is easily lost" and without it "English poetry will not often please." Fielding is inferior to Richardson because "Characters of manners are very entertaining; but they are to be understood by a more superficial observer, than characters of nature, where a man must dive into the recesses of the human heart"; and even *Paradise Lost*, after discussion of all its greatness, can be conclusively put down by appealing to readers, none of whom, it is said, "ever wished it longer than it is." Finally, by way of a last example of this persistently affective approach, good criticism must always show how the literary work affects readers: "There is no great merit in telling how many plays have ghosts in them, and how this ghost is better than that. You must shew how terrour is impressed on the human heart."

Recent scholars who have undertaken to summarize Johnson's poetic theories, disagree about the extent to which he carried out the program for a systematic criticism that he states in *Rambler* 92—"It is . . . the task of criticism to establish principles; to improve opinion into knowledge"—but they do agree that Johnson's critical touchstone was the response of the reader. W. R. Keast says, in what remains the authoritative statement of the matter, that Johnson understood "literature

as a mode of activity" to be approached not as "ideal form but
[as] . . . human acts to be judged in relation to the agency of
their production and appreciation." If not elaborated into a
tight system, this affective view was still, according to Keast, "a
coherent view of literature and a coherent body of assumptions
concerning both its practice and its evaluations." A later writer
on the subject of Johnson's criticism, Leopold Damrosch, Jr.,
also argues, in *Johnson's Criticism*, that "to locate and organize
Johnson's principles . . . is not in the end the best way of getting
at what he does best." He sees Johnson's best criticism as more
ad hoc and empirical than does Keast, but he too finds it consistently reader oriented, even in its contradictions: "The usual
reason for his real or apparent self-contradictions is his admirable effort to respond fully to specific works."

Johnson does on many occasions, of course, get the responses of actual readers wrong, as when he said, for example,
that *Tristram Shandy* did not last because its novelty was quickly
lost, that Fielding would be seen as "a barren rascal," or that
"we learn from Othello this very useful moral, not to make an
unequal match." But these are lapses only, which by their very
wrongness reveal Johnson's warm involvement, immediate
and personal rather than lofty and theoretical, in the books he
is discussing. And Damrosch is exactly right when he says in
"Samuel Johnson and Reader-Response Criticism" that most
often "Johnson's criticism is rich in evocations of what readers
really feel." One of the most striking qualities of his critical
writing is the way that again and again he puts his finger, emphatically, exactly, on what we all do take to be the immediate,
honest response of most readers, including ourselves, to a particular passage or book. No one, we believe, ever really did wish
Paradise Lost longer, Thomson's sense in *The Seasons* does often
get lost in a cloud of words, a reader *would* soon hang himself
if he read Richardson for the story rather than the sentiment,
and the mixture of tragedy and comedy as he says in the "Pref-

ace to Shakespeare," never really bothered anyone who lives in "the real state of sublunary nature, which partakes of good and evil, joy and sorrow. . . ."

Remarks like these, and they are frequent, so refresh us with their honesty and apparent good sense that they partially conceal what is also regularly the case, that in reporting what the common reader experiences in his reading, Johnson, to use his own and I think rather accurate words, often "improve[s] opinion into knowledge." The kind of critical authoritarianism that could lie hidden beneath the mask of the common reader escapes in a little scene in which Goldsmith was asked "what he meant by *slow*, the last word in the first line of 'The Traveller,'

'Remote, unfriended, melancholy, slow.'

Did he mean tardiness of locomotion? Goldsmith, who would say something without consideration, answered, 'Yes.' [Johnson] was sitting by, and said, 'No, Sir; you do not mean tardiness of locomotion; you mean, that sluggishness of mind which comes upon a man in solitude.' " What Goldsmith meant is not at all certain, and the author's view of the matter, considered or unconsidered, has at least as much authority as Johnson the reader's; but Johnson forcefully imposes his own preferred, and admittedly more interesting, meaning, in a way that dramatizes what he often did under the guise of the common reader. He was, however, sensitive to the danger, for he well understood, as he explains in *Rambler* 93, that "Criticks, like all the rest of mankind, are very frequently misled by interest." Even the great Addison, he continues, "is suspected to have denied the expediency of poetical justice, because his own Cato was condemned to perish in a good cause."

While acknowledging the power of the new general reading public of printed books and representing some of its commonsense attitudes, Johnson's common reader is not quite an exact picture of the actual reader of his time, nor is the common

reader a mere mask for Johnson's own authoritarian critical
views, though these too can regularly be heard in the uncom-
monly forceful and precisely phrased responses attributed by
Johnson to his reader. As usual, Johnson in constructing the
common reader was making a complex best of the actual situation print gave him: a strange, distant, diverse, and in some
ways threatening group of readers with great power over him
as a writer and over letters in general. He accepted this as the
fact of writing in a print culture, but then, rather than damning
the degenerate age, he proceeded to construct an image of the
common reader that dramatized the best that could realistically
be expected from such a democratic social group, both appealing to and calling into being their good sense, their fundamental humanity, their awareness of permanent social and experiential truths. In this way he told his actual readers that they
knew, or could know, out of their innate abilities and the culture they shared with other human beings, living and dead, a
great many truthful things about letters, and that books in turn
could help them to know interesting and useful things about
themselves and the world. Appealing to and speaking through
"the common sense of readers, uncorrupted with literary prejudices," he finessed the old aristocratic literary order with its
assumption of the superiority of educated, refined, even innate
taste, and its neoclassical intellectualized rules of genres, unities, decorum, and the absolute authority of ancients, all of
which he parodied in the figure of the professional but imper-
cipient critic Dick Minim in *Idlers* 60 and 61, "who talked of language and sentiments and unities and catastrophes." Letters,
Johnson uses his common reader to insist, was neither an ar-
cane mystery nor the province of only the learned and well
born, but was readable books which could be understood and
enjoyed, with a little aid from a critic like himself, by literate
persons willing to use their reason and honestly consult their
own experience. Working in this fashion, he proceeded to per-

suade his readers that by applying their good sense and common humanity, they knew, or at least could know, what was important about Homer, Virgil, Shakespeare, and the other literary classics; that they could read accurately and judge meaningfully literary works like *Paradise Lost, Absalom and Achitophel*, and Gray's *Elegy*; that they understood the essential issues of such technical questions as meter and the relation of sound to sense; genres such as pastoral, ode, comedy, and tragedy; poets, biography, and literary fame; and the nature of literary criticism itself.

The degree to which many of the new readers may have required and been enlightened by this kind of critical reassurance and tactful guidance may be estimated from some words of James Lackington, the proprietor of the Temple of the Muses bookstore, which while perhaps overstated to advertise the usefulness of his own trade (the style does *not* convey a determined sense of accuracy) nonetheless give us an idea of what kind of uneasiness with books might have still been considered credible late in the eighteenth century. As a young cobbler's apprentice in Bristol, Lackington wrote in his memoirs, he and a friend, both literate, wanted to read books, but "so ignorant were we on the subject, that neither of us knew what books were fit for our perusal, nor what to enquire for, as we had scarce ever heard or seen even any *title pages*, except a few of the religious sort, which at that time we had no relish for . . . we were ashamed to go into the booksellers' shops; and . . . there are thousands now in England in the very same situation: many, very many have come to my shop, who have discovered an enquiring mind, but were totally at a loss what to ask for, and who had no friend to direct them."

Johnson's common reader had fairly obvious tactical uses for letters. It lessened the writer's isolation in the print situation by providing him with at least an image of the audience he was addressing, and it gave dignity to his work by representing the au-

dience not as an ignorant group of wretches craving only novelty and crude excitement but as an understanding and
intelligent group of men and women capable of appreciating
well-written books and basic literary questions. Not only did
the figure of the common reader acknowledge the actuality
and power of the new audience for books, but it was also a most
tactful way of improving the actual reader, while not seeming
to do so. But in the invention and development of the common
reader, as in many other aspects of Johnson's literary activities,
such as the role of the author and the aura of the literary text,
the solution of practical problems led inevitably to more universal literary principles that established the nature of letters
and its place in the new capitalistic, industrial society.

The official and accepted image of the literary audience is
never finally a historical fact, as Walter J. Ong tells us in his famous essay, "The Writer's Audience Is Always a Fiction," but
an idea of an audience that materializes in the fictional audiences of works like *The Canterbury Tales, The Decameron, A Mid-
summer Night's Dream*, or Dryden's *Essay on Dramatic Poesy*. All of
these famous fictional audiences from earlier writings are still
listeners. They are also few in number, and, except in Chaucer,
are entirely upper class. A reading audience of *hypocrites lecteurs*
is more difficult, less interesting probably, to portray fictionally
than an audience of listeners, though it has been successfully
done, most famously in *Don Quixote*, and in more modern
works like Nabokov's *Pale Fire*. But fictitious audiences of readers need not always take overt form. Every author, Ong argues,
manipulates his readers into a certain stance, and thereby a
certain response, not by materializing them but by setting them
up in an explicit relationship to the text and author like that established by Victorian addresses to the "dear reader," or Hemingway's unspoken stylistic insistence that the reader knows in-
timately the scene described and therefore needs only minimal
details, as in the opening of *Farewell to Arms*—"In the late sum-

mer of that year we lived in a house in a village that looked
across the river and the plain to the mountains."

What is essentially at stake in the device of the fictional audience is the interpretative will, the power to control the meaning of a work by defining its audience and their response, and
not only authors play the game of defining the audience. The
most famous audience in English literature, that of Shakespeare's plays, provides a salient instance of who makes the audience, how it is done, and something of why it is done. The
socially ambitious Shakespeare's own images of a theatrical audience in *Hamlet* or *The Tempest*, for example, are always of aristocratic groups in noble settings. The mere approach of ground-
lings like the drunken Caliban, Stephano, and Trinculo in *The
Tempest* is enough to end the noble revels celebrating the be-
trothal of Prince Ferdinand and Miranda, the daughter of the
Duke of Milan. But Shakespeare's Puritan contemporaries, the
avowed enemies of stage plays, portray in their polemics all
public theater audiences, his included, as made up entirely of
just such whores, cutpurses, lazy apprentices, and idle swag-
gerers. The Puritans, interestingly enough, had their way, and
down to the present day the popular image of Shakespeare's
audience is of a brutal and rowdy bunch of "nut-cracking Eliz-
abethans" whose control of the public theaters explains what
have been thought to be undesirable vulgarities in the plays. In
our own time, scholars have revalued the plays as high art, perfection in all their parts, by, among other devices for raising
their status, discovering, first, an audience which was a true
cross section of the English people at their moment of greatness (Harbage), and, more recently, an audience of intellectual
"privileged" playgoers (Cook) capable of understanding the
complex interpretations modern criticism and production
have given the plays.

Ralph Cohen provides another extended case history of the
way audiences have been used to determine literary meaning

in his remarkable history of the ways in which a succession of critics and educators from Johnson's own time well into the present century have collectively shaped attitudes of readers toward Thomson's *Seasons*. By describing confidently what readers do or should experience in reading the poem, the critics have, Cohen shows in close and totally convincing detail, not only controlled the interpretation of the poem but objectified their own literary, and social, values.

When seen in the long tradition of literary audience-making, Johnson's common reader is not just a reflection of an actual historical audience of readers, nor merely an attempt to control the interpretation of books, nor only a way of overcoming the isolation of reader and author. The reader is all of these things, but ultimately he is also a way of attributing to letters, as if its nature were a prior fact, a certain kind of existence and worth that in part corresponds to the realities of print culture, and in part realizes a conception of what letters at its best might be. Clarence Tracy, in his definitive study of Johnson's common reader, points out that because the reader is often defined negatively—*i.e.*, in terms of what he or she does not understand: Latin, metaphysical conceits, technical terms, the subtleties of learning—Johnson's fictitious audience remains always "a little bloodless." But still, though remaining always somewhat as vague and faceless as actual readers were to authors in an age of print, the common reader, Tracy goes on to point out, has the basic qualities of Enlightenment rationalism:

> when one has stripped away from a real person his layers of acquired knowledge and experience, his particular manners and customs, . . . and all his other similar wrappings, what is there left of him? What was left for Johnson was the basic man who was so much the preoccupation of seventeenth and eighteenth century thinkers, man deprived of innate ideas, of traditions, and of superficial differences owing to time, place and culture, man, in short, reduced to the level on which all men's minds work alike.

The advantage possessed by the concept of the common reader was universality; what pleases him is what will please everybody everywhere, except readers who have been unable to shake themselves free from personal bias and ephemeral interests."

Using this kind of common reader as his touchstone, Johnson constantly discredits critical views of a limited and localized kind to imply for literature something close to universals in subject matter and constants in style. The details and particulars of a literary work—the streaks of the tulip—should be neither extensive nor specific because what pleases and instructs readers are said in *Rambler* 36 to be "just representations of general nature," large, universal truths acknowledged by all: "poetry has to do rather with the passions of men, which are uniform, than their customs, which are changeable." Art is moral in what it teaches not because it contains some didactic tag or homiletic exhortation, but because the nature it imitates is itself grandly moral in its direction and displays for the reader "transcendental truths, which will always be the same." The "ornaments" or style, in literature as in architecture, are everywhere useful only to the extent that "they obtain an easier reception for truth," and "metaphorical expression . . . is [always] a great excellence in style, when it is used with propriety, for it gives you two ideas for one;—conveys the meaning more luminously, and generally with a perception of delight." Of poetic language in the most general sense, the "Preface to Shakespeare" says, there is "in every nation, a stile which never becomes obsolete," and it is to be found in all languages at the same linguistic point, "above grossness and below refinement, where propriety resides." Literary genres are not to be identified by local formalities but by "their effects upon the mind" in the largest possible sense: "every dramatick composition which raises mirth is comick"; tragedy is ultimately no more than "a poem of more general dignity or elevation than comedy"; pastorals are simply "images of rural life." A poetical work may contain a number of "minute circumstances and arbitrary decorations" but finally, *Rambler* 139 pronounces, it must always be structured in accordance with the unchanging "law of poetical architecture . . . solid as well as beautiful," so that "nothing stand single or independent, so as that it may be taken away without injuring the rest; but that from the foundation to the pinnacles one part rest firm upon another." Johnson recognizes that meter or modulation of numbers and its ability of "acting at once upon the senses and the passions" are at the heart of poetry, but in describing metrical effects in *Rambler* 88 he dispenses with "the dialect of grammarians," because "the ear is sufficient to detect dissonance," and concentrates on the essential issues, as true in one time as another: "That verse may be melodious and pleasing, it is necessary, not only that the words be so ranged as that the accent may fall on its proper place, but that the syllables themselves be so chosen as to flow smoothly into one another."

Examples could be multiplied, but enough have been given to indicate the way in which Johnson attributed to his common reader responses to literary works that implied in them existence of something fairly close to those absolutes of nature that are grounded in the reader's heart, and therefore in the bases of human existence. Books are true if they ring true to common readers' deepest sense of things. Readers are delighted by those works that put basic human truths in striking and unusual ways, give them variety of form, produce new examples, and enforce them with vigor and elegance. The reader's judgment, responding to truth and force of statement, alone can finally be trusted to identify a work as a literary classic, and since the popularity of writers rises and falls in the short run, canonicity can be established, says the "Preface to Shakespeare," only by reverence paid by readers to "writings that have long subsisted," at least, says Johnson, for a century, the time needed for them to assume the "dignity of an ancient." Transforming the social slur suggested by the word "common" into the meaning of "essentially human," or "universal," while still keeping in play its reference to the actual literary audience of his time, Johnson used the phenomenology of his fictitious reader to project a literature that expresses what is most universal, unchanging, and central in human life in forms and in a language that are permanently meaningful. In this cosmic view of letters, the old neoclassical criticism and the exact stylistic specifications of courtly letters, such as the requirement of single plots and the unity of time, or the prohibition against mixing tragic and comic scenes, become as in *Rambler* 156 only "the accidental prescriptions of authority . . . confounded with the laws of nature." The false authority of such "accidental prescriptions" was demystified by submitting the old literary laws to the close examination of reason, as, most notoriously, in the "Preface to Shakespeare," where they are triumphantly refuted by a type of practical criticism based on the "actual" responses of common readers in order to reinforce the truth of Johnson's own "common-sense" views.

Despite the confidence with which Johnson demolished the poetics of courtly letters and described his own common reader's responses to literature, he sometimes knew and acknowledged the limitations and ultimate relativity of any poetics, including his own. Individual readers are capricious and variable in judgment; different languages set up different stylistic standards and concepts of correct diction; the process of time, *Rambler* 106 shows, constantly changes the canon—"Parnassus has its flowers of transient fragrance, as well as its oaks of towering height, and its laurels of eternal verdure"—and writers will always, *Rambler* 121 tells us, find new things to say and new ways to say them: "in the boundless regions of possibility, which fiction claims for her dominion, there are surely a thousand recesses unexplored, a thousand flowers unplucked, a thousand fountains unexhausted, combinations of imagery yet unobserved, and races of ideal inhabitants not hitherto described." Nature itself, which Johnson's criticism declares to be the object of the poet's "just representation," is, he well understood, a "boundless ocean of possibility," while art is an incomplete and changing way of describing what is never fixed or still: "The works and operations of nature are too great in their extent, or too much diffused in their relations, and the performances of art too inconstant and uncertain, to be reduced to any determinate idea. It is impossible [says *Rambler* 125] to impress upon our minds an adequate and just representation of an object so great that we can never take it into our view, or so mutable that it is always changing under our eye, and has already lost its form while we are labouring to conceive it." Poetry and letters are no more susceptible to the laws of criticism, he goes on, than nature is to the forms of poetry: "Definitions have been no less difficult or uncertain in criticism than in law. Imagination, a licentious and vagrant faculty, unsusceptible of limitations, and impatient of restraint, has always endeavoured to baffle the logician, to perplex the confines of distinction, and burst the inclosures of regularity. There is therefore scarcely any species of writing, of which we can tell what is its essence, and what are its constituents; every new genius produces some innovation, which, when invented and approved, subverts the rules which the practice of foregoing authors had established."

This *longue durée* of letters and its object, nature, is another special version of what Johnson's social and psychological loss of bearings, intensified here as elsewhere by the vast amount of information and profusion of books made available by print, always predisposed him to see beneath familiar and solid-seeming surfaces of life. In society's "chaos of mingled purposes and causalities" and a world where "every thing is set above or below our faculties," Johnson surely knew, what Keast wisely says, that "probability rather than demonstration is the utmost attainable by the critic." But skepticism and relativism, as we have seen before, were never congenial modes of thought or bases of action for Johnson, even though consideration of the human situation in any area regularly brought him to these positions. He personally disliked Hume and Swift— "he was not a man to be either loved or envied"—both of whom saw the world as uneasily as he did but reacted to their knowledge with, in the latter case, a despairing and sometimes a brutal cynicism, and, in the first, with what seemed, at least to Johnson, too calm and tolerant an acceptance of the limits of knowledge.

His own position is more Lockean in its combination of acceptance of an inability to know the ultimate truth of things with a determination to order rationally what is known, but the emotional tone is very different. Johnson never can put aside his doubts nor quell his fear that beyond things there is nothing, and, always with a perturbed and partial awareness of how provisional were the meanings he constructed or defended, he constantly tried to fend off chaos by erecting firm social and literary orders. Words *are* and *mean* because they are recorded in the *Dictionary* in the way that writers have used them. Literature is and means what it does because common readers perceive it this way in the depths of their being. From our vantage point in time, we can see that the poetics Johnson constructed out of and around his common reader is rickety as a philosophic system and fundamentally contradictory in its root assumptions that poetry tells truths about a "general nature" that is at the same time known to be too vast and metamorphic for human comprehension or accurate description. Furthermore, Johnson's poetics, for all its pretense of absolute empiricism, is no less historically determined than the neoclassical criticism it displaced or the thoroughgoing romanticism it anticipated. But these criticisms are all after the fact, the social fact that

Johnson established for letters by means of the common reader. After him, in place of the limited aristocratic groups addressed by Dryden and Pope, there was a literary audience of readers as extensive as mankind, responding out of its deepest being to a literature that told powerfully the great eternal truths of human life. What can be known through letters will be known, Johnson established, by common readers. They will perceive, honor, and preserve those works in which their reason and their experience recognize familiar, established human truths. Though alone with the text, isolated from one another and separated from the author, readers nonetheless can, though "uninstructed by precept, and unprejudiced by authority," still, as Johnson says in *Rambler* 52, understand the literary work "in questions that relate to the heart of man" with an existential knowledge far more "decisive than learning."

CHAPTER VII

THE PLACE AND
PURPOSE OF LETTERS IN
PRINT SOCIETY

The Actual and the Imaginary Library

There was no necessity in print, as Pope and others charged, to make "blotterature" rather than literature. If the mass-production methods and market orientation of the print business encouraged the printing of a great deal of ephemeral junk, it also made it possible, by way of example, for an editor and pamphleteer to write *Robinson Crusoe*, and for a printer, Samuel Richardson, at the request of two booksellers, to put together a manual on writing familiar letters that became the novel *Pamela*, to which corrections were at times made directly in type, on the composing stick. The power of print to make literary works of high quality begins to seem almost purposeful when we consider the part print played in creating the Johnsonian *oeuvre*. "When we turn to Johnson's writings," Hugo Reichard says, "we find that only some of them seem immaculately his. . . . Saliently, the very writing that takes up the most space in the canon and that gives Johnson most of his income issues from him by induced labor," and that labor, as we have seen, was most often induced by printers and publishers.

Print not only helped to create literature by encouraging individual writers like Johnson and particular literary works like *Pamela*, but by bringing together in one place and in one time, as in a great universal library, the books of former times and many places, it constructed the collection that would eventually crystallize into the canon of romantic literature. The major

classical texts had already been printed before the eighteenth
century, in the original languages and in translation, but now
they were reprinted, translated again, and widely disseminated
in improved scholarly editions. A good deal of Anglo-Saxon
writing—though not yet *Beowulf*—and the Norse and Icelandic
sagas were also printed for the first time. Chaucer, Langland,
Gower, and other medieval writers were either first published
or reprinted in authoritative editions. All the major English
poets were edited and printed at this time. The minor Renaissance dramatists were collected and published in sets by Dodsley and others. Bishop Percy collected the old ballads. In addition to numerous English and other European works, various
Arabic and oriental texts were printed as well. René Wellek has
analyzed in detail the huge accumulation of literary works
printed in England in the eighteenth century, and has concluded that during this time, "mankind and its poetry were surveyed, quite literally from 'China to Peru.' The main materials
for a history of English literature were assembled, the wide
background of the poetic activities of other nations was
sketched in, and all awaited only the shaping hand of the genuine historian."

This accumulation of books, old and new, made available by
print, which ultimately had profound consequences for knowledge in general and letters in particular, materialized in the actual libraries of the time, such as Johnson's own excellent but
disordered collection, the Harleian collection that he helped to
catalogue, the King's Library where he and George III discussed the state of letters, and the growing national library in
the British Museum where various private collections, including eventually George III's, were being assembled. Libraries of
the time seldom exceeded 50,000 volumes, and 100,000 ap-
proximates the outside number, but this was a bibliographic
magnitude sufficient to change the society's conception of
knowledge. Instead of the 20 manuscripts that Chaucer's Clerk

dreamed of someday owning, or the static collection of a few permanent classics that courtly letters idealized as the eternal Ancients, the large and constantly growing libraries of printed books that appeared in the eighteenth century both realized and imaged the Enlightenment's vast and continuing increase of information. The variety and extent of these new collections, like some great encyclopedia projected into architectural space, engendered new scholarly methodology and new ways of thinking about truth. No longer tied to a scrupulous Talmudic poring over a limited number of absolutely authoritative wisdom texts, the scholar working in these extensive new collections had to turn over many books saying many things, to approach questions of fact historically and comparatively, to establish truth rationally and scientifically, and to at least consider, as did the leading English philosophers of the time, Berkeley and Hume, the skeptical possibility of many truths rather than one. Johnson's mind was if not exactly at home in, then still familiar with, this epistemological scene, and he projected it beyond the limits of actual libraries to an imaginary library, where the darker meanings of vast accumulations of printed books were fully realized. Others might praise without qualification the opportunities for scholarship and the discovery of truth offered by the new collections, but not Johnson. "No place," he begins in *Rambler* 106,

> affords a more striking conviction of the vanity of human hopes, than a publick library; for who can see the wall crouded on every side by mighty volumes, the works of laborious meditation, and accurate enquiry, now scarcely known but by the catalogue, and preserved only to encrease the pomp of learning, without considering how many hours have been wasted in vain endeavours, how often imagination has anticipated the praises of futurity, how many statues have risen to the eye of vanity, how many ideal converts have elevated zeal, how often wit has exulted in the eternal infamy of his antagonists, and dogmatism has delighted in the

gradual advances of his authority, the immutability of his decrees, and the perpetuity of his power? . . .

Of the innumerable authors whose performances are thus treasured up in magnificent obscurity, most are forgotten, because they never deserved to be remembered, and owed the honours which they once obtained, not to judgment or to genius, to labour or to art, but to the prejudice of faction, the stratagem of intrigue, or the servility of adulation.

Nothing is more common than to find men whose works are now totally neglected, mentioned with praises by their contemporaries, as the oracles of their age, and the legislators of science. Curiosity is naturally excited, their volumes after long enquiry are found, but seldom reward the labour of the search. Every period of time has produced these bubbles of artificial fame, which are kept up a while by the breath of fashion, and then break at once and are annihilated. The learned often bewail the loss of ancient writers whose characters have survived their works; but, perhaps, if we could now retrieve them, we should find them only the Granvilles, Montagues, Stepneys, and Sheffields of their time, and wonder by what infatuation or caprice they could be raised to notice.

It cannot, however, be denied, that many have sunk into oblivion, whom it were unjust to number with this despicable class. Various kinds of literary fame seem destined to various measures of duration. Some spread into exuberance with a very speedy growth, but soon wither and decay; some rise more slowly, but last long. Parnassus has its flowers of transient fragrance, as well as its oaks of towering height, and its laurels of eternal verdure.

It is as if Piranesi had drawn the library of the printed book, showing in grand stairs and soaring structures that lead to nowhere and rest on nothing the skepticism, even nihilism, and the latent fear that this enormous increase in information carried with it. Johnson's psychic disposition to emptiness and hopelessness unerringly and inevitably led him, here as elsewhere, to peer into the darker shadows of the library, and to make out there "the vanity of human hopes," that long vista of historical time in which one knowledge is inevitably replaced by newer knowledges, where enormous labors of thought and writing are soon forgotten except as entries in the catalogue, where great arguments that once exercised all the learned minds of the time have lost their meaning or sunk into silence altogether, and where the high hopes of writers along with their reputations are lost forever in a continuous Heraclitean stream of literary fashion that does not often allow true excellence to survive much longer than pompous folly. In this vision of the eighteenth-century universal library wth its ever-lengthening ranges of printed books, as in other imaginary libraries such as Swift's picture of the royal library in St. James's Palace in *The Battle of the Books* where the ancients fought the moderns and lost, or in Pope's description in *The Dunciad* of Colley Cibber's library of dulness with its groaning shelves of heavy native authors—"the classics of an age that heard of none"—polite letters' dream of a limited number of books excellently written, speaking eternal truth, at last disappeared. In this huge echoing space the voices of the king commanding Johnson to write and Lord Chesterfield asserting linguistic *droit de seigneur* over *droit d'auteur* trail away into silence. Nor in subsequent centuries as collections have increased astronomically has this fear of the library created by print ever disappeared entirely. The Whiggish historical view of all print and more books as uncomplicated progress has only partially been able to conceal a fear that George Gissing, speaking in *New Grub Street* of the British Museum collection, calls "the valley of the shadow of books," and that the Argentine writer J. L. Borges, himself a librarian, extrapolates in his story "The Library of Babel" to the ultimate disappearance of knowledge in an infinite library containing all possible books, that is, all possible combinations of type.

Actual and imaginary libraries such as these are important parts of our culture, one of the few points at which we can actually examine print society's conception of knowledge and its organization. There are other places as well at which the "knowledge tree" becomes visible—encyclopedias, some philosophies (Aristotle, for example, or Kant), academies of arts and sciences, school curricula and university departmental structures—but the library is particularly revealing because it contains the primary sources of information—printed books—dictates the methods by which they can be approached and studied, and schematizes their principal modes of organization in the shelving arrangements and the catalogue. The library focuses the intellectual world and provides a paradigm of consciousness, what a society knows and how it knows it. Not to be a category in this official scheme of knowledge, as alchemy or astrology no longer are, or to get into the wrong classification group, the "practical," say, rather than the "fine arts," or to get the wrong name, belles-lettres rather than "literature," has fatal consequences for any mode of knowledge and its practitioners. The social importance of being a branch of the "knowledge tree" could not be better illustrated than in the history of what happened in the eighteenth century to the intellectual concepts of poetry, letters, and literature in the library that print created and in the scheme of knowledge it totally reorganized.

In the vast spaces of Johnson's library of "the vanity of human hopes," the traditional concept of poetry, along with other categories of knowledge, lost its distinct outlines and its firm place in the larger intellectual scheme. When Boswell asked Johnson, point blank, "What is poetry?" Johnson's structuralist, even poststructuralist, reply—"Why, Sir, it is much easier to say what it is not. We all *know* what light is; but it is not easy to *tell* what it is"—is the view of someone who has read a great many books, reflected on their differences, and concluded that definitions of poetry, like anything else, can no longer be made by reference to some prior essence but only in terms of similarity and contrast in a context, an intellectual system, or a library. When faced with the necessity of defining poetry positively in

the *Dictionary*, he did little better: "poems, poetical pieces."
Even his more positive remark in the "Life of Pope" about the
nature of poetry—"if Pope be not a poet, where is poetry to be
found?"—relies on example rather than definition and,
though the question may be rhetorical, the interrogative phras-
ing still keeps the skeptical possibility in play. The doubts extended to, in *Rambler* 125, for example, full-fledged skepticism
about any of the poetic absolutes, such as genres, that were ax-
iomatic to courtly letters: "There is therefore scarcely any species of writing, of which we can tell what is its essence, and what
are its constituents; every new genius produces some innovation, which, when invented and approved, subverts the rules
which the practice of foregoing authors had established."
Johnson saw individual poems as solid and specific enough,
though he recognized that their reputations and meanings
changed with the passage of time and that they therefore required the editorial care of scholars with historical and linguistic knowledge of the period in which they were written; but
when he thought of poetry as a whole, as if looking at all the
books assembled in one section of his imaginary library, he
conceived not of some fixed object, some eternal pre-existent
necessary category of writing, like "letters" or "literature" or
"belles-lettres," but, as in his description of the fate of the books
in his imaginary library, a continuing historical process. "Literature" was not a fact for Johnson, says Keast, in a way that
precisely summarizes what the library told Johnson about
knowledge, but "a mode of activity," and Johnson himself
often explained in various contexts why it was necessary to
think of letters as always changing. Poetry, though it depends
in his view for its ultimate value on the degree to which it justly
represents the truths of "general nature," which are, he often
said, unchanging, is not itself nature but a man-made thing
which can never do more than approximate general nature
and which constantly changes in its effort to reach its unreach-
able goal. What poetry is at any given point cannot therefore be

determined by any logical analysis of some poetic essence, but only by a historical process in which individual poetic works are constantly being compared and revalued by readers and by the society at large in terms of the degree to which they seem to continue to tell the truth about important human matters. His position is subtle and complex, and it will be better to let him make his own Lockeian argument in full as he does in his "Preface to Shakespeare." The passage, though it ends with the praise of an ancient, could serve as an introduction for humanists to the scholarly use of a large modern library of printed books:

> To works, however, of which the excellence is not absolute and definite, but gradual and comparative; to works not raised upon principles demonstrative and scientifick, but appealing wholly to observation and experience, no other test can be applied than length of duration and continuance of esteem. What mankind have long possessed they have often examined and compared, and if they persist to value the possession, it is because frequent comparisons have confirmed opinion in its favour. As among the works of nature no man can properly call a river deep or a mountain high, without the knowledge of many mountains and many rivers; so in the productions of genius, nothing can be stiled excellent till it has been compared with other works of the same kind. Demonstration immediately displays its power, and has nothing to hope or fear from the flux of years; but works tentative and experimental must be estimated by their proportion to the general and collective ability of man, as it is discovered in a long succession of endeavours. Of the first building that was raised, it might be with certainty determined that it was round or square, but whether it was spacious or lofty must have been referred to time. The Pythagorean scale of numbers was at once discovered to be perfect, but the poems of Homer we yet know not to transcend the common limits of human intelligence, but by remarking, that nation after nation, and century after century, has been able to do little more than transpose his incidents, new name his characters, and paraphrase his sentiments.

These comparative, historical, and social views of the value, existence, and study of poetry are exactly the kinds of understanding that fit the actual libraries created by print, containing books from different times and cultures, books which said many different things in many different forms, books which in their aggregate broke down old concepts of knowledge and queried older understandings of letters. Johnson's notorious attacks on almost any kind of dogmatism in letters—the necessity of the unities, the elegance of pastoral, the superiority of blank verse to rhyme, the laws forbidding the mixture of literary kinds such as comedy and tragedy—realize critically the kind of literary skepticism that the availability of many books encouraged, and even forced. Conversely, his equally notorious empiricism—close readings of what poems actually say and how, comparison of one work to another, judging literary value by the responses of "actual" readers, following out the history of the reception of books—is a positive response to the same kind of bibliographical experience.

But a random collection of empirical observations was not what an age much given to organizing fact into theory and coherent systems moved toward, nor was it what Johnson, even with his fundamental distrust of systems, finally settled for. Eventually the old conception of courtly letters and the wisdom texts of its ancient classics were superseded in the eighteenth century by new understandings of letters that took into account and gave shape to the vast supply of information now available in printed books and library collections.

Catalogues, Encyclopedias, and Knowledge Trees:
Organizing the Library

If Johnson looked into the shadows of the library and saw there, as he did in so many other places, the possibility of meaninglessness that has haunted the Gutenberg project from its beginning, his age, including himself much of the time, and

subsequent ages as well, have more often optimistically found
in print's universal library the place where mankind's dream of
boundless prelapsarian knowledge can at last be realized. Not
only are vast amounts of information conveniently assembled
there in books, and in books about books, but print with its
logic of systematization orders information, thus making it usable by placing it firmly in a structure of knowledge. In "Some
Conjectures about the Impact of Printing," Elizabeth Eisenstein describes this general tendency of print to organize information into knowledge as an aspect of print's general *esprit de
système* operating beyond the internal order of individual works
to structure the entire library by a process of "combinatory intellectual activity." Once print made numerous books available,

a given purchaser could buy more books at lower cost and bring
them into his study or library. In this way, the printer provided
the clerk with a richer, more varied literary diet than had been
provided by the scribe. To consult different books it was no longer
so essential to be a wandering scholar. Successive generations of
sedentary scholars were less apt to be engrossed by a single text
and to expend their energies in elaborating on it. The era of the
glossator and commentator came to an end, and a new "era of intense cross referencing between one book and another" began.
More abundantly stocked bookshelves increased opportunities to
consult and compare different texts and, thus, also made more
probable the formation of new intellectual combinations and per-
mutations. Viewed in this light, cross-cultural interchanges fostered by printing seem relevant to Sarton's observation: "The
Renaissance was a transmutation of values, a 'new deal,' a reshuf-
fling of cards, but most of the cards were old; the scientific Renaissance was a 'new deal,' but many of the cards were new." Combinatory intellectual activity, as Koestler has recently suggested,
inspires many creative acts. Once old texts came together within
the same study, diverse systems of ideas and special disciplines
could be combined. Increased output directed at relatively stable
markets, in short, created conditions that favored, first, new com-

binations of old ideas and, then, the creation of entirely new systems of thought.

As an example of combinatory intellectual activity, Eisenstein offers the assemblage in the Renaissance of an ahistoric system of magic by bringing together "Hermetic, cabbalistic, Gnostic, theurgic, Sabean and Pythagorean writings into a 'hermetic corpus.' " A more humble example of combinatory activity in the library, but one that makes more obvious the way in which print made combinatory activity necessary and inevitable, is the library catalogue. In the description of his imaginary library, Johnson considered its catalogue, in which alone the fame of many older books was preserved, important enough for particular notice. That interest reflects his own expert knowledge of catalogues and the realities of the eighteenth-century librarian who was faced with an accumulation of books built up by print over three centuries that had to be sorted out if the library was to be usable. If the librarian devised a way of shelving his old books so that they could be found by locating them, by way of one historical example, by faculties, he was still faced with the problem of what to do with the constant accession of new books. Even if librarians found room to insert new books into the old categories, they were still in difficulty. Just where in the old order should they go? How should the old books be rearranged to provide for the insertion of the new? And what should be done with new kinds of books, novels for example, that were impossible to fit into the old systems?

The cataloguing problem in eighteenth-century libraries provides an unusually direct insight into the way in which technology (print) can affect culture (the structure of knowledge). Print does not determine the exact nature of the outcome, but it sets up the situation and forces a response to it in accordance with print logic, in this case a systematic organization of information into a rational structure of knowledge. Edward Miller's description of the catalogue problem still troubling the British Museum in the 1830s, when a battle of the catalogues took place, gives an excellent view of the practical cataloguing problems posed by large libraries:

> There was still widespread discussion within the Department of Printed Books and in literary circles on the merits or otherwise of the catalogues available to the public in the Reading Room. The readers were still using an interleaved copy, in twenty-three folio volumes, of the printed catalogue of the old library, which had been prepared between 1807 and 1810 by Ellis and Baber. Into these interleaved copies had been transcribed the titles of a large proportion, but by no means all, of those books which had been received since the completion of the printed catalogue, amounting, in all, to some 30,000 additional titles. . . . There were in existence two such interleaved copies of the catalogue, one, as has been said, for the use of readers, the other for the use of the staff. Both these copies, but particularly the Reading Room copy, were showing marked signs of the heavy use to which they were exposed. In addition, there was increasingly less space available on many of the pages to insert the accessions slips in their correct place within the alphabetical sequence. Many errors had also been found arising from the practice of employing some of the attendants, without proper supervision or instruction, on the highly intricate task of incorporation.

As a scholar and professional writer, dependent on being able to locate information, Johnson well understood the increasing practical necessity of catalogues. He constantly browsed in the library, to get an idea of what books were available, and, in a passage quoted before but important enough to this context to bear repeating, he remarked to Richard Cambridge, who had commented on his strange "desire to look at the backs of books," that "when we enquire into any subject, the first thing we have to do is to know what books have treated of it. This leads us to look at catalogues, and at the backs of books in libraries." Consulting the catalogue of any actual European library at this time, he would have found numerous arrangements: alphabetical shelf lists by title or author, unalphabetized listings by individual original collections—for example, Sloane or Cotton—categorization by bibliographical format—folios, quartos, octavos—or even subject indexes like the German *Realkatalog* or the French *catalogue raisonné*. The printed book obviously encouraged systematic, abstract organization of the library collection but offered many variant possibilities of arrangement. Printed books, for example, have titles, which suggest possibilities of grouping by general subject; they have publication dates so that chronology becomes a feasible method of organization; and they have authors so that all the works of a single writer can be assembled, and all the works of all the authors put in alphabetical order.

If the library is an image of knowledge at a given time, the catalogue, which determines the library's organization, is an official scheme of that knowledge, the objective statement, an enactment and concretization, of the intellectual categories that constitute true knowledge and their relation to one another. This is always a very sensitive and important social matter, and in the modern world, control of the official catalogue system— British Library or Library of Congress, for example—gives real power over the paradigm of knowledge in the society, comparable to control over the meaning of words in the dictionary, or over education through the departmental structure of the modern university. For a particular intellectual category to lose its classification in the catalogue is equivalent to official decertification as knowledge, and to have the wrong classification—"fiction," by way of an actual example close to our main interest, rather than "literature"—is almost equally fatal.

The power to make the central library catalogue is a social power with important consequences worth great struggle. In the British Museum, for example, public hearings, parliamentary committees, and a titan of a keeper, Panizzi, were required to establish finally, and then only by the mid-nineteenth century (1849), the principles, the famous 91 rules, governing the main catalogue. The story of the deep political and bitter social struggle over the question of whether the printed index was to be alphabetical, with full bibliographical descriptions, or to be alphabetic and brief, or to be arranged by category dramatizes not alone the general folly of mankind and the cantankerous personalities of scholars and librarians, but the importance of this matter to society at large, no matter how imperfectly the participants may have understood the real intellectual and social stakes.

But Panizzi's battle at the British Museum lies beyond the eighteenth-century print-forced changes in letters we are presently considering. The great eighteenth-century struggle for the power to determine the categories and structure of knowledge took place not in the library, and not in England, but in the writing and publication in various editions and formats from mid-century on of the monumental *Encyclopédie* of Diderot and d'Alembert. An encyclopedia is a condensed library, an organized summary of the knowledge of the age, and print was as deeply and formatively implicated in the history of the *Encyclopédie* as it was in the construction of the great public library. The exact ways in which print affected the *Encyclopédie* have been instructively worked out by Robert Darnton in his *The Business of Enlightenment, A Publishing History of the "Encyclopédie,"* where he has shown in precise and fascinating detail, drawing on the records of the Société Typographique de Neuchâtel, the extraordinary ways in which the printing business from start to finish affected the development and spread in the *Encyclopédie* of Enlightenment views, and print views, "that knowledge was ordered, not random; that the ordering principle was reason working on sense data, not revelation speaking through tradition; and that rational standards, when applied to contemporary institutions, would expose absurdity and iniquity everywhere."

The last version of the *Encyclopédie*, the vast *Encyclopédie méthodique*, abandoning what was by then considered a meaningless alphabetical organization, attempted the utopian, but characteristically eighteenth-century Gutenberg projéct of arranging all its information in categories and by faculties to produce an exact image of the "circle of knowledge" promised by the very word *encyclopédie*. *Un superbe ouvrage et la vrai Encyclopédie*, its promoter, C.-J. Panckoucke called it. The equivalent of a library catalogue, and an image of the structure of knowledge an encyclopedia provided, was what d'Alembert in the "Preliminary Discourse" to the original *Encyclopédie* called a "genealogical tree of the arts and sciences" or a "Mappemonde," a schematic arrangement of all knowledge as a knowledge tree. The part of the knowledge tree dealing with arts and letters will be reproduced later in these pages.

One of Johnson's early employments as a young professional newly come to London was to help catalogue the library of Robert and Edward Harley (first and second Earls of Oxford), and his description of the project provides a good practical example of the uses of knowledge trees and their close relations to library catalogues. The Harleian library with its 50,000 books, 350,000 pamphlets, and over 7,000 volumes of manuscripts, plus many prints and other items is a good example of the new world of books the printing press was constructing in the library. After Oxford's death in 1741, the books and pamphlets had been bought on speculation by the bookseller Thomas Osborne for £13,000. He needed a catalogue to sell this large number of books to prospective buyers. Seeing an opportunity to capitalize further on public interest in this notable library, he decided to sell the catalogue for 5 shillings a volume rather than giving it away. To prepare the catalogue, he engaged the scholar William Oldys, and later hired Johnson to help him. It was hack work of the dreariest kind, carried on, Johnson noted bitterly, without amanuenses; but in his characteristic way of always doing his best once involved, he became intrigued by the problem of cataloguing and flung himself into the project with great energy and skill. He wrote a general account of the library, published in late 1742, to encourage sales of the forthcoming catalogue. In these *Proposals* he argues that the catalogue will not be just the usual sale list but an "uncommon" classification, with full bibliographical description of the books, which would be a credit to the Harley family and to England, a monument of scholarship, and a stimulant to book collecting, well worth, he is careful to add, the price of 5 shillings a volume Osborne will charge. "The books," he tells the prospective customers, will be "distributed into their distinct classes, and every class ranged with some regard to the age of the writers; . . . every book . . . accurately described; . . . the peculiarities of editions . . . remarked, and observations from the authors of literary history occasionally interspersed; . . . this catalogue . . . may inform posterity of the excellence and value of this great collection, and promote the knowledge of scarce books, and elegant editions."

Osborne was apparently not much interested in this kind of scrupulous bibliography, and when he later spoke roughly to Johnson about the slowness with which the project was proceeding, Johnson knocked him down with a heavy folio and stood triumphant with his foot on his chest, the author rampant over a defeated bookseller.

The *Proposals*, which later became the "General Account" prefaced to the catalogue, deserves to be printed as a part of Johnson's criticism more frequently than it is, for it represents the general scheme of knowledge as he understood it, and it was his attempt to construct a complete knowledge tree. But in the end he only divided the books into various categories without attempting to do more than indicate the order and relation of these categories. Religious writings, including bibles and theology, stand first, in the place of honor, as Sacred Literature, followed by secular writings such as religious and civil history, then poetry, geography, and "chronology"—this once familiar category containing, for example, Isaac Newton's *Chronology of Ancient Kingdoms* and John More's *Table from the Beginning of the World to the Year of Christ 1593*. Johnson then goes on to voyages and travels, laws, physic, philosophy, criticism, mathematics, tactics, architecture, fortification, painting, and even horsemanship and fencing. The actual printed catalogue was, however, arranged with far fewer classifications than Johnson's grand scheme, and an index of titles supplied in the middle of the volume is organized in still different classifications. Johnson and Oldys were really not very systematic cataloguers, probably could not be, given the size of their task and the speed with which they had to work. Furthermore, abstract schemes, though they interested him, were never very congenial to Johnson. The catalogue is still extremely interesting as an objective form of Oldys' and Johnson's conception of the cultural scheme of knowledge, and constructed as it was in the middle of practical business circumstances and the interests of noble collectors of books, it reminds us again how closely our conception of knowledge is intertwined and interacting with other social activities and concerns.

Robert Darnton, in his essay, "Philosophers Trim the Tree of Knowledge: The Epistemological Strategy of the *Encyclopédie*," sees the making of conceptual schemes of knowledge such as Johnson's as a formalization of a much more basic and central human activity: "Pigeon-holing is ... an exercise in power." "All social action," he goes on, "flows through boundaries determined by classification schemes. ... All borders are dangerous. If left unguarded, they could break down, our categories could collapse, and our world dissolve in chaos. Setting up categories and policing them is therefore a serious business. A philosopher who attempted to redraw the boundaries of the world of knowledge would be tampering with the taboo. Even if he steered clear of sacred subjects, he could not avoid danger; for knowledge is inherently ambiguous." Darnton's purpose, in this article and elsewhere, is to follow the "serious business" of the revolutionary restructuring of the totality of knowledge by writers in the eighteenth century and its revolutionary social consequences in 1789. For our purposes here, however, we can narrow the focus of observation to a single area, the arts, and to a specific category, poetry, and their redefinition during the eighteenth century.

The Place of Letters in the Scheme of Knowledge: Poetry, the Arts, and Literature

The Nine Muses and the Seven Liberal Arts were little more obsolescent as systems of knowledge in a print culture than was the still-standard view in the first half of the eighteenth century of "literature" or "letters" as a broad category of all writing of excellence on serious topics, for which the models and rules of composition had been set for all time by the classics. Within letters, poetry—including dramatic poesy—was still, as it had been since Aristotle, distinguished by its fictional qualities from history, a record of fact, on one hand, and by its specificity from philosophy, an abstract scheme of reality, on the other hand. But the categories were not watertight, and whenever Johnson used the word "literature" or one of its compounds such as "literary history" or "literary transactions," he still referred to all the many kinds of writing worthy to be included in the realm of polite letters. "The patrons of literature," he says in his proposals for printing a catalogue of the holdings of the Harleian library, "will forgive the purchaser of this library [the bookseller Osborne] if he presumes to assert some claim to their protection and encouragement," and using the word in a somewhat different but still very general sense, he regularly speaks of people having "much" or "great literature," meaning wide reading knowledge of many kinds of books. In the *Dictionary*, literature is defined simply as "learning, skill in letters." René Wellek, who has carefully traced the historical development of the word "literature" in his essay, "What is Literature?" describes its normal eighteenth-century meaning in a way which fits Johnson's usage exactly: "literature is used very inclusively. It refers to all kinds of writing, including those of erudite nature, history, theology, philosophy, and even natural science."

The vast library that print constructed and Johnson imagined as "the vanity of human hopes," made impossible these older, looser, more generous, less compartmentalized conceptions of literature. In the circumstances of the new libraries, and the many books they brought together, the old conception of polite letters simply got lost in the vastness of time and the quantity of information, or simply became useless, as it did in Johnson's inability to answer positively Boswell's question "What is poetry?" But as new classification systems were designed to meet the need to organize the increasing amount of information in the libraries, a new conception of "literature" gradually appeared and took its place in a different configuration of knowledge.

Library catalogues did not lead the way in establishing the new print-based conception of "literature" and giving it a place in the new rational scheme of knowledge. We can perhaps detect an unsteady movement toward the category of "literature" in the catalogues of the British Museum, where about 1790 Ayscough proposed a "synthetical arrangement" of the books in which Category III would be, "Poetry, Novels, Letters, Polygraphy," the last term referring, in a way that reveals a continuing inability to think the category through systematically, to any collection of individual works bound together. And by 1838 belles-lettres, which still remains an elegant variation for literature, occupied a section in the reading room.

Knowledge trees are more suggestive of the kind of historical change in the conception of letters that was actually taking place. In *The Advancement of Learning*, Francis Bacon's influential scheme of knowledge offers the outlines of the older, more traditional arrangements: poesy belongs to a category of human, as distinct from divine, learning. Within human learning it derives from the faculty of imagination and is placed, in the ancient manner, between history, derived from memory, and philosophy, derived from reason. Poesy has three branches, narrative, representative, and allusive, which form a scale measuring the distance of the work from reality, narrative being realistic and literal, while allusive is fictional and allegorical. Bacon's famous description of poesy as "feigned history" renders precisely the view of the meaning and purpose of poetry that largely held sway until the eighteenth century:

> The use of this feigned history [i.e., poetry] hath been to give some shadow of satisfaction to the mind of man in those points wherein the nature of things doth deny it, the world being in proportion inferior to the soul; by reason whereof there is, agreeable to the spirit of man, a more ample greatness, a more exact goodness, and a more absolute variety, than can be found in the nature of things. Therefore, because the acts or events of true history have not that magnitude which satisfieth the mind of man, poesy feigneth acts and events greater and more heroical. . . . So as it appeareth that poesy serveth and conferreth to magnanimity, morality, and to delectation. And therefore it was ever thought to have some participation of divineness, because it doth raise and erect the mind by submitting the shows of things to the desires of the mind; whereas reason doth buckle and bow the mind unto the nature of things.

In Ephraim Chambers' *Cyclopaedia* (1728)—which Johnson knew well in connection with his *Dictionary*, as he also knew Bacon—knowledge has become more complicated but the scheme is, at least from a logical point of view, little improved. Knowledge is divided by Chambers into the natural and artificial, and the latter in turn into the internal and external. The external is further subdivided into the "real" and the "symbolical," and "Fables-called Poetry" are a part of the symbolical along with "Words . . . called Grammar," "Armories-called Heraldry," and "Tropes and Figures-called Rhetoric."

Like Bacon and Chambers, neither Johnson's *Proposals* nor the Harleian catalogue has a category of anything much like what we would now call "literature." There is "poetry," of course, and the index has a section titled *Litterae Humaniores*, but this turns out to contain only grammars. It is clear that no more than their predecessors did Johnson and Oldys understand "literature" in the modern sense of a category of writing composed of all the works of the imagination, regardless of genre—though, interestingly enough, Johnson said in 1778 that he had made a list for Mrs. Montagu of "all Daniel Defoe's works of imagination." But in the Harleian catalogue, poetry, both classical and modern, remained a category of verse, while under the heading *artes* we find painting, architecture, sculpture, and music—not dance—plus a *mélange* of useful technical skills such as hydraulics, horsemanship, calligraphy, shorthand, glass blowing, and, not surprisingly for a man of print, typography.

Only in Diderot's and d'Alembert's tree in the *Encyclopédie, Système Figuré Des Conoissances Humaines*, as it appears in the first edition of Volume I (1751), do we begin to see something like the conception of literature and the arts that has actually taken shape as real in the modern world. No doubt the enormous effects of this publication on general understanding has had a good deal to do with the spread and establishment of this particular conception of the arts and of letters as fact. The overall scheme acknowledges and follows Bacon in locating the origins of various types of understanding in mental faculties;

but imagination is removed from its ancient place between memory (history) and reason (philosophy) to the far right end of the scale (Memory-Reason-Imagination) where it is elaborated in the following way:

IMAGINATION.

There are curiosities here, a bit odd to the modern mind, such as the sacred-profane division, the inclusion of engraving among the arts, the retention of Bacon's old category of the "parabolic," and the treatment of the dramatic, including "pastoral," as a separate category from the other types of poetry; but in the main this is the schematic arrangement of literature and the arts we still know and take for granted as fact. "Poetry" or "making" is still not an unfamiliar general term for the category of what we more often call the arts, which are all expressions of the imagination realizing its powers in a number of "sister arts." If the arts are not for us still the same precise group appearing in the *Encyclopédie*, we are accustomed to changes within the category, the twentieth century having added, for example, photography and film, even as earlier ages added gardening, and dance. Similarly, though the subcategories in each of the arts—epic, madrigal, epigram, and novel as species of narrative poetry, for example—may seem odd to us nowadays, we can recognize in both the daring and the rightness of including the novel here in the mid-1700s, the kind of constant change in this area that allows, for example, *à la* Frye, romance, comedy, tragedy, satire, and irony now to appear inevitable.

But the overall structure proposed by Diderot and d'Alembert still holds, for the philosophers schematized in their knowledge tree the actual historical "combinatory activity" that led to what its primary historian, Paul Oskar Kristeller, calls in a famous article of that title, "The Modern System of the Arts." Here Kristeller tracks the long growth of the modern concept of the fine arts from antiquity to its first complete statement in the Abbé Batteux, *Les beaux arts réduits à un même principe* (1746), through its spread throughout the modern world through the *Encyclopédie*, and its metaphysical legitimation by the German philosophers of aesthetics, particularly Baumgarten and Kant, who made the beautiful, as the distinctive mark of art, an *a priori* mental category. In this historical process, poetry gradually took its place in a general category of the fine arts, which were at first distinguished from other cultural activities and their products by the end they sought, nonutilitarian pleasure, and the means they employed to achieve it, the imitation of nature in its more beautiful compositions. Within this concept of the arts—though Kristeller does not follow the story out at this level—verbal art gradually, and logically in view of its primary definition as the kind of writing having its source in the imagination, expanded to the larger category of "literature" which came over time to include all imaginative writing— plays, poems, novels, essays—produced everywhere and at all times by the human imagination.

René Wellek has followed this process by tracking the historical changes in the meaning of the word "literature." "Only very slowly," he reports, "was the term narrowed down to what

264   PLACE AND PURPOSE OF LETTERS

we today call 'imaginative literature': the poem, the tale, the play in particular." Although the *OED* gives 1822 as the first date for this latter meaning, Wellek quotes George Colman in 1761—"Shakespeare and Milton seem to stand alone, like first-rate authors, amid the general wreck of old English literature"—and Wordsworth is pretty clearly using "literature" in the modern sense when he remarks in the observations prefixed to the 1800 second edition of *Lyrical Ballads* that he hesitates to undertake a systematic defense of the "class of Poetry" because it would require, among other things, "retracing the revolutions, not of literature alone, but likewise of society itself." Literature in this sense was already Goethe's *Universalpoesie* of all mankind, and by the time of the second edition of *Lyrical Ballads*, Wordsworth in defining true poetry in his preface could phrase simply and precisely one of the basic principles around which the modern conception of literature has been constructed: "It may be safely affirmed that there neither is, nor can be, any *essential* difference between the language of prose and metrical composition." He then goes on to fix literature firmly in the overall social scheme of knowledge by differentiating it as one of the arts from what has remained its defining opposite in the world and its scheme of knowledge: "much confusion has been introduced into criticism by this contradistinction of poetry and prose, instead of the more philosophical one of poetry and matter of fact, or science."

A History of Letters:
THE LIVES OF THE POETS

The idea of poetry as one component of a larger category of imaginative art was not entirely unfamiliar to Johnson, and while he never expounded the theory in a systematic way, he did link some of the major arts in conventional ways at various times. Familiar with the ancient tradition of *ut pictura poesis*, he can say in his *Proposals* for the Harleian catalogue that "Painting is so nearly allied to poetry, that it cannot be wondered that those who have so much esteemed the one, have paid an equal regard to the other." Architecture, which he liked, also provided him with easy parallels to poetry, though he thought "fine allusions, and bright images, and elegant phrases" more proper to poetry where "all these ornaments are useful, because they obtain an easier reception for truth" than for architecture where "a building is not at all more convenient for being decorated with superfluous carved work." And though he could say at age seventy-one that he had never "been affected by musical sounds" before hearing "some solemn musick being played on French horns" in a funeral procession, he shows in *Ramblers* 86, 88, and 92 that he well understood the relation of poetic meters to music. It is, however, Roger Lonsdale's considered opinion in his biography of Burney that Johnson "made little effort to conceal his scorn and suspicion of music and musicians. Hawkins recorded Johnson's remark that music 'excites in my mind no ideas, and hinders me from contemplating my own'; and he added his own suspicion that 'music was positive pain' to Johnson. Similarly Boswell heard Johnson's opinion that music 'was a method of employing the mind, without the labour of thinking at all.' Even harsher was the statement attributed to Johnson that 'no man of talent, or whose mind was capable of better things, ever would or could devote his time and attention to so idle and frivolous a pursuit.'" Statuary, he thought only a little better of: "Painting (said he) consumes labour not disproportionate to its effect; but a fellow will hack half a year at a block of marble to make something in stone that hardly resembles a man. The value of statuary is owing to its difficulty. You would not value the finest head cut upon a carrot."

Boswell's friend, Henry Home, Lord Kames, had, however, in his *Elements of Criticism* (1762)—the most famous poetics of the day, at least in Britain—assembled something very like the modern system of the arts, with particular attention to the place of poetry in the scheme. The category of what he already calls "the fine arts," was, with two additions to Batteux's catalogue of the arts, familiar to Kames, for he speaks of the pleasures arising from the cultivation of "poetry, painting, sculpture, music, gardening, and architecture." Johnson, who had thought once of writing a *history* of criticism, not a poetics, was not entirely scornful of Kames—"a pretty essay, and deserves to be held in some estimation"—but then he adds quickly, "though much of it is chimerical." On another occasion when Goldsmith wittily said of Kames, "It is easier to write that book, than to read it," Johnson defended Kames, arguing that "The Scotchman has taken the right method in his 'Elements of Criticism.' I do not mean that he has taught us any thing; but he has told us old things in a new way"; but then he quickly qualifies this praise, too: "We have an example of true criticism in Burke's 'Essay on the Sublime and Beautiful.' " Johnson's preference for an affective type of criticism that describes an immediate, emotional response to art and nature—and one that argues, as Burke's does, that words are a better medium for the sublime than pictures—over a systematized logical account of true taste fits well with his general views that poetry has a *history* rather than an *essence*, or a place in a logical structure of knowledge. While Johnson could say in *Rambler* 36 that "it is probable, that poetry is nearly of the same antiquity with rational nature," attempts to fix it exactly, in a library catalogue, a knowledge tree, or a systematic poetics, or in any philosophical fashion based on the identification of a universal poetic essence or an abstract logical scheme of all knowledge, were uncongenial to him. His historical view led away from *poetry* to a concept of *letters* much like Kristeller's history of the arts: "The various arts are certainly as old as human civilization, but . . . in the course of history . . . [they] change not only their content and style, but also their relations to each other, and their place in the general system of culture, as do religion, philosophy or science."

A history orders and validates cultural things as effectively as does a coherent philosophical system. Both are primary intellectual strategies, or combinatory intellectual activities, of western culture, and both have been used from the Greeks to the present to legitimate the existence, to order in time, and to link the constituent parts of any chosen subject. History, like philosophy, though in different ways, strengthens the reality of its subject by isolating it from other aspects of reality, defining it and attributing to it certain qualities that society considers to be distinguishing marks of the real, such as coherence, cause-and-effect linkage, and the power of some quality to maintain itself or persist, even while changing, in time. But while similar in cultural purpose and at least in some of their ways of functioning, the philosophic and historical mentalities have traditionally been opposed ways of thinking about and ordering the world, one abstract and idealizing, the other experiential and committed to a changing world; one hypothesizing an ideal scheme of things to justify the actual deductively, the other moving inductively through the actual to seek whatever general laws may be, usually at best, hypothesized. The explosion of printed information in the eighteenth century fostered a vast increase in both philosophic and historical activity, for the age of the philosophe was also the age of the historian, many philosophers, particularly the more skeptical, say, Voltaire or Hume, being also historians. Given Johnson's characteristic radical doubts, he inevitably had little faith in abstract philosophic schemes, and his combinatory efforts gave letters a new place in print culture by assembling the information print made available into a literary history, *The Lives of the Poets*.

The class of writings Johnson called poetry and we, *mutatis mutandis*, call literature, had no history, at least as we define the term, in England, and not much more in France or Italy, until the later eighteenth century. There had been earlier lists of writers such as Leland's *Laborious Journey* (1549) and John Bale's *Summarium* (1548) which listed famous clerks in all studies. There were also mythological literary histories, like Sidney's, which followed Boccaccio's fourteenth-century *Genealogy of the Gentile Gods* in tracing poetry back to Apollo, Orpheus, Moses, and King David, and like Bale traced poetic origins to mythical heros like Osiris and Samothes Gigas, the brother of Homer! Later writers were no more interested in disentangling poetry from other forms of writing or organizing the materials available to them in an orderly historical pattern. Fuller's *Worthies of England* (1662), Aubrey's *Brief Lives* (printed only in 1813), and Wood's *Athenae Oxonienses* (1691–1692) provide brief biographies of writers with others and arrange them in such quaint categories as counties of origin or enrollment at Oxford. True literary history came, René Wellek argues in his pioneering *Rise of English Literary History*, only with an accumulating awareness of the distinctiveness of poets, poems, and periods; a sense of the development from one author and one period to the next; and a recognition of the importance of the social milieu, intellectual environment, spiritual atmosphere, and the quality of different ages, languages, and nations.

These attitudes are all made possible, or at least furthered, by the availability of large numbers of printed books, and as Lawrence Lipking shows in his summary book on eighteenth-century histories of the arts, *The Ordering of the Arts in Eighteenth-Century England*, it was not until the period between 1762 and 1790 that England was provided for the first time with histories of the various arts: Walpole and Reynolds on painting, Hawkins and Burney on music, and Warton and Johnson on poetry. Warton's *History of English Poetry* takes chronological priority over Johnson's *Lives of the Poets*, Warton's first volume of three appearing in 1774; but despite the grand evolutionary

scheme announced in its preface—"to pursue the progress of
our national poetry, from a rude origin and obscure beginnings, to its perfection in a polished age"—he does not deal
with Old English writings, nor does he get beyond the beginnings of the Elizabethan period. What he does mainly, although his book contains interesting remarks about primitivism and romance, is to provide a chronology, a bibliography,
and an extensive anthology of quotations. Wellek, who prefers
Warton over Johnson as the first true literary historian, con-
cedes that his "main success was unfortunately not in the actual
writing of a history, but rather in his ability to organize into an
orderly scheme the materials accumulated by his predecessors
and by his own researches." But Johnson in his *Lives of the Poets*
(1779–1781) constructed a literary history that though it begins only about 1600, and is primarily organized as a series of
biographies, established the place of letters as a deep-running
continuity in the social life of the English nation, through the
lives of its poets and their audiences.

   As was usual with Johnson's works, print played a large part
in the generation and development of *The Lives of the Poets*, as
if to manifest its deeper involvement with the subject matter
and the form of literary history. Boswell tells us that the king
commanded Johnson to write "the literary biography of this
country." But the monarch, and the aristocratic society he sym-
bolized, had in fact lost authority over letters, and the power to
define its place in the world by writing its history or the lives of
its writers had passed into other hands. At any rate, Johnson
did nothing on the work until on 29 March 1777, while he was,
he said, at his prayers, he was visited by three old friends and
publishers, Tom Davies, William Strahan, and Thomas Cadell,
representing a conger of 36 London booksellers and publishers, who proposed to him that he should "write little Lives, and
little Prefaces, to a little edition of the English Poets." Johnson
was intrigued by the idea, having earlier written a number of

literary lives, such as those of Savage, Cave, and Sir Thomas
Browne. He had also proposed several others, for example, a
life of Chaucer, and often declared that "the biographical part
of literature . . . is what I love most." He accepted on the spot
and set a surprisingly low fee—about which, however, he never
complained—of 200 guineas, to which the conger later added
another 200 guineas. The prefaces were wanted by the publishers, one of them, Dilly, told Boswell, for "an elegant and accurate edition of all the English Poets of reputation, from
Chaucer to the present time." Behind this noble concern for
letters was also a very practical concern for property. After the
Donaldson decision, perpetual rights in most of the poets proposed for the collection were no longer legally valid, and another Scottish publisher was now printing the small, cheap
Apollo Press editions of *The British Poets* (eventually there were
109 volumes) and selling them in the London market through
the agent, John Bell. No longer protected by law, the London
booksellers were reduced to trying to maintain what they now
piously called their "honorary copyright" by declaring that the
Scottish books were poorly printed and inaccurate. They proposed to produce a sumptuous edition—"the whole will be conducted with spirit, and in the best manner, with respect to authourship, editorship, engravings, etc., etc."—to reaffirm their
rights over the poets by the only means still available to them,
the costliness, comprehensiveness, quality, and scholarship of
their books. To add the weight of that great authority on poetry, Samuel Johnson, to the booksellers' series would have
been, as Edward Dilly said, "a very valuable addition, and
stamp the reputation of this edition superiour to any thing that
is gone before." In other words, Johnson's scholarly authority
would transfer over and lend validity to the booksellers' claims.

This publishing rivalry was only another skirmish in the ongoing literary battle, which Johnson's history of poetry would
help to settle, about who controlled poetry. The general read-

ing public? The people who could afford to buy the cheap Scottish editions? The more limited set of readers of taste and means who would be the market for the expensive and elegant London edition? The booksellers? Samuel Johnson the author? And, as if to declare that the London publishers and their conceptions about limited audiences and perpetual copyrights no longer controlled the literary future, their plans began at once to go awry. The original plan was for an edition containing all the major poets from Chaucer to their own times, but the size and cost of such an edition—Bate has thoroughly examined the question in his *Samuel Johnson* and estimates that it would have come to approximately 100 volumes—was too much for them, and they reduced the plan to cover only the period between 1660 and the time of writing. They then scaled this down further by excluding all living poets, concerned that the sales of existing editions might be harmed either by the new edition, or by what Johnson might say about the authors. Finally the conger proposed to do only 47 poets, and Johnson then added a few names—James Thomson, Blackmore, Watts, Pomfret, and Yalden—to bring the number to 52. In the end the total edition came to 68 volumes: 56 contained the poetry, 10 were composed of Johnson's prefaces, and 2 were devoted to an index.

Managing to sound somehow, at least to my ear, oddly like one of the Peachums in *The Beggar's Opera*, Mrs. Thrale says of Johnson's writing of *The Lives*, "He loved to be set at work." But once he started work, the project began to grow in size and in importance for him, and what had been intended as only short prefaces, a page or two containing a few salient facts, became biographies of the English poets, a history of English poetry, and a monument establishing the dignity of letters in the world. The pattern is apparent in the writing history of *The Lives* but even clearer in its subsequent printing history. The short prefaces originally proposed by the booksellers were, as

introductions to the individual volumes, to be only adjuncts to
the poetry; but, as many of the introductions grew in size, they
took on life of their own and, with Johnson's urging, they were
eventually printed between 1779 and 1781, not as prefaces, but
independently as the first ten volumes of the edition. By 1783,
and frequently since, they were being reprinted alone, without
any visible connection to the collections of poetry, which have
long been forgotten, that they were supposed to introduce.
The lives of the poets as written by a poet had broken free of
booksellers and even of poems. Titles reveal the same pattern.
The first four volumes appearing in 1779 were titled *Prefaces,
Biographical and Critical, to the Works of the English Poets.* Later
separate editions became *The Lives of the Most Eminent English
Poets; with Critical Observations on their Works,* and in time this
was transformed into the much grander and more meaningful
title we now know best, which states directly and without en-
cumbrance the primary fact of literature, *The Lives of the English
Poets.*

The title suggests biography, but together the biographies
gave us our first history of English letters. Just why Johnson expanded short prefaces into a free-standing literary history can
only be guessed. In his "Advertisement" to *The Lives* he says
only that he was "led beyond" his original plan "by the honest
desire of giving useful pleasure." But whatever the motives
may have been, the book as it finally took shape offered a powerful and influential statement about all the major literary
questions that troubled letters in an age of radical change.
What is poetry? Who writes it and why? What are the right
ways to read and the effects of reading it? What is its function
in the social world? But the critical question it most obviously
answered was, put crudely, who owns poetry, or, more circum-
spectly, where does poetry originate and what determines its
nature? Both in the writing and publishing history, and in the
composition as a grouping of poetic biographies, as well as in

what is said directly, *The Lives of the Poets* answered this question in the same way that Johnson had in the *Dictionary* answered the question of who controls and makes language. Not the king, not the nobles, not the booksellers and printers, not even the audience of common readers—though they are flattered into thinking themselves all-powerful even while they are being cleverly instructed—but the writer is the basic fact of letters.

This, as I have said, to some degree anticipates romantic poetry and its visionary poets with creative imaginations, but Johnson's poet is different from the romantic artist. His powers are more limited and he lives in a historical scene of complex social change, not amid beneficent nature or in transcendent realms of truth. In poetry as in life, he may say in the "Life of Cowley," "truth indeed is always truth, and reason is always reason; they have an intrinsick and unalterable value, and constitute that intellectual gold which defies destruction," but he regularly places his writers in a world of contingency where poets are made by chances such as Cowley's happening on a copy of Spenser as a child, and where the history of poetry contains such meaningless events as that involving John Philips, the author of *The Splendid Shilling*, sitting at school "hour after hour while his hair was combed by somebody, whose service he found means to procure."

By centering his history of letters on the lives of poets, and recounting those lives with full anecdotal detail, Johnson insured that there will always be some degree of randomness, some absence of consistent purpose, or at least any purpose easily understood, in the story of letters he tells. Samuel Butler wrote his satire on the Puritans, *Hudibras*, to win favor and pension from the restored king, but somehow, despite the brilliance and high reputation of the work, the court, for reasons Johnson does not understand and therefore does not explain in his "Life of Butler," never got around to rewarding him.

When Wycherley eventually arranged for Butler to meet the Duke of Buckingham, with a view to attracting his support for the poet, his Grace, happening to spy "a pimp of his acquaintance . . . trip by with a brace of Ladies, immediately quitted his engagement, to follow another kind of business." These are only some of the more bizarre and petty oddities, contradictions, and inconsistencies to be found in Johnson's literary history. There are far greater mysteries. Milton the man, as Johnson presents him, was a regicide, and a vain and a spiteful man, but somehow, and Johnson the moralist is very uneasy about this, "The poet, whatever be done, is always great." Waller wrote a panegyric on Cromwell when he was alive, but then sang the virtues of Charles Stuart when he regained his throne; and when the king mentioned that the poem praising *him* was inferior to Cromwell's, Waller replied easily, "Poets, Sir, succeed better in fiction than in truth." This brings on Johnson's strong indignation and a little excursion on the proper end of poetic fictions being "the conveyance of truth," but Waller's constant adjustments of his attitudes and his poetry to the necessities of the world, fully described by Johnson, elude his moral grasp, and as they slide by they provide momentary glimpses of accidents, discontinuities, and mysterious gaps between poets and their poetry, and the world and its moral system. Even when Johnson traces a distinct pattern in, say, the improvement of taste and of poetic language over time, a full conclusion is never entirely reached, for if Denham can be praised for "having done much" in this respect, we are instantly told that "he left much to do." David Bromwich puts his finger on precisely this eccentric tone of *The Lives* when he says that Johnson's "own practice teaches that the drama of biography and criticism together is the test they offer to our admiration."

The Lives has regularly been criticized for the looseness of its narrative and the unsystematic nature of its poetic. But it would be a mistake to allow modern expectations of tightly organized histories and logical poetics to obscure Johnson's real achievement in *The Lives* of combining the hitherto scattered pieces of English literary lore, and working them into a structure of biography, social history, and criticism sufficiently firm to constitute for the first time a history of English letters.

In keeping with the commission from the booksellers, *The Lives* includes only those authors who wrote at least some poetry. Although Johnson did not include several earlier lives he had published of writers who published no poetry, like Sir Thomas Browne, he did include previously written lives of some, Savage but not Shakespeare, who *were* poets. But within the biographies of poets he included, Johnson freely discusses other literary genres, Swift's prose, Dryden's and Congreve's plays, Pope's letters, Milton's polemical pamphlets, and Addison's essays, to cite only a few examples of other literary types that are included without any sense of inappropriateness in what is finally a history of English letters, not just poetry. Only the novel is obviously excluded.

Strictly speaking, the biographies covered only the period extending from Milton and Cowley to Gray and Lyttleton, a span of little more than a hundred years, but extensive discussion of Donne and the other metaphysicals, as well as more limited references to other earlier poets, English, European, and classical, shadow forth a larger and longer setting. And in the continuous activity of mental and scholarly sorting, pulling down and comparing one poet's writing with another, establishing chronological priority and tracing influence, Johnson, as he wrote, gradually provided a broad sense of the development of all European letters. To discuss Milton led inevitably to a consideration of Homer, Virgil, Ariosto, and Spenser, what each borrowed from the other, what the requisites of epic were, and how each writer fulfilled the epic contract. A consideration of Butler's *Hudibras* extended inevitably to Rabelais and Cervantes, and the satire of Rochester carried back to Horace and out to the edges of letters and an obscure "poem called *Nihil* in Latin by Passerat, a poet and critick of the sixteenth century in France." It is impossible to read *The Lives* without feeling the presence of the long line of European letters from Homer and the Greeks onward.

But the main plot involves English poetry from the early seventeenth to the latter eighteenth century. Beginning in his "Life of Cowley" with the poets to whom he gave the name "metaphysical" and described as learned but singular men who wished "only to say what they hoped had been never said before," Johnson traced the development of "correctness" in subject, style, and meter through Denham and Waller—"The critical decision has given the praise of strength to Denham, and of sweetness to Waller"—to its culmination in Dryden and Pope. Dryden he praised for enriching the language with "a variety of models," and went on to say, "To him we owe the improvement, perhaps the completion of our metre, the refinement of our language, and much of the correctness of our sentiments." But it was Pope, who "professed to have learned his poetry from Dryden," who for Johnson achieved the summit of poetic art. After giving Dryden's mind and art high praise, Johnson compared him to Pope by remarking that while Dryden "poured out what the present moment happened to supply" and thought no more of it, "Pope was not content to satisfy; he desired to excel, and therefore always endeavoured to do his best; he did not court the candour, but dared the judgment of his reader, and, expecting no indulgence from others, he shewed none to himself. He examined lines and words with minute and punctilious observation, and retouched every part with indefatigable diligence, till he had left nothing to be forgiven." Pope's polished, perfected art represented for Johnson the heights of poetry, and though still unwilling to define poetry in any limiting way, he does say that

Pope will take us as far in that direction as we can go: "if Pope be not a poet, where is poetry to be found?"

Johnson did not believe, as we do, that a major poetic shift was taking place during his generation from Pope's correctness to a style that has since been typified as preromantic or the poetry of sentiment, and called the "literature of power" by De Quincey, or the "poetry of process" by Frye. What Johnson smelled was decadence, not new beginnings, in a group of nearly contemporary poets who wrote, he felt, "with unnatural violence" and in irregular forms such as ode and blank verse about pleasures of the imagination, ancient bards, night thoughts, and solitary reflections on nature and humble life. Of Young he noted that his excellence "is not exactness, but copiousness," of Akenside that "He remarked little, and laid hold on nothing," of Gray that "he has a kind of strutting dignity," and of Collins that he suffered particularly from the surplus of imagination that was the radical weakness of all these poets: "He . . . employed his mind chiefly upon works of fiction and subjects of fancy, and by indulging some peculiar habits of thought was eminently delighted with those flights of imagination which pass the bounds of nature, and to which the mind is reconciled only by a passive acquiescence in popular traditions. He loved fairies, genii, giants, and monsters; he delighted to rove through the meanders of inchantment, to gaze on the magnificence of golden palaces, to repose by the waterfalls of Elysian gardens."

Johnson never gave way on his central position that poetry has no essence: "To circumscribe poetry by a definition," he repeats in his "Life of Pope," "will only shew the narrowness of the definer." Each of the lives is composed of a biography, a description of the poet's writings, and, finally, an analysis of his style; and as these various discussions of the art of writing in *The Lives* accumulate, part by part, a reasonably coherent history that has something definitive to say about most of the leading facts of modern literature takes shape. As it does so, poetry and letters become solidly real in the lives of those who write, and in the social worlds of court and garret in which they move, and in a formal sense as well, as if letters was gradually being realized and coming to exist in its own right. The "local poem" appears in Denham, criticism is finally stabilized by Dryden, the ode passes through a succession of developments. We may not now agree with Johnson's judgment about the absence of sincerity in pastoral poetry, particularly in *Lycidas*, but in focusing on sincerity he locates, as he so often does, a permanent issue in literature. It is remarkable how consistently Johnson identifies and clears away the confusion surrounding such perennial technical literary questions as the function of metaphor, the place of the caesura, the basic importance of sound patterns, the relation of meter and meaning, the appropriate level of diction, or the organization of the fable. He is no less perceptive about grander theoretical questions such as the nature of fancy and imagination, the place of wit in poetry, the necessity of a unified structure, the moral function of letters, the importance of novelty, the distinction between the sublime and the beautiful, the problems of translation, and the value of imitation. He understood very well that each age has a dominant literary form: "there has prevailed in every age a particular species of fiction. At one time all truth was conveyed in allegory; at another, nothing was seen but in a vision; at one period, all the poets followed sheep, and every event produced a pastoral; at another they busied themselves wholly in giving directions to a painter." He knew and explained how consistently poets imitated one another and in doing so suffered from an "anxiety of influence": hearing that Goldsmith had complained "that he had come too late into the world, for that Pope and other poets had taken up the places in the Temple of Fame," Johnson responded understandingly, "It is difficult to get literary fame, and it is every day growing more difficult."

He provided fundamental definitions of all the major genres—
tragedy, comedy, epic, satire, romance, burlesque, ode, pastoral, elegy. Even about the novel, which he saw as a species of
comic romance, he had some penetrating things to say. And
for each genre he defined the proper effects on the reader and
the means of achieving them.

It is never organized into a tight philosophic system, and it
contains big contradictions, as many modern critics have
pointed out, but anyone unfamiliar with literature, in 1780 or
still today, could get from Johnson's *Lives*, with the possible exception of a few key romantic ideas like symbolism or organic
form, the basic literary nomenclature, and the central points
around which letters in the age of print has been organized.
And as they acquired this information, common readers of *The
Lives* would assimilate with it a sense that while poetry may not
have a metaphysical essence, letters does have a historical continuity and a loose formal existence. The history and the poetics interact, to reinforce actively the reality of one another in
Johnson's practical criticism, which is concentrated in the third
section of each of the lives. Here, Johnson's poetic principles
are used to analyze and judge the historical poems. One of the
lasting qualities of *The Lives* is the steadiness with which poetic
standards are brought to bear on great literary texts, *Paradise
Lost*, metaphysical poetry, *Absalom and Achitophel*, *The Rape of the
Lock*, *Gulliver's Travels*, *The Seasons*, *Elegy Written in a Country
Churchyard*. And with each interpretation, the reality of English
writing thickens with the orderly piling up of substantial poetic
facts. When Johnson finishes, the works *are* there, dense and
meaningful, and English poetry had become English letters.

"Art and the equipment to grasp it are made in the same
shop," writes the anthropolologist, Clifford Geertz, in his article "Art as a Cultural System," and any theory of art is, therefore, in Geertz's view, "a theory of culture and not an autonomous enterprise." This is, though unintended, an excellent

description of Johnson's literary history, where letters is not theory or ideology, such as Sidney's golden world replacing the brazen world of nature, or the neoclassical idealization of the Ancients, but is as immediately real as the lives of those who write poetry in actual times and places, as solid as the intricate poems that are read and responded to by living people. In Johnson's history, poems and poetry are deeply enough involved with culture to raise questions about their involvement in individual lives, in the social and moral realms, and with the governing truths of a particular society. From a strictly theoretical or aesthetic point of view, many of the personal details that Johnson includes in his biographies, the ghastly mix-up of Dryden's funeral, the sharp quarrel between Addison and Steele about limiting the size of the nobility, a close account of the money Pope made from his translations, the hideous particulars of Swift's madness, tell us little about poetry. But these same matters, which are one of the parts of *The Lives* that have always most interested and delighted readers, validate the poetic lives, the poetry, and the critical theories by grounding them in the real stuff of life. The very irrelevance of many of the details to any logical pattern actually strengthens a historical enterprise that can admit the incongruities of actual life which, so at least Anglo-American culture believes, never does absolutely conform to any neat scheme. Poets and poetry, *The Lives* is always showing us, participate in the fullness, including the meaninglessness, or at least the absence of any tight logic, of actual living, and thereby become letters.

The theory and the criticism of the poetry appearing in the context of each life work in much the same way. Seldom getting very abstract, the criticism demonstrates the solidity and complex reality of poetry that can be analyzed in specific ways, never removing very far from the accidents and chances which shape writing: an author's habitual mode of composition, the poetic fashions of the time, the history of the transmission of the manuscripts and printed texts, publishers' contracts and sales, the circumstances, both economic and personal, of the writer. Criticism and theory never float free in some realm of pure philosophy but are also tied, in ways we have earlier examined in detail, to the open and obvious responses of readers of poems. The audience is not so dramatically present in Johnson's history of poetry as are his very real poets and their writings, but the common reader is consistently there in the background judging the value of poetry by his common sense, "uninstructed by precept." We see the reader finishing *Paradise Lost* with little reluctance—"None ever wished it longer than it is"—and hear the reader joining Johnson in praising Gray's most famous poem—"In the character of his *Elegy* I rejoice to concur with the common reader." We feel with readers the repellent grossness of Pope's and Swift's physical imagery— "such as every other tongue utters with unwillingness, and of which every ear shrinks from the mention"—watch readers delightedly enjoying *Gulliver*—"a production so new and strange that it filled the reader with a mingled emotion of merriment and amazement,"—and on and on. Readers roaring with pleasure at *The Beggar's Opera*, learning manners from Sir Roger de Coverly, feeling "gratitude" for Denham's smooth verse. The constant presence of readers in the rhetoric of *The Lives*, along with frequent descriptions of actual publics such as those who subscribed to Pope's *Homer*, or were aroused by Swift's Irish propaganda, or learned by heart the songs of *The Beggar's Opera*, adds greatly to the reality of the poetry in *The Lives*. Here, as in the real world, letters never exists in a vacuum. It is written by real people, embodied in real texts, and it is read by readers who get bored, are delighted with novelty and often miss the point, but in the long run ask the kind of critical questions "that relate to the heart of man," distinguishing the true from the false and conferring fame on those works they perceive as having permanent value.

Of course, the first reader is always Johnson, only partially hidden behind his fictional common reader, and his personal involvement with his story adds a great deal to the reality of his literary history. He admits that he doesn't know what a particular line means. Having married a widow, he is annoyed at Milton for insisting on marrying only virgins, and, as a Jacobite, he thunders at the wickedness of the regicide. Suffering deeply from melancholy and existential doubts, he viciously attacks Swift for defending against similar despairs with sneers and cynicism, and then turns round and quotes the Dean's dying words with full sympathy and understanding: "It is all folly; they had better let it alone." He contradicts himself, hurries over subjects and poets that don't interest him, hastens to conclusions when he is bored and tired, fills up bare spaces in his writing with long quotes from other writers, lists of writings, and his own earlier words on the subject, and often doesn't bother to pull the pieces together very tightly. But even these defects sometimes work to keep us aware that letters exists by virtue of being written, read, and responded to vigorously by real people with particular interests like himself.

CHAPTER VIII

THE SOCIAL CONSTRUCTION OF ROMANTIC LITERATURE

The History of Literary Systems

Romantic art, including literature, has presented itself for about two hundred years now, in terms of transcendencies, locating its origins, finding its language, and explaining its functions in the deeps of the unconscious self, the cosmic struggles of Apollonian and Dionysiac energies, the ancient myths of Edenic past and apocalyptic future, darkling Oedipal wrestlings with precursor poets and, most recently, the emptiness of the abyss. Centered in these worlds of spirit, romantic literature offered itself to the world, with at least some success, as a manifestation of an unchanging and distinctively human psychic essence, an epistemological and linguistic absolute, a *Universalpoesie*, the true voice of mankind appearing in all cultures at all times. In the course of the nineteenth century, these concepts came to seem so real and so true as to be unquestionable, facts rather than concepts. As this happened, literature concealed its social origins and denied its social existence, becoming a group of sacred texts that, as the products of the imagination speaking its primary language of metaphor, symbol and irony, manifest essential humanity.

But, as we have entered a postindustrial society, and as electronics has begun to replace print as the basic mode of communication in the late twentieth century, literature increasingly appears less and less a fact of nature and more and more a single episode in a much longer history of letters in western society. There are hints that if we knew enough to construct meaningful comparisons with the literary systems of other ad-

vanced cultures—a true comparative literature, that is—literature would be revealed to be even less a cultural or human absolute, and more a social product of a particular time and
place. As the ideology of romantic art has ceased to command
belief, it has become inescapably obvious that literature, along
with the other arts, is a part of culture, existing in the day-to-
day world as both a subjective concept and a set of objective social realities. Literature, that is to say, increasingly appears as
the social reality that I have called "letters."

As a socially constructed reality, letters like other institutions
such as the family, state, law, and church has a history of development, adjustment, and change closely involved with the major events in western history. This history appears on the largest scale as a succession of radically different literary systems.
Postclassical western culture, though it has had a variety of
styles and modes—metaphysical poetry or symbolism, for example—has constructed only three of these complete literary
systems by bringing together in a coherent, though loose, manner the various aspects of letters—the poet, the approved way
of writing, the theory, and so forth—and securing for the literary system a place in the world in some working relationship
to the rest of the social establishment. First, the old oral poetry
of the singer of tales, the scop, bard, and jongleur, which celebrated in formulaic verse and song heroic exploits and tribal
values, in the mead hall or the castle of the feudal lord. Second,
the primarily oral but scribally modified system of courtly letters which began with Dante's appearance, guided by the classical poet Virgil, in *The Divine Comedy* as a new type of poet and
flourished as an art of aristocratic gentlemen-amateurs in the
new Renaissance courts of Italian princes and European sun
kings. Third, "literature," the literary system of the age of print
and industrial capitalism. Literature originates in romantic artists with special powers—imagination, genius, sensitivity—who
create fictions more profound than the scientific statements of

natural law in works of art of full formal perfection. Literature resists the crudity of machinery, money, narrow rationalism to make reason and the will of God prevail. With its shift of emphasis from the poet to the work of art, and its acceptance of fundamental doubts about language and the possibility of meaning, modernism is increasingly treated as a radical break with high romanticism and as, therefore, the beginning of a fourth major literary system. The movement in this direction is very strong and it may well in the end prevail, but from the point of view of a truly *social* history of literature, it appears to many scholars, including myself, that modernism merely continues with a different emphasis, and less cultural confidence, some of the central positions of the old print-based literary system of industrial capitalism: an assumed hostility between art and society, the privileged meaning accorded the work of art, the conception of the "fine arts" as a group of related "higher" activities, and the independence of the art work from the social world.

Revolutionary structural changes in the literary system have come infrequently and, it would appear, only in conjunction with fundamental changes elsewhere in society. Feudal lords, divine-right kings, and parliamentary democracies, as well as oral, scribal, and print cultures, have been associated with different systems of letters. We are nervously curious at present about these major literary shifts since our social order and its primary mode of communication feel like they are changing, and our literary system has been showing signs of radical instability, not just romantic excitation, for some time now. The various types of criticism that have been lumped under the term "deconstruction," with their announcements of the death of the poet, the indeterminacy of the text, and the demystification or "unpacking" of all other romantic dogma, such as influence, genre, and tradition, dramatize the effects of more fundamental social changes on literary beliefs and their threat to the existence of romantic literature. In these circumstances of radical literary change, if we are not to stand helplessly by thinking that the end of the world has come, or opportunistically conceive that anything goes since all things can change, it becomes necessary that we have some broad social conception of why and how such radical changes occur, and how and why a literary world is put back together again. The dynamics of unmaking and making letters real in the world, organizing it in a structured system or social institution, and establishing its particular place in the world as a part of the overall meaning—making activity of culture—has been the study of the preceding pages with their exploration of the various ways in which new literary values were established and made believably real in eighteenth-century England and the life of Samuel Johnson. But the activity of making letters, or any other socially constructed reality, is ceaseless. Perhaps in conservative primitive societies some equivalent of our literary system, if any, changes as slowly as the family or the system of education. But in a volatile society such as that of the modern western world, the rate of technological change forces constant modifications of culture, and letters is constantly assimilating new realities where it can, and accommodating itself to the change where it must, in order to keep the literary system in at least some kind of working relationship with the rest of what is believed and done. Some brief consideration of the primary ways in which Johnson's definition, worked out over a lifetime, of letters in a print culture—the writer, the text, the audience—was modified and adjusted to create romantic literature, will serve to round out this model of the manner in which letters is socially constructed and constantly reconstructed. A consideration of two works, Wordsworth's *Prelude* and Balzac's *Lost Illusions*, which are paradigmatic of the larger changes taking place in letters in the early nineteenth century, will provide insight into the ongoing activity of literary change and the ways in which romantic literature was socially constructed in the age of print.

Wordsworth's PRELUDE and High Romanticism

By and large, the literary values that Johnson established as social fact on a print basis, as opposed to theorizing, have remained fundamental to letters in western society since his time. The troubled writer whose intense psychic efforts to give personal meaning to a threatening world are enacted in and validate his writings; the monumentalized, highly stylized texts that are the source of linguistic authority; universal audiences reading and understanding literature out of their human nature; and a history of changing letters made up of writers, their poems, and their styles: these have all been and remained, in one form or another, structural concepts of literature from Johnson's time nearly to ours. But they have constantly been elaborated, adjusted, combined, and recombined in a never-ceasing modification of literary surfaces. Some of the major changes, principally those we call romanticism and modernism, were so extensive as to change the face of letters almost entirely, nearly concealing the fact that romantic and modern literature have remained variants of a more basic literary system framed by print and adapted to the realities of capitalist society.

The Johnsonian scene of writing differs greatly from the dominant scene of romantic writing. Few writers very much resemble Johnson. Scott writing himself out of debt, Trollope with his watch in front of him putting down so many words before going off to the post office, George Orwell with his plain view of how and what to write. But the main line of English writers comes forward from Wordsworth's *Prelude*, which has, more than any other single work, given ideal form to the romantic poet and the true work of literature, and defined the high function and place of both in the world.

The Johnsonian and Wordsworthian scenes of writing seem at first to be diametrical opposites at all the critical points. Johnson's author is a large-minded person who happens by chance to be directed toward poetry, while Wordsworth's poet is a visionary selected for his sacred task by unseen mighty powers. There could hardly be a more startling or more meaningful contrast in the conception of poetic vocation than Boswell's description of how Johnson tried desperately to escape becoming a writer for Cave, but was forced in the end to write to earn his bread, and Wordsworth's description of his poetic initiation when on a magnificent morning, on a broad fruitful plain surrounded by laughing sea and bright mountains, he knew he had been chosen as a poet:

> I made no vows, but vows
> Were then made for me; bond unknown to me
> Was given, that I should be, else sinning greatly,
> A dedicated spirit.

Wordsworth might stress in his criticism that the poet was "a man speaking to men," using "the real language of men in a state of vivid sensation," and that poetic powers were only heightened imaginative perceptions of what is felt to some degree by all men, but in *The Prelude*, the poet is a singular hero who does "work of glory," and is constantly renewed, despite periods of doubt and confusion, by visionary "spots of time" which reassure him "that the mind Is lord and master, and that outward sense Is but the obedient servant of her will."

The story of the poet's life and the setting for his poetry are as radically different in the two works as the vocation of the poet. Johnson's story is a literary variant of the middle-class myth of the poor but talented young man coming from the provinces to the capital city with only a few pennies in his pocket and a manuscript, *Irene*, under his arm to win fame and fortune in the great world. Wordsworth reverses the journey, beginning *The Prelude* with the poet escaping the city—aided, we should perhaps remember, by the bequest in 1795 of £900 from Raisley Calvert—casting only "A backward glance upon the curling cloud Of city smoke," before plunging deep into a leafy, green bower, and then moving deeper into nature, returning to the Lake Country with its simple scenes of rural life, going down into the memories of childhood, and backward into the English past. Johnson's plot enacts the actual movement of capitalist society and its people at a time of accelerating urbanization and industrialization. Wordsworth's plot blazes a reverse path taken in reaction to urbanization and industrialism. In *The Prelude*, as elsewhere, romanticism turns from bourgeois society, with its rational ways of thought and its machines, to seek what was believed to be a more authentic and satisfactory being in the depths of nature, the past, gothic or primitive, and the primary energies of the human mind.

Johnson's famous remark that "when a man is tired of London, he is tired of life" indicates his continuing love affair with the city streets and districts, the taverns, dining rooms, printers' shops and booksellers' stores, the tea and conversation of many drawing rooms and the constant bustle of urban activity. "Such was his love of London, so high a relish had he of its magnificent extent, and variety of intellectual entertainment, that he languished when absent from it," and on learning that he was probably fatally ill on a visit to his native Lichfield, he left at once to reutrn and die in the great city. "The town," he rightly said, "is my element; there are my friends, there are my books. . . ." But for Wordsworth, who recounts his painful experience of London in Book VII of *The Prelude*, the city is Vanity Fair, the "monstrous ant-hill on the plain Of a too busy world," where every face is a mystery, every crowd a "Parlia-

ment of Monsters." Here "imaginative power" languishes
within the poet and the poetic mind is overwhelmed by,

> blank confusion! true epitome
> Of what the mighty City is herself
> To thousands upon thousands of her sons,
> Living amid the same perpetual whirl
> Of trivial objects, melted and reduced
> To one identity, by differences
> That have no law, no meaning, and no end—

The city for Johnson, nature for Wordsworth, do not merely
reflect different tastes of different men, but stand at the center
of their conceptions of letters, opposing symbols of the true
subject matter and source of poetry, the places where the poet
lives and writes, images of the function of poetry in the world.
For Johnson, whose characteristic stance in the *Life* is in conversation with others and who wrote always for the public, letters is social, urban in the fullest sense. The truths it provides,
never absolute, are established as "just representations of general nature" only by long-continued agreement in the city of
mankind. Its primary subject matter is neither pastoral nor
particular, the "streaks of the tulip," but universal human passions and their social consequences among people living together. Its styles and types change over time with changes in
understanding, shifts in fashion and modes of life. Its existence as a distinct mode of discourse is social and takes objective
shape as a large *public* library or a history like *The Lives of the
Poets* where the actual lives of writers and their social circumstances provide the settings for writings that are bought and
judged by common readers and changeable publics.

Wordsworth's characteristic stance in *The Prelude* is, despite
his frequently expressed desire for communication with all
other living creatures through a shared essential humanity,
one of nearly complete solitude, never more so than in the

spots of time when the meaning of existence is intensely perceived. He is alone, usually having left his companions behind, when a huge mountain rises over his head as he rows out on the lake; when he sees a girl walking in the wind on a distant lonely mountainside; or when he emerges from the clouds on Snowdon to a clear view of the heavens and the faint sound of the mighty waters of ocean. Isolate, he feels in nature, in the sharp distanced images of humble lives—old soldiers returned from the wars, ancient leechgatherers—and in his own poetic mind and memories, the working in the world of some awesome power, never perceived quite clearly enough to be definitely named, and therefore variously called God, Spirit, Mighty Forms, or, at Snowdon, "the perfect image of a mighty mind." Ultimately, as modern critics like Geoffrey Hartman have taught us to see, Wordsworth dispenses with nature and rural life as mediations of the transcendental truth and finds in the mind of the poet alone the power, "when the light of sense goes out," to commune with and participate in the majestic intellect that gives meaning to the visible world. Poetry then replaces nature, or becomes "a power like one of Nature's," that tells the world, and those who live in it that all and everything are joined, harmonious, interacting; that life has ultimate though unknown purpose, and therefore that each of its parts is instinctly, symbolically, meaningful and that there are benevolent metaphysical powers at work in the universe, shaping life by speaking in and acting through all its parts.

Wordsworth's romantic poetics is based on his romantic metaphysics. Poems are not statements of a social meaning in a carefully calculated style like Johnson's, but are themselves verbal forms of natural being: simple rather than elaborate, organically unified rather than rhetorically structured, original rather than novel, making use of symbol and metaphor rather than allegory and simile, carrying feeling rather than ideas, and existing in ambiguity and mystery rather than seeking truths established by social agreement and long endurance.

The whole of literature is for Wordsworth a mystical body— "Poets, even as Prophets, each with each Connected in a mighty scheme of truth"—that has as its purpose to tell humanity that life can be good because "the mind of man becomes A thousand times more beautiful than the earth On which he dwells. . . ." Perhaps the differences between the Johnsonian and the Wordsworthian views of poetry appear most summarily in their views of its history. For Wordsworth the life of poetry is in the subtitle of *The Prelude*, "the growth of a Poet's mind." For Johnson the history of poetry is *The Lives of the Poets*. The difference can also be felt in the characteristic anecdotes connected with each. The essential Wordsworthian story is his report of having to reach out, while walking, and, such is his subjective power, grasp a tree in order to convince himself that anything outside his mind is really there. The Johnsonian incident took place at Harwich where he struck "his foot with mighty force against a large stone, till he rebounded from it," while saying to Boswell of Berkeley's idealism, "I refute it *thus*."

The list of Johnson-Wordsworth oppositions could be almost endlessly extended. Wordsworth chooses Milton as the true poet, while Johnson, disliking Milton, takes Pope. Johnson's audience for poetry is the common reader, while Wordsworth's true audience is, as Abrams says, commenting on romanticism's expressive theories of poetry and the consequent concentration on the poet, "reduced to a single member, consisting of the poet himself." It should be noted in this regard that *The Prelude* though begun in the 1790s was not, except for a few excerpts, published until after many revisions and the poet's death in 1850. It was addressed to one "dear friend," Coleridge, to whom, on a hill in the Lake Country it was eventually read. Only Dorothy and a few chosen friends like De Quincey heard or read portions of it while Wordsworth was alive.

In this and similar ways, Johnson's world of the writer in print circumstances trying to assemble a world became Wordsworth's romantic visionary. The romantic scene of writing as it appeared in *The Prelude* provided the mythic form of romantic letters. As such, it has shaped the life of writing so powerfully that generations of writers have lived in the scene that Wordsworth established in his poem as the setting and reality of the poetic life. Isolated from society, exiled from and hostile to the world of industrial capitalism, they have spoken in poetry the truth and beauty known only to the imagination, defended the authentic human self with its ancient ways of thinking and feeling against science and crude utilitarianism, and created perfect works of art, organic in structure, crystalline in form.

Johnsonian letters and Wordsworthian romanticism were a part of that great social change in which the old aristocratic order and its agrarian way of life were destroyed in the French and the Industrial Revolutions. Even as the old courtly letters had been the literary system of the hierarchical society, romantic literature became the literary system of industrial capitalism, but with a very different conception of its social function. Where courtly letters had legitimated the *ancien régime*; and Johnson had, while establishing the dignity of writers and writing, acknowledged their dependence on print and their existence in the town; romanticism, coming at a later stage of industrial capitalism when its power and effects seemed increasingly threatening, shaped itself in opposition to bourgeois society. Wordsworth dramatized this antagonistic role in *The Prelude* not only by the choice of a natural setting for a poetic life but by, after a first flush of enthusiasm, rejection of the French Revolution and of the London metropolis, both of which perverted true nature. The path he takes in escaping the city and rejecting the modern world, including suppressing the Annette Vallon affair, predicts the subsequent history of romantic literature with its idealization of the old ways of life, the countryside and simple rural life, childhood and primal emotions, myth and animism. Championing older, often primitive, ways of living, thinking, knowing, and feeling, romantic literature has been constantly at odds with the actualities of social life, and the defender—as it is put in a most penetrating study of the change, Raymond Williams' *Culture and Society, 1780–1950*—"of certain human values, capacities, energies, which the development of society towards an industrial civilization was felt to be threatening or even destroying."

The rejection of capitalist society and its rationalistic thought in favor of older idealized felt values of community and imagination ironically provided romantic literature with a firm, though not a centrally important, place in modern culture as the defender in art of certain "higher" values and more humane ways of feeling. But this strategy, insofar as it was ever planned, had its costs, for it involved literature in a fundamental social contradiction by placing its aesthetics and metaphysics in direct opposition to its actual social circumstances. This rub has been felt heavily and consistently in ways that are revealed by the persistently difficult relationship of romantic literature and print technology. Print has in fact been so much the medium of romantic literature that it can properly be called the literary system of print culture. We could not, to give a few examples of what we have already looked at in detail, have our present literary system if the printing press had not made available the library of canonical texts, ancient and modern, that is the substantial fact of romantic literature; imparted to those texts the typographical fixity which enables us to think of them as literary monuments, urns and icons, existing perfect and unchanged in their own right; and established the public market for books which freed writers from patronage and allowed them to consider themselves individual creative artists making meaning out of chaos by writing out of the depths of their own beings, rather than being servants of the established social order. These same connections of romantic literature to print technology appear from another angle in the dependence of Wordsworth's basic assumption about poetry, as different as they appear from Johnson's, on the literary realities that Johnson and print between them made and established as social fact: the independence and dignity of the author, the ideal reality and authority of the literary work, and an audience of universal common readers who respond to poetry out of their unchanging and essential humanity. Cowper may himself have threatened in a letter (10/31/79) to "thresh" Johnson's "old Jacket till [he] made his Pension Jingle in his Pocket" for his criticism of Milton, and to Blake, in *An Island in the Moon*, Johnson may have looked like "the Bat with Leathern wing Winking & blinking" in the cave of the *ancien régime*, but in the social history of literature, Johnson was the first writer to meet the realities of industrial society. The right of the poet, to offer one more last important example, to define the true language of a man speaking to men, which Wordsworth assumes, was objectified, not merely claimed, by the ability of print to produce a dictionary and by the booksellers' willingness to finance the venture in expectation of profits; by the social needs of an ambitious man to make his name in the world as an author, and the existential needs of a marginal man with radical doubts about the meaning of anything to create, order, and fix meaning in language; and by a host of human accidents, borrowed books, improvident Scottish assistants, and the careless words of a noble lord.

There have always been arguments that despite its overt rejection of capitalist society, romantic literature is synchronized with it in a general though somewhat concealed way by, for example, its celebration of poetic transformations of certain basic bourgeois values such as individualism, vision, and innovation. Probably the broadest perception of the radical relationship of a universal romantic literature that included in itself all the works of the creative imagination to the realities of industrial capitalism was phrased by Marx and Engels in the first section, "Bourgeois and Proletarians," of *The Communist Manifesto*:

> The bourgeoisie has through its exploitation of the world market given a cosmopolitan character to production and consumption in every country. . . . In place of the old wants, satisfied by the production of the country, we find new wants, requiring for their satisfaction the products of distant lands and climes. In place of the old local and national seclusion and self-sufficiency, we have intercourse in every direction, universal inter-dependence of nations. And as in material, so also in intellectual production. The intellectual creations of individual nations become common property. National one-sidedness and narrow-mindedness became more and more impossible, and from the numerous national and local literatures, there arises a world literature.

The general connection of capitalist economics and literary culture that Marx and Engels point out here can be traced more exactly in the linkage of the print infrastructure to the literary superstructure provided by Walter J. Ong in his "Romantic Difference and the Poetics of Technology." Ong quotes Carl Woodring as saying that, unlike Turner and Whitman, Wordsworth "was never to find romance in steam locomotives." But Wordsworth's poetry, like other romantic poetry, Ong argues, "manifests a feeling of control over nature" that is also a prime characteristic of industrialism. This control, Ong continues, appears in literature as a romantic conception of knowledge that derives ultimately from the amount and form of information print made available. Until the eighteenth century, society was organized around the "commonplace," a few formulary general truths—Pope's "What oft was thought" or Johnson's "just representations of general nature"—that emphasized the known and the familiar. With the coming of a full-scale print culture, however, vast amounts of knowledge became available and were locked firmly in place, so that what was known need no longer all be memorized, and on this secure basis the search for the new and different could proceed. Romantic literature, in Ong's view, was the poetic form of this modern print-based search for the remote, mysterious, inaccessible, exotic, and bizarre. "Oddly enough," he eloquently concludes, "romantic poetic was the poetic of the technological age . . . romanticism and technology can be seen to grow out of the same ground, even though at first blush the two appear diametrically opposed, the one, technology, programatically rational, the other, romanticism, concerned with transrational or arational if not irrational reality . . . each grows in its own way out of a noetic abundance such as man had never known before. Technology uses the abundance for practical purposes. Romanticism uses it for assurance and as a springboard to another world."

Balzac's LOST ILLUSIONS: *Social Romanticism*

The main line of romantic literature has, however, totally rejected any connections with the society and the technology it radically criticizes, ignoring the contradiction that Marshall McLuhan in his *Gutenberg Galaxy*, itself a romantic attack on print, phrases with great precision and equal distaste. In the era of print, McLuhan says, "literature [is] at war with itself and with the social mechanics of conscious goals and motivations. For the matter of literary vision [is] collective and mythic, while the forms of literary expression and communication [are] individualist, segmental, and mechanical." There are writers and critics who have understood and talked about this contradiction, but George Gissing's novel, *New Grub Street* (1891), is one of only a few English works that explore in any detail how deeply, even contrarily, literature and the life of writing have been affected by print. The printing press has always been a machine, but it remained a fairly simple machine through the first quarter of the nineteenth century. After that time its power increased exponentially as the rotary press was invented, the steam engine was used to drive it, type-setting machines like the linotype appeared, cheap pulp paper in long continuous rolls was manufactured, and lithography and photographic plates mechanically reproduced printed images. Gissing had little interest in technology, but he felt and recorded the increasingly enormous power of this print-machine technology to impose its logic on the literary world and its workers. Of one of his writers, he remarks that she "was not a woman, but a machine for reading and writing." And he foresees the day when the human writing machine will be replaced with even more efficient machinery: "before long some Edison would make the true automaton: the problem must be comparatively such a simple one. Only to throw in a given number of old books, and have them reduced, blended, modernised into a single one for today's consumption."

That day may actually have arrived only with the word processor, but it seems already to have been the lived fact in the writing scene of Gissing's Victorian England. Jasper Milvain, the ambitious journalist who writes on any subject for the magazine editor Fadge, makes his way up the ladder of the publishing world by mechanically tailoring his style of writing to the public taste: "just take two lines of some good prose-writer, and expand them into twenty." Marian Yule wears out her life in "the valley of the shadow of books," the great library of the British Museum created by print, where she reads endlessly, takes voluminous notes, and then assembles this raw material to produce articles, which her father, the failing scholar Alfred Yule, appropriates and passes off as his own work. It is in the person of his alter ego, the novelist Edwin Reardon, that Gissing shows most extensively the ways that the print machine extends itself into writing and the life of the writer. Poverty recruits him, like Johnson and Savage many years before, as a laborer in the literary factory, which imposes its work rhythms on him so completely that he finds himself "ticking off his stipulated quantum of manuscript each four and twenty hours." The marketplace automatically sets the romantic subject matter of his novels and the rotary motion of the printing press extends through the circulating libraries which require "three-decker" novels that maximize profits by engineering suspense. Reardon does the best he can under these circumstances to avoid writing potboilers, but in the end his novels are written even as they are printed, mechanically.

Irving Howe very aptly has called Gissing "the poet of fatigue." Exhaustion, hopelessness, and helplessness, in writing and in love, are the distinctive notes of *New Grub Street*, which may explain this fascinating novel's relative neglect. For a full-scale and fully energized portrayal of "social romanticism," the direct confrontration, which the Marxists have done so much to develop and explain, of romantic literature with capitalist society and its print technology, without softening either the essential romanticism or the industrial capitalism, we must turn to France, which, for interesting reasons, has remained extremely sensitive to the relationship of art with the social world. A brief comparison of Rousseau's *Confessions* to Boswell's *Life* will at least suggest some of the reasons why this has historically been the case.

It is one of the great ironies of literary history that Rousseau's *Confessions* (published 1782–1789), the French equivalent, *mutatis mutandis*, especially allowing for the different temperaments of the men involved, to Boswell's *Life of Johnson*, should be the story of a patronage writer with revolutionary political and social views, while Johnson's story is that of a paid writer for the marketplace, scorning, or almost scorning, patronage, but expressing extremely conservative political and social views. Logically, Johnson was the kind of conservative who should have been fully supported by patronage, while the truly radical Rousseau ought to have gotten nothing from the old regime. But logic and life, here as elsewhere, have little connection, and while Johnson scraped by, Rousseau, though he ended in poverty and disfavor, was, once he became famous, the darling of the salons, the object of concern of the king and Madame de Pompadour, the beneficiary of gifts and exquisite lodgings from great nobles and their wives, who competed for the honor of having him read them his works and helping him get them past the genial censor, the famed Malesherbes. Even George III at one point, probably for political reasons, pensioned Rousseau, and Rousseau himself seems to have seen no contradictions between the way he lived, how he published, and what he wrote. Despite publishing his books abroad for financial and political reasons, constantly struggling with customs officers and censors, having *Emile* publicly burned in Geneva and his life and living threatened because of writings like the "Origin of Inequality" and the "Savoyard Vicar," he could still remark at the beginning of Book IX of his *Confessions*, covering the year 1756, that "I have always felt that the position of an author is not and cannot be distinguished or respectable, except insofar as it is not a profession. It is too difficult to think nobly, where one thinks only in order to live."

If Boswell's *Life* is *the* story of the professional writer in the age of print, *The Confessions* is *the* story of the patronage writer in the age of print, and it should be enough to cure even the most recidivist Miniver Cheevy of any antiquarian longings for a return of patronage. Of course, Jean-Jacques, insecure, mercurial, sensitive to the point of paranoia, shy and, at least at some times, almost clinically introverted was not the ideal character type for a social situation that made even really tough writers like Diderot and Voltaire cringe at times. But Rousseau's sensitivity serves as an accurate register of the extraordinary stresses felt by all patronage writers who had, like himself, to stand for hours making conversation before and after very late dinners, to try to avoid offending either of two great ladies of the court struggling with one another for sole possession of a philosophe, to work in a patronage job as a secretary in the legation at Venice for a venal, stupid, and lazy aristocrat whose neglect of business made it impossible for Rousseau to find any time to write, to wonder if it would offend his patrons if he paid the gardener at a little house they had provided him. It inevitably did. Perhaps the quintessential patronage story might be Rousseau's description of how after naming his dog "Duke" he had second thoughts, since he was living in a house provided by a duke, and, not sure but thinking there was a slight possibility that he might offend, then changed its name to "Turk." Safe enough, but a malicious friend immediately forced him, under the guise of a pleasant joke, to tell the so amusing story at the next conversation at the duke's palace, thus ensuring the offense that had originally been only a possibility, by the very means that had been taken to avoid it.

In the contradictions of his situation, Rousseau is a characteristic figure of the author in eighteenth-century France, where, because of the power of the centralized state and the comparative efficiency of its bureaucracy, writing and the institutional arrangements through which it had to work were at odds with another. In the French world of letters, at least until the changes of 1789, and to a considerable extent afterward, the new ideas and conceptions of writing that were associated with the print revolution were still channeled and controlled by practices like patronage, censorship, and the required royal *privilege* to print that were appropriate to the *ancien régime* and its courtly system of letters. The cultural historian Robert Darnton has described the extensive contradictions of this scene of writing in a number of detailed books and articles about the publication of the *Encyclopédie*, the printing business and its technology, and the government control of publication.

His is a wonderful recreation of the French eighteenth-century world of writing and printing in all its human, technical, and bureaucratic detail, and it is also a strange human story of pirated editions and blackmailing printers, of police spies on writers whose incredibly complete dossiers contain sophisticated literary judgments of their subjects, of the high-pressured financing of the Enlightenment and of ritual cat massacres expressing the hatred of apprentices and journeymen printers for their bourgeois. But at root in all these situations, Darnton argues in *The Literary Underground*, there was a conflict between, on the one hand, what we have called "print logic" and, on the other, what he calls "the corporate organization of [French] culture." The difficulty with the cultural arrangement for the new writers, he explains, "was not simply an economic matter . . . it contradicted the basic premises under which the young writers had flocked to Paris in the 1770s and 1780s. They had come with the conviction that the republic of letters really existed as it had been described in the works of the great philosophes—as the literary counterpart to the 'atomic' individualism of Physiocratic theory, a society of independent but fraternal individuals, in which the best men won but all derived dignity, as well as a living, from service to the common cause." But where in England, as a result of the activities of Johnson and others, literary culture shifted in response to the new print circumstances and the expectations they aroused, France got the kind of tangle of conservative patrons and radical writing that Rousseau lived in, and there, Darnton continues, "experience taught" all the new young writers "that the real world of letters functioned like everything else in the Old Regime: individuals got ahead as best they could in a labyrinth of baroque institutions. To have an article published in the *Mercure*, to get a play accepted by the *Comédie Française*, to steer a book through the Direction de la Librairie, to win membership in an academy, entry into a salon, or a sinecure in the bureaucracy required resorting to the old devices of privilege and protection, not merely the demonstration of talent." The results of these conflicts in literary culture were not only the radicalization of large numbers of French writers, but also, by virtue of the sharp contrast between literary institutions and expectations, an awareness on the part of these writers of the extent to which social arrangements were an important part of the life of writing and the realities of letters. Even after 1789 when things improved but did not entirely change, because of the pervasive presence of the French state in social life, French writers, far more than the English, retained this political consciousness about writing. The differences between the ideology of romantic literature and the social realities of the actual literary situation, which could be and usually were ignored in English-speaking countries, or rejected outright in the Wordsworthian fashion, rubbed hard against the French writers— hard enough to sensitize them to the social realities of their profession. It is not, therefore, surprising that the great example of tough, social romanticism should be the work of a French royalist, Balzac. In *Lost Illusions* romantic writers cannot leave the world behind with a Wordsworthian turn into nature but must remain locked into and unable to disengage from a struggle to the death with capitalist technology and economics, bourgeois business and politics.

In his usual thorough sociological manner, Balzac in *Lost Illusions* traces the many ways in which gold and print combine to corrupt literary values in the early industrial age. The first volume, *The Two Poets* (1837), set in provincial Angoulême, describes the practices in an old-style print shop and its destruction by some very up-to-date competitors who bring to the provinces the latest in technology and sharp business practices. The third volume, *The Trials of the Inventor* (1843), returns to Angoulême to record the invention of cheap paper and the bilking of its inventor by rapacious commercial interests. In the famous second volume with its grimly ironic title, *A Great Man of the Provinces in Paris* (1839), Balzac shows us in fascinating and lurid detail the extensive effects of an infrastructure of print business, capitalist economics, and parliamentary politics on the superstructure of romantic literary culture. In Paris, where money is "the answer to every riddle," literary fame is no longer the reward of the writer's genius, but a commercial product that "costs twelve thousand francs in reviews and three thousand francs in dinners." To the publishers and booksellers on the Rue Serpente, books are "like cotton bonnets to haberdashers, a commodity to be bought cheap and sold dear." Finance is far more important in bookmaking than story or style, for as the canny old publisher Dogereau puts it, "When an editor publishes an author's first novel he has to risk sixteen hundred francs for printing and paper. It's easier to write a novel than to find such a sum." Printing had long replaced the aristocratic patron with the great publisher, but as the successor of the great printer-patrons of early print society, Aldus, the Estiennes, or a Société Typographique, Balzac gives us the capitalist Dauriat: "Maybe I'm not quite a Maecenas, but literature owes me some gratitude: I've already more than doubled the price which manuscripts fetch."

Each of the major genres is debased in turn by the cash nexus. Poetry is the name of Dauriat's greatest fear, and he emphatically instructs his clerks to avoid it: "Whenever anyone brings manuscripts for me, you'll ask if they are in verse or prose. If they're in verse, get rid of them straight away. Verse will ruin the book trade." At the opera, the economically based sexual and social rivalry in the boxes is so fierce that mention is made of the performance only to remark that the last act is set in hell. The drama has degenerated to vaudeville and melodrama in theatres where the play is of far less importance than the legs and bosoms of the actresses, the applause of hired claques, the puffing journal reviews paid for with various favors, and the backing of the wealthy merchants who keep the actresses.

The work of Addison and Johnson in England, Lessing and the Schlegels in Germany, and of the philosophes in France had made newspaper and magazine journalism a respectable minor genre of literature, and in Balzac's Paris the journal has become the most influential form of writing. But its original purpose of educating a growing literate public has by now been grossly perverted in a world in which "every man bribes or is bribed." The pages of the journals are filled with advertisements extorted from merchants by threat of blackmail, with direct personal attacks on the publisher's opponents and support of his allies, with reviews of books and plays designed to sell the works of the writer's friends and damn those of his enemies. Along the way, everyone gets his cut: the journalists get review copies of books and complimentary theater tickets, both of which are resold at discount; the backers of journals get support for their political interests; and the editors manipulate and speculate in the company stock.

Criticism, which largely takes the form of reviews in journals, has become a major literary genre, but it is only a slightly disguised form of bookselling. "Janus is the tutelary deity of criticism and the symbol of genius. Only God is triangular." In an amazing passage that every critic should have by heart, the writer Lousteau explains brilliantly how this Janus criticism works. You begin your review article, he remarks, by dividing literature into two groups, the "literature of ideas" and the "literature of imagery." The literature of ideas expresses the genius of the French language and of revered older writers, Voltaire, Diderot, Lesage. The literature of imagery is weak modern writing in imitation of Scott and the Anglo-German school, "composed of scenery and word-pictures and metaphor and dramatic situations." The novel under review is then discredited by showing in detail that it belongs to the literature

of images. The author and his publisher, thoroughly alarmed
at having the names of the mighty dead flung at them, hasten
to assuage the critic with flattery and cash. The critic then
writes another review in which he explains that it is his duty to
"examine every work in all its various aspects," and that he now
wants to show that the novel under discussion is an example of
"the ultimate achievement of the literary art [which] is to impress the idea on the image." Out of all these changes of tack,
Lousteau concludes, "Your week will have earned you four
hundred francs as well as the pleasure of having told the truth
somewhere or other."

Balzac, the Piranesi of print culture, binds together all these
scenes of the decline and fall of literature with the adventures
of the young romantic poet, Lucien Chardon. Sensitive, hand-
some, dashing, amorous, convinced of his own genius, poor
and ambitious, Lucien in Angoulême imagines "scenes of calm
and pure poetry" and dreams visions "of the wonders of Art,
the noble triumphs of genius and the shining wings of glory. A
tear glistened in the poet's eye. . . ." Carrying with him his sonnets, the *Marguerites*, and his historical novel in the manner of
Scott, *The Archer of Charles IX*, he accompanies his mistress, the
wealthy, proud, and dull Madame de Bargeton, to Paris. The
city is no longer Wordsworth's "monstrous ant-hill on the
plain" but the exciting, vital center of all artistic activity to
which the provincial writer now comes to realize his genius:
"Here is the habitat of writers, thinkers, poets. Here only can
the seeds of fame be sown. . . . Here only can writers find, in
the museums and art collections, the immortal works of past
genius to warm and stimulate the imagination. Here only vast
libraries, always open, offer knowledge and sustenance for the
mind. In short, in Paris, in the very air one breathes and the
smallest details of existence, there is a spirit which permeates
and makes its impress on the creations of literature." After his
mistress abandons him, Lucien lives for a time the life required

by the romantic myth, a Left Bank garret, hunger, long hours in the library reading, and total dedication to art. But poverty matters no more to the romantic poet than historical fact to his mythology: "Plautus the great writer of comedies was a mill-hand. Machiavelli wrote *The Prince* in the evenings after spending the day in the company of workmen. Even the great Cervantes, who had lost an arm at the battle of Lepanto while making his contribution to that famous victory, and was called a 'disreputable old crock' by the scribblers of the time, unable to find a publisher, had to wait ten years before he could get the second part of that sublime work *Don Quixote* into print." In time success does come, but not in quite the way the myth predicts. The *Marguerites* are bought by Dauriat for 3,000 francs, but the publisher has no plans to print the poems. He simply intends to bribe Lucien for a favorable review of one of Dauriat's authors. *The Archer of Charles IX* becomes a minor classic after Lucien's death, but only because it has been almost completely rewritten by more talented friends. Lucien himself· has, it gradually becomes apparent, very little talent, only a certain knack for writing lively scenes of Parisian life which appear as *feuilletons* in the journals. Lacking the "savage energy of real talent or the grim will-power of ambition," fascinated by the clothes, the food and wines, the women and the power that Paris offers, he moves from one journal and one political party to another, selling his pen to various groups until at last he overreaches himself and returns in disgrace to Angoulême. He later goes back to Paris as a minor character in another Balzac novel, *Splendors and Miseries of a Courtesan*, to die in prison by his own hand after failing to bring off an unattractive swindle.

"A world in which the superfluous is indispensable" is Balzac's description of Parisian social and literary life where everything is show and pretense, and very little is real. The money god of capitalist society is the power that debases both literature and writers: "Great God! Gold at all cost! . . . Gold is the only power which this society worships on bended knees." But gold and print, the two forces that corrupt literature are the same, for hard gold coin has been mostly replaced with paper, sometimes the printed banknote, more often the promissory note. Payment for anything and everything is almost never in cash, but in promises to pay at some future time, three months, six months, a year. Since human needs are always immediate, however, this paper always has to be discounted at once to pay another debt or to buy something urgently desired. As it passes from hand to hand the face value of the paper constantly diminishes through a series of discounts until it becomes entirely worthless. The complex way greed gradually leaches any reality out of the paper of promissory notes and, simultaneously, of the literature, which is another kind of substitute for reality, is brilliantly summarized in the history of a book company, the firm of Fendant and Cavalier, one of those many publishing houses founded without capital. Paper manufacturers and printers, anxious to sell their products, extend credit to the publishing house, while their authors are paid for their manuscripts with bills drawn for six months, a year, or longer. After publication the printed books themselves are usually discounted and used as another form of paper money to pay debts within the print world. "Reckoning on two or three successes, the profit from the sound propositions paid for the bad ones, and they kept going by grafting one book onto another. If all their operations were dubious or if, by bad luck, they happened upon good books which could only be sold after being savoured and appreciated by the real public; if the discounts levied on their bills were onerous, if creditors of theirs became bankrupt, they calmly filed their petitions [of bankruptcy] without turning a hair, being prepared in advance for such a result."

This paper chain of increasingly discounted promises to pay, connecting the nothingness of a firm founded without capital to the non-existence of bankruptcy is the master plot of *Lost Illusions*, and literature, like everything else, follows the path, soon ceasing to be worth the paper it is written on. Its books are literally cheapened by Fendant and Cavalier who exchange promissory notes for manuscripts, pay bills with books at reduced prices, and remainder cut-rate books on credit. In the bookseller Dauriat's shop and elsewhere in Paris it is ultimately difficult to distinguish books from other kinds of financial paper. Books are used to pay reviewers in lieu of cash, to settle bills and demand notes, and are exchanged for meals, sex and other favors. Literature is actually only one medium of exchange in a vast network of credit, and its continuous discount in the market parallels depreciation of more serious kinds. To make money, poetry gives place to cheap best-sellers, criticism to self-serving book reviews, responsible journalism to venal advertising and vicious propaganda. Writers become greedy, vain, deluded fools like Lucien or cynics like Lousteau who write only for their own advantage. Paper gets cheaper and cheaper, and the discovery in the third novel of a vegetable pulp, rather than linen, paper that can be made at low cost in the limitless amounts and sizes required by a world of paper promises to pay, looks forward to a society and a literature with still less connection with any reality.

Lost Illusions portrays the ruin of romantic literature and the destruction of its mythology in the realities of print culture and capitalist society. Literature in any meaningful sense cannot, Balzac says, survive in such a setting. Even the true poet, not a self-deluded scribbler like Lucien, but Balzac's idealized romantic visionary, Louis Lambert, becomes fatally diseased in Paris and retires from the city to go mad and die. Only the complete withdrawal from the world, vowing poverty and despising fame, of the *Cénacle*, a small group of writers who abandon poetry and fiction for philosophy, history, and sociology, offers the slightest hope for the survival of meaningful writing. Balzac persuaded several of his poet friends, including Gautier, to write some of Lucien's sonnets, the *Marguerites*, but none of them has any real poetic power. Lucien himself has no real poetic talent. Only one of his poems has life, and the circumstances of its composition suggest what Balzac considered to be the actual unromanticized scene of writing in modern print culture. Utterly disgraced and totally broke, Lucien sits through the night facing the body of his dead mistress, the actress Coralie, writing a lively drinking song to get the money to bury her:

> Rions! buvons!
> Et moquons-nous du reste.

In the end, Balzac was perhaps finally himself the best image of what he understood writing and literature now to be, the only writer with both the "savage energy of real talent" and "the grim will-power of ambition." "I've become," Maurois quotes him saying, exhausted and near the end of his life, "a sort of word-machine, and I think I must be made of iron." When he first arrived from the provinces in Paris as a young writer—carrying like Lucien's *Marguerites* his classical tragedy, *Cromwell*, Balzac actually worked for a time in a "novel factory," turning out to order parts of Gothic and historical novels in the manner of Scott. When he left this work, he took its production-line methods and the factory "speed-up" over to his own writing for the rest of his life. Work, work, work: to bed in the evening and then up at midnight, dressed in his famous gown, smoking his water pipe, constantly drinking black coffee, the "nocturnal Homer," as Maurois styles him, wrote until morning. Visits to friends' houses in the country led only to closed rooms where the writing continued ceaselessly. And on it went, a story in a night, a novel in a few weeks, endless revision of proofs, ever more plans for an ever grander *oeuvre*.

The Balzacian word-machine was driven by desire, even

greed, for the things produced by the factories of industrial capitalism: jewel-studded canes, fine books, thick carpets, carriages, cashmere covers for huge beds for seductions, furniture, vases, china, vintage wines, linens, and on and on. The debts could only be met, if at all, by writing; and the writing itself was, as Georg Lukàcs has called it, a primitive accumulation of ideological capital. In a letter to his future wife, Madame Hanska, in 1834, Balzac sounds like an intellectual version of his miser Gobseck, collecting ideas not things, as he lists all that he will gather into his *Studies of Morals*: "a complete picture of society from which nothing has been omitted, no situation in life, no physiognomy or character of man or woman, no way of living, no calling, no social level, no part of France, nor any aspect of childhood, old age, middle age, politics, justice or war." But gradually, working within, not outside of, the acquisitive materialistic bougeois world he so savagely criticized, the raw materials were transformed into Balzac's *Comédie Humaine*, "that Empire," his great biographer names it, "on which intelligence never sets."

Conclusion: Cultural Poetics and Johnson's
Three-Legged Chair

The Life of Johnson, The Prelude and *Lost Illusions* provide a brief history of the responses of letters to the beginnings of capitalist society, and between them they constitute a paradigm of the primary views of the place and function of literature in the social world over the last two hundred years. Johnson offers a common-sense compromise in which the author lives in and accepts the world, while making the best he can out of the literary arrangements offered, such as a copyright law or the new powers of the democratic reading audience; Wordsworth's is the standard high-romantic position, turning away from what is conceived of as a hostile social world to seek elsewhere for values that will maintain poetry and humanity in alien surroundings; Balzac's is the stand of the literary revolutionary who, realizing the inescapable and destructive power of the primary modes of production over culture, knows that romantic escape is impossible and determines to fight grimly to achieve the little that can be won.

But the similarities of the three works and the understanding of literature they reveal may finally be more interesting than their differences. In them literature, or letters, or poetry, has no locus, no hard factual existence in a set of texts, no preexistence in some ideal form, but is in the midst of the full social world a working part of human life—a way that people find their livings and seek dignity in the world. They give letters a human context and provide it with an understandable and purposeful place in the social world, sharing in its historical change. That place in the social world is conceived in all three works as being not merely some utilitarian activity but an ongoing and worthy effort to achieve by literary means the continuing end of society itself: to construct a human world with meaning and purpose. This culture-making activity takes place in all three works against a background of social change, imaged in Boswell and Balzac chiefly as print technology and its market practices, and in Wordsworth as the industrial city and the French Revolution, but in all cases the larger change is so radical as to require and bring into play a new kind of literature, with different kinds of authors, texts, and audiences. The new kind of literature is depicted openly as a varying response in all of its parts to this profound change in the social world in an attempt to maintain and further by these literary means certain humane values which would be otherwise in danger of extinction. These portrayals of literature, in a time of the greatest stress, frankly offer us primary examples, as well as models for our own time, of a cultural poetics in which literature openly appears not as a given fact of nature or culture but, in the process of being made, as an invention, a socially constructed reality designed like other such cultural realities as art, philosophy, history, and science to give purpose and meaning to life.

These same books also remind us that literature, like the family, the state, human sexuality, or cuisine, is, as a cultural artifact, not a thing but an ongoing social activity. The energy and direction of that activity can be observed nowhere to better advantage than in the life of Samuel Johnson, with Boswell standing always, like a *Doppelgänger*, just behind him. In a time much like our own of intense social and technological change, Johnson the writer's need for some kind of existential stability and meaning in his life and work show in real terms—meeting the king, defying Lord Chesterfield, struggling with madness, constructing a dictionary—just what the stakes are that are always involved in the making of a literary or any other kind of cultural system. There are social theories of literature as deterministic as Taine's view that it is only another industrial product "like vitriol or sugar," and as dreary as those kinds of sociology-of-literature studies that prove, with statistics, that, for example, the largest percentage of seventeenth-century writers was made up of the second sons of clergymen. But, even in a time when we much need, in criticism and elsewhere, to return literature to the world and affairs of living men and women, before it disappears forever into the contemplation of nothingness, taking with it not only our livelihoods but that extraordinary body of written images of humanity that have been assembled and called literature, there is no necessity to be bound to narrow and small-minded sociological views. Johnson and Boswell, like Wordsworth and Balzac, create and act in a great social theater of literary life. The high charge in even its small details, the deep commitment of the actors, the daring personal risks they take, the intensity and skill with which they play out their parts, the intricacy and power of the many people, ideas, and energies, the interplayed fullness of social life, all make real a human world of letters with an important place and function in the lived reality. Make it real, too, in the face of what is always feared—chaos, meaninglessness, and nothingness. This kind of literary life, as Johnson and Boswell lived and wrote it, shares many of its activities not only with the skeptical philosophies of its own time but with many of the characteristically twentieth-century philosophies such as the sociology of knowledge, cultural anthropology, phenomenology, structuralism, existentialism, and the general term increasingly applied to all these approaches, constructivism. To all of these theories, as well as the deconstructions that haunt them all, I am much indebted, but the mode of existence of people in the world that they hypothesize is perhaps best caught in still another image of Samuel Johnson, which can end, even as his meeting with the king began, this effort to describe the social construction of letters in the age of print.

On Wednesday, 8 March 1758, Doctor Charles Burney, the author of the famous *History of Music* and the father of the more famous novelist Fanny Burney, visited Samuel Johnson in his house in Gough Square, just off Fleet Street. After dinner, Boswell tells us, Johnson took Burney up to the garret where the *Dictionary* had been assembled. (The room, restored after being burned out in the bombing raids of 1941, is still preserved in the Johnson museum that the house has become.) In the garret, Boswell reports, Burney "found about five or six Greek folios, a deal writing-desk, and a chair and a half. Johnson giving to his guest the entire seat, tottered himself on one with only three legs and one arm." This remarkable chair achieved some notoriety, and Northcote, the biographer of Sir Joshua Reynolds, provides a description of how Johnson managed his uneasy seat on an occasion when Reynolds, with the sculptor Roubiliac, went to visit the great cham: "Johnson received him with much civility, and took them up into a garret, which he considered as his library; where, besides his books, all covered with dust, there was an old crazy deal table, and a still worse and older elbow chair, having only three legs. In this chair Johnson seated himself, after having, with considerable dexterity and evident practice, first drawn it up against the wall, which served to support it on that side on which the leg was deficient." Apparently the chair was Johnson's habitual working seat over some considerable period of time, and a gentleman who visited him during the period between 1758 and 1760 when he was writing his *Idlers*, "always found him at his Desk, sitting on [a chair] with three legs; and on rising from it, he remark'd that Mr. Johnson never forgot its defect, but would either hold it in his hand, or place it with great composure against some support, taking no notice of its imperfection to his visitor. . . . It was remarkable in Dr. Johnson, that no external circumstances ever prompted him to make any apology, or to seem even sensible of their existence."

For Miss Reynolds, the painter's sister, who recorded this scene, the broken chair was an indication of Johnson's shameful poverty before he was given a pension by the crown, but every scholar will also recognize it as one of those awkward pieces of furniture, inevitable in the life of reading and writing, that is easier to adjust to and forget than to find the time to get fixed. Prop it against the wall, balance on it, hold it up with your hand, manage somehow, but don't lose the time that would be involved in the tedious business of locating a replacement, finding a repairer, getting it carried to his shop, discussing repairs and price, arranging for its return. Much too complicated and boring; it doesn't matter anyway. The three-legged chair is exactly the kind of detail that makes us feel at home with Johnson, finding in him familiar human motives and a life deeply involved with the solid supports and deficiencies of everyday things and experiences. He is our literary hero of reality, the modern writer in the age of print, speaking with confident authority of and living with literary things as they really are, and yet, no matter how easily he may carry it off, his vigorously authoritative writings, his commanding authorial personality, and his conception of letters rest no more four-squarely upon some final, factual reality than did his three-legged chair upon the floor of his study.

APPENDIX

LETTERS AS A
SOCIALLY CONSTRUCTED REALITY:
A SCHEMATIC VIEW

Theory has not been emphasized in the preceding pages, but the empirical description of the substantial facts of the literary history offered there has been structured by a theory of letters and literature as socially constructed realities. It may be that there are some readers who would like to see the theory openly spelled out and logically ordered, and it is hoped that the following bare-bones axioms of a social theory of letters will satisfy these interests. I begin with some familiar points of general social theory as the context for the social view of letters that such a theory seems to me to entail.

The humanly perceived world is made up of nature and culture.

Nature is assumed to be a world of fact, operating according to its own laws, prior to and independent of human observation and the scientific descriptions which try, asymptotically, to approximate it.

Over and against the feared infinity and meaningless repetition of the natural world, culture provides a human world of order, substantial reality, purpose, and meaning. Culture is the total social world that people make, the sum of socially constructed languages, institutions, beliefs, values, roles, histories, and on and on, in which human beings live and which they accept as reality for the most part.

Culture exists both objectively as a set of artifacts, like cities, institutions, rituals, roles, cosmologies and philosophies, and subjectively as a perceived reality, believed by individuals born into the culture, and particularly into its language, to be as real and permanent as nature.

As real and permanent as culture appears to individuals, it is radically unstable, and its reality and plausibility must constantly be reinforced by a variety of means such as new forms of legitimation, explanations of historical or natural events that question a culture's basic values, tighter integration of the various parts of a culture, and adjustment to new circumstances.

Culture is never made but always making, an activity, really, rather more than a thing, though always seeking the durable status of a thing.

The cultural world that people construct often includes sacred or privileged texts, oral or written, such as genealogical poems, tribal epics, bibles, and so forth, that legitimate social values and help to organize and explain the culture in meaningful ways.

As a functioning part of culture, these texts share the master purpose of culture to construct a meaningful human world, and they often reveal in a paradigmatic fashion how, why, and what is done.

In some advanced societies, these "wisdom texts" form the nucleus for a more extensive and specialized social system of writing and interpretation of texts, or of speaking and memorizing in oral societies, that, for example, categorizes literary types, sets the role and defines the skills of the writer, constructs a theory of writing, and provides a literary education.

The definition of the poet, of the literary text, of the audience, and the accepted place of letters in the social world are crucial elements of different literary systems and may be considered the major structural components of literary systems.

The different names of letters—poetry, letters, *belles-lettres*, literature, *Dichtung, Schrifttum,* and the numerous other terms of other languages—are not different words for the same transcendental object but the marks of various historical concepts of writing, or literary systems, and their place in the social world.

Western literary history begins to be recorded with the assumption by Aristotle in his *Poetics,* and in Plato's various objections to poets and poetry, of a distinctly literary activity, and the formulation of a loosely systematic view of its origins, its form, its types, and its social purposes.

Aristotle's definition of letters is not a scientific description of some cultural given, or innately human, literary essence—which is the way his views, for example, of tragic catharsis, or of tragedy and comedy, are regularly read—but a social construct, a systematic definition and assemblage of the parts of writing, appropriate to and believable in his own place and time.

Subsequent social arrangements of letters in the West—often marked by the powerful statement of a poetic ideology by some master critic such as Horace, Dante, Sidney, Pope, Wordsworth, Eliot, or Frye—are not simply continuations or further refinements of earlier literary theories. The presence of the old is always felt in the new in this conservative social activity. But the old takes its place in a new configuration, now in a theory of imitation, now in a theory of novelty. The path of change is historical, not usually logical, and for that reason neither letters nor its interpretation, criticism, can be said to progress as science is believed to in its study of a prior nature.

Like other changing parts of culture such as the family or the state, letters too changes in response to shifting social circumstances, most obviously to the kind of social structure that employs writers—tribal, feudal, monarchical, democratic—and the mode in which they express themselves—oral, manuscript, print, electronic.

Through all of its historical changes, until the romantic era, letters continued to manifest its social function through a close association with and support of the established order, ethical, religious, governmental.

Romantic "literature," appearing in Europe in the course of the eighteenth century as one of the fine arts, broke with this long tradition of subordination to other institutions in the social order and offered itself as an independent activity of the spirit, prior to and independent of other parts of culture.

Romantic literature offered itself as an essence, the direct and true voice of a deep and timeless humanity heard in all ages and places.

What we call "literature" is, however, a highly specialized romantic and modern system of letters, principally legitimated by Wordsworth in England, which defines the literary text as poetry or fiction, explains literary activity in terms of its origin in a psychological faculty of the creative imagination, and posits its social role as a truly human voice criticizing the destructive activities of bourgeois capitalism and scientific rationalism.

While direct support of and dependence on the main line of dominant social values, and their institutional forms, may be considered the normative social function of letters, romantic literature over the last two hundred years has made a place for itself in society as a social institution in its own right, with its own explanatory philosophy (literary criticism), a distinctive group of texts (the literary canon), a set of well-defined social roles (author, critic, teacher, editor, etc.), a place in the educational system as one of the humanities, and in the "knowledge tree" as one of the arts.

To individuals born into modern western culture and its languages, literature appears, like other social realities, in all its objective forms as a given fact, a part of "what is," as real as the things of nature, and it becomes fixed in their subjective conception, consciousness, of the world as an unchanging and unchangeable part of reality.

But, as a part of culture, not as part of a serene unchanging nature moving according to eternal laws hypothesized by science, literature is always radically unstable and unpredictable.

Man-made and having no absolute existence in its own right, it has no exact location where it is totally fixed, no essence by which it can be defined, and no point where it achieves complete coherence.

Dependent for its believability and its functioning on its congruence with other social beliefs, values, and practices, literature is fluid and constantly changing as the world around it changes.

Literature, constantly destabilized by these social pressures, as well as by such erratic psychological forces as the desire for novelty, forgetfulness, or ignorance, is always in the process of being changed, made real in the world in different ways, linked up in different configurations and defined from some new angle.

This process of social adjustment is constant, but it becomes unavoidably noticeable and deeply disturbing at times like the present when radical social and technological changes, from print to electronics, are calling the old romantic literary values into question, by revealing their arbitrariness, and forcing new and extreme adjustments, perhaps even a new kind of letters replacing romantic literature.

Like Lot's wife, literature continues to exist by constantly moving forward in a dialectic movement between its objective "reality" and subjective conceptions of it: the world shapes the individual's conception of literature, the individual changes literature to suit new needs.

The literary system is always falling apart, always evaporating be-

fore our eyes, always in very real danger of ceasing to exist, but letters
is also always being put back together again, and its continued existence, its components and their organization, and its place in society depend on continuing literary activities, the kinds of poems and novels
written, the type of literary theory and interpretation developed, the
structure of literary education in the schools.

While these social constructions can never be judged as absolutely
true or false, neither are they merely opinions, one of which is as good
as any other, for they can be pragmatically understood and evaluated
in terms of whether they further, however indirectly, the culture's primary purpose of making real and believable a structured and meaningful world.

There are many ways of achieving this end, which, as the historical
case of romanticism shows, are not confined to some form of direct
support of the political and religious *status quo*, though this would appear to be the normative relationship of letters to its parent society.

All literary history is inevitably revisionary history reinterpreting
past events to support present theories, and neither the history nor the
theory offered in this book can be exempt from the judgment of
whether it contributes positively to the cultural function of letters.

BIBLIOGRAPHY

AARSLEFF, Hans. *From Locke to Saussure, Essays on the Study of Language and Intellectual History.* University of Minnesota Press, Minneapolis, 1982.

ABRAMS, M. H. *The Mirror and the Lamp: Romantic Theory and the Critical Tradition.* Oxford University Press, New York, 1953. 292 (25)

ADAMS, Hazard, ed. *Critical Theory Since Plato.* Harcourt Brace Jovanovich, New York, 1971.

ALKON, Paul K. "Johnson and Chronology." *Greene Centennial Studies, Essays Presented to Donald Greene in the Centennial Year of The University of Southern California.* Eds. Paul J. Korshin and Robert Allen. University of Virginia Press, Charlottesville, 1984, pp. 143–71.

ALSTON, R. C., and Crump, M. J., eds. *Eighteenth-Century Short-Title Catalogue, The British Library Collections.* 113 fiches. British Library, London, 1984.

ALTICK, Richard D. *The English Common Reader, A Social History of the Mass Reading Public 1800–1900.* University of Chicago Press, Chicago, 1957. 69 (30)

ARBER, Edward, ed. John Milton, *Aeropagitica.* Alexander Murray, English Reprints, London, 1868. 72 (24)

ARENDT, Hannah. *The Human Condition.* University of Chicago Press, Chicago, 1958.

AUSTEN, Jane. *Jane Austen's Letters to Her Sister Cassandra and Others.* Ed. R. W. Chapman. 2 vols. Clarendon Press, Oxford, 1932.

AYLING, Stanley E. *George the Third.* Collins, London, 1972. 25 (196)

BACON, Francis. *The Advancement of Learning and New Atlantis.* Ed. Arthur Johnson, Oxford Paperback English Texts, gen. ed. John Buxton. Clarendon Press, Oxford, 1974. 260 (2:4)

BALDICK, Chris. *The Social Mission of English Criticism, 1848–1932.* Clarendon Press, Oxford, 1983.

BALZAC, Honoré de. *Lost Illusions.* Trans. Herbert J. Hunt. Penguin Books, Harmondsworth, 1971. 304 (202, 206, 273, 274), 305 (372),

306 (374, 376, 286, 191), 307 (191, 195, 166, 185), 308 (417), 310 (472, 450)

BARTHES, Roland. "The Death of the Author." In *Image-Music-Text*, ed. and trans. Stephen Heath, pp. 142–48. Fontana/Collins, Glasgow, 1977. 72 (142)

BATE, Walter Jackson. *The Achievement of Samuel Johnson*. Harcourt Brace, New York, 1961.

—— *The Burden of the Past and the English Poet*. Harvard University Press, Cambridge, 1970.

—— *From Classic to Romantic, Premises of Taste in Eighteenth-Century England*. Harper Torchbooks, Harper and Row, New York, 1961. 173 (95)

—— *Samuel Johnson*. Harcourt Brace Jovanovich, New York, 1975. 89 (521)

BELANGER, Terry. "Publishers and writers in eighteenth-century England." In *Books & their Readers in Eighteenth-Century England*, ed. Isabel Rivers, pp. 5–25. St. Martin's Press, London, 1982. 10 (21), 48 (6, 6)

BENJAMIN, Walter. "The Work of Art in the Age of Mechanical Reproduction." In *Illuminations*, ed. Hannah Arendt, trans. Harry Zohn, pp. 217–51. Schocken Books, New York, 1969.

BERGER, Peter. *The Sacred Canopy*. Doubleday Anchor Books, New York, 1969. 50 (9)

—— and Luckmann, Thomas. *The Social Construction of Reality, A Treatise in the Sociology of Knowledge*. Doubleday Anchor Books, New York, 1967.

BLOOM, Edward A. *Samuel Johnson in Grub Street*. Brown University Press, Providence, 1957.

BOSWELL, James. *The Correspondence & Other Papers of James Boswell Relating to the Making of the Life of Johnson*. Ed. Marshall Waingrow, vol. 2 of *Boswell's Correspondence*, gen. ed. F. W. Hilles. McGraw-Hill, New York, n.d. 121 (164), 163 (246)

—— *Life of Johnson*. Ed. George Birkbeck Hill, rev. L. F. Powell. 6 vols. Clarendon Press, Oxford, 1934–50. 18 (2:259), 26 (2:33, 35, 40), 39 (2:33, 40, 40), 42 (2:319), 43 (3:15), 70 (1:143), 75 (2:233), 78

(1:457), 81 (1:413), 82 (2:209, 210; 1:414), 83 (2:435; 1:397, 397), 89 (2:297), 91 (1:107), 92 (1:131, 134, 134), 95 (4:34; 1:204; 4:236), 96 (3:33, 42; 1:331), 97 (2:119), 99 (3:162), 100 (1:438), 101 (2:259), 103 (1:443), 104 (1:455, 258), 105 (1:264, 261, 374), 106 (4:116; 2:317; 1:429), 109 (1:425), 110 (1:25), 111 (4:183, 406; 3:155; 2:166), 112 (2:446; 3:71), 113 (3:228), 118 (1:30), 130 (1:35), 131 (1:94, 277), 133 (1:99, 96), 134 (1:99), 135 (1:163 n.1, 35), 137 (1:483, 483), 141 (1:213, 437; 2:351; 3:53; 2:469, 153, 102, 250), 142 (2:106, 93; 3:295), 143 (3:295, 296; 2:87), 144 (2:106), 145 (4:374), 154 (3:332), 162 (3:351), 163 (1:152; 4:408), 173 (3:270), 175 (1:219), 176 (1:224), 177 (3:280; 1:204), 178 (4:236), 183 (1:287), 202 (1:259, 261), 205 (2:139), 206 (2:139; 4:236), 207 (1:144), 208 (3:272), 210 (2:271), 211 (1:57; 2:344), 212 (1:435), 213 (2:226; 4:308), 214 (2:365; 3:284), 215 (1:48), 216 (1:40; 4:409; 2:440), 219 (1:458; 3:37; 2:185), 226 (1:200), 227 (1:192; 2:49, 90), 229 (3:253), 230 (3:280), 235 (2:439; 3:174), 246 (3:38), 252 (2:365), 265 (2:439; 4:22; 2:439), 266 (1:394; 2:89), 269 (3:109), 270 (1:425; 3:110, 111, 110), 278 (2:358), 289 (3:178; 4:374), 314 (1:328; 328 n.1), 315 (1:328 n.1)

BOWLES, William: see Boswell, *Correspondence.*

BRADY, Frank. *James Boswell: The Later Years, 1769–1795.* McGraw-Hill, New York, 1984. 119 (64, 90), 144 (63)

BROADHEAD, Glenn J. "Samuel Johnson and the Rhetoric of Conversation." *Studies in English Literature,* 20 (1980), 461–74. 207 (461)

BROMWICH, David. "The Uses of Biography." *Yale Review,* 74 (1984), 161–76. 274 (175)

BRONSON, Bertrand H. *Johnson Agonistes.* Cambridge University Press, Cambridge, 1946.

—— "Strange Relations: The Author and His Audience." In *Facets of the Enlightenment, Studies in English Literature and Its Contexts,* pp. 298–325. University of California Press, Berkeley and Los Angeles, 1968. 221 (299)

—— "Thomas Chatterton." In *The Age of Johnson,* ed. F. W. Hilles, pp. 239–56. Yale University Press, New Haven, 1949. 85 (249)

BROOKE, John. "The Library of King George III." *The Yale University Library Gazette*, 52 (1977), 33–45. 25 (42)

BUTLER, Marilyn. *Romantics, Rebels and Reactionaries, English Literature and its Background 1760–1830.* Oxford University Press, Oxford, 1981.

BYRD, Max. "Johnson's Spiritual Anxiety." *Modern Philology*, 78 (1981), 368–78.

"Caldwell Minute": *see* Taylor, F.

CARLYLE, Thomas. *On Heroes, Hero-Worship and the Heroic in History.* Ed. Carl Niemeyer. Bison Books, University of Nebraska Press, Lincoln, 1966. 115 (154, 179, 181), 116 (154, 170, 182, 180, 181)

CHAYTOR, H. J. *From Script to Print.* Heffer and Sons, Cambridge, 1945. 71 (1)

CHESTERFIELD, Philip Dormer Stanhope, Earl of. "The Language of Ladies," *The World*, 101 (Dec. 5, 1754). In *Letters and Other Pieces*, ed. R. P. Bond, pp. 280–85. Doubleday, New York, 1935. 202 (282)

CHRISMAN, Miriam Usher. *Lay Culture, Learned Culture: Books and Social Change in Strasbourg, 1480–1599.* Yale University Press, New Haven, 1982.

CLIFFORD, James L. *Dictionary Johnson: Samuel Johnson's Middle Years.* McGraw-Hill, New York, 1979.

—— *Young Sam Johnson.* McGraw-Hill, New York, 1955.

COCHRANE, J. A. *Dr. Johnson's Printer, The Life of William Strahan.* Harvard University Press, Cambridge, 1964.

COHEN, Murray. *Sensible Words, Linguistic Practice in England 1640–1785.* The Johns Hopkins University Press, Baltimore, 1977. 190 (79), 192 (78)

COHEN, Ralph. *The Art of Discrimination, Thomson's "The Seasons" and the Language of Criticism.* Routledge and Kegan Paul, London, 1964.

COLEMAN, D. C. *The British Paper Industry, 1495–1860: A Study in Industrial Growth.* Clarendon Press, Oxford, 1958.

COLLINS, A. S. *Authorship in the Days of Johnson, Being a Study of the Relation between Author, Patron, Publisher and Public, 1726–1780.* Robert Holden, London, 1927. 31 (202)

CONNELY, Willard. *The True Chesterfield.* Cassell, London, 1939.

COOK, Ann Jennalie. *The Privileged Playgoers of Shakespeare's London, 1576–1642.* Princeton University Press, Princeton and Guilford, 1981.

CRADDOCK, Patricia B. *Young Edward Gibbon, Gentleman of Letters.* The Johns Hopkins University Press, Baltimore, 1982.

DAMROSCH, Leopold, Jr. "Samuel Johnson and Reader-Response Criticism." *The Eighteenth Century,* 21 (1980), 91–108. 228 (103)

—— *Samuel Johnson and the Tragic Sense.* Princeton University Press, Princeton, 1972.

—— *The Uses of Johnson's Criticism.* University Press of Virginia, Charlottesville, 1976. 227 (21)

DARNTON, Robert. *The Business of Enlightenment, A Publishing History of the "Encyclopédie" 1775–1800.* Harvard University Press, Cambridge, 1979. 254 (539)

—— *The Literary Underground of the Old Regime.* Harvard University Press, Cambridge, 1982. 302 (22)

—— "Philosophers Trim the Tree of Knowledge: The Epistemological Strategy of the *Encyclopédie.*" In *The Great Cat Massacre and Other Episodes in French Cultural History,* pp. 191–214. Vintage Books, New York, 1985. 257 (192)

DAVIS, Natalie Zemon. "Printing and the People." In *Society and Culture in Early Modern France,* pp. 189–226. Stanford University Press, Stanford, 1975.

DIDEROT, Denis: *see Encyclopédie.*

—— *Lettre sur les aveugles à l'usage de ceux qui voient* (1749) and *Lettre sur les sourds et muets* (1751). In *Diderot's Selected Writings,* ed. L. C. Crocker, trans. Derek Coltman. Macmillan, New York, 1966.

DISCH, Robert, ed. *The Future of Literacy.* Prentice-Hall, Englewood Cliffs, N.J., 1973.

DOWLING, William C. "Boswell and the Problems of Biography." In *Studies in Biography,* ed. Daniel Aaron. Harvard English *Studies,* 8, pp. 73–93. Harvard University Press, Cambridge, 1978.

—— *The Boswellian Hero.* University of Georgia Press, Athens, 1979.

DOWLING, William C. *Language and Logos in Boswell's "Life of Johnson."* Princeton University Press, Princeton, 1981.

EAVES, Morris. "Romantic Expressive Theory and Blake's Idea of the Audience." *PMLA*, 95 (1980), 784–801.

EDINGER, William. *Samuel Johnson and Poetic Style.* University of Chicago Press, Chicago, 1977.

Eighteenth-Century British Books, Author Union Catalogue. Compiled by Robinson, F.J.G.; Averly, G.; Esslemont, D. R.; Wallis, P. J., 5 vols. Dawson Publishing, in association with Avero Publications, Folkestone, Kent, 1981.

EISENSTEIN, Elizabeth. *The Printing Press as an Agent of Change*, 2 vols. Cambridge University Press, Cambridge, 1979. The single-volume paperback edition, 1980, is cited for quotations. 53 (105)

—— "Some Conjectures about the Impact of Printing on Western Society and Thought." *Journal of Modern History*, 40 (1968), 1–56. 12 (15), 250 (7), 251 (9)

ELIOT, T. S. "Tradition and the Individual Talent." In *Critical Theory Since Plato*, ed. Adams, pp. 784–87. 157 (784, 785)

ELLEDGE, Scott. "The Naked Science of Language, 1747–1786." In *Studies in Criticism and Aesthetics, 1660–1880*, eds. Howard Anderson and J. S. Shea, pp. 266–95. University of Minnesota Press, Minneapolis, 1967. 200 (274)

ELLIS, Frank H. "Johnson and Savage: Two Failed Tragedies and a Tragic Hero." In *The Author in his Work, Essays on a Problem in Criticism*, eds. Louis L. Martz and Aubrey Williams, pp. 337–46. Yale University Press, New Haven, 1978.

Encyclopédie, ou Dictionnaire raisoné des sciences, des arts et des métiers, par une société de gens de lettres. Ed. Denis Diderot and others, 35 vols. Paris, 1751–1780. 261 (xliv)

ESDAILE, Arundell. *The British Museum Library.* George Allen and Unwin Ltd., London, 1946. 26 (189), 44 (19)

FEBVRE, Lucien and Martin, Henri-Jean. *The Coming of the Book: The Impact of Printing 1450–1800.* Trans. David Gerard. NLB, London, 1976.

FIEDLER, Leslie. "What Shining Phantom: Writers and the Movies." In *Man and the Movies*, ed. W. R. Robinson, pp. 304–23. Penguin Books, Baltimore, 1969. 73 (305)

FLEEMAN, J. D. *Preliminary Handlist of Copies of Books Associated with Dr. Samuel Johnson*. Oxford Bibliographical Society, Bodleian Library, Oxford, 1984.

—— "The Revenue of a Writer, Samuel Johnson's Literary Earnings." In *Studies in the Book Trade, In Honour of Graham Pollard*, eds. R. W. Hunt, I. G. Philip *et al*. Oxford Bibliographical Society, Bodleian Library, Oxford, 1975, pp. 211–30. 103 (223)

FOLKENFLIK, Robert. "Macpherson, Chatterton, Blake and the Great Age of Literary Forgery." *The Centennial Review*, 18 (1974), 378–91. 86 (379)

FOTHERGILL, Brian. *The Strawberry Hill Set: Horace Walpole and his Circle*. Faber and Faber, London, 1983.

FOXON, David. "Pope and the Early Eighteenth-Century Book Trade." Lyell Lectures, typescript, 1975.

FRANKL, Paul. *Principles of Architectural History: The Four Phases of Architectural Style, 1420–1900*. Ed. and trans. J. F. O'Gorman. MIT Press, Cambridge, 1968.

FREED, Lewis. "The Sources of Johnson's Dictionary." Ph.D. dissertation, Cornell University, 1930.

FRYDE, E. B. "Lorenzo De' Medici, High finance and the patronage of art and learning." In *The Courts of Europe, Politics, Patronage and Royalty, 1400–1800*, ed. A. G. Dickens, pp. 77–98. Thames and Hudson, London, 1977. 40 (96)

FRYE, Northrop. *Anatomy of Criticism, Four Essays*. Princeton University Press, Princeton, 1957. 98 (90)

FUSSELL, Paul. *Samuel Johnson and the Life of Writing*. Harcourt Brace Jovanovich, New York, 1971.

GEDULD, Harry M. *Prince of Publishers: A Study of the Work and Career of Jacob Tonson*. Indiana University Press, Bloomington, 1969.

GEERTZ, Clifford. "Art as a Cultural System." *Modern Language Notes*, 91 (1976), 1,473–99. 279 (1497, 1488)

—— "Thick Description: Toward an Interpretive Theory of Culture." In Geertz, *The Interpretation of Cultures*, pp. 3–30. Basic Books, New York, 1973.

GENÊT, Jean. *The Balcony*. Trans. Bernard Frechtman. In *Seven Plays of the Modern Theater*, introduction by Harold Clurman, pp. 269–370. Grove Press, New York, 1962. 127 (353)

GIBBON, Edward. *Memoirs of Edward Gibbon* (1796). Ed. Henry Morley. George Routledge & Sons, London, 1918.

GINGER, John. *The Notable Man, The Life & Times of Oliver Goldsmith*. Hamish Hamilton, London, 1977.

GISSING, George. *New Grub Street*. Ed. Bernard Bergonzi. Penguin Books, Harmondsworth, 1968. 245 (46), 298 (138, 214)

—— *The Private Papers of Henry Ryecroft*. Archibald Constable, London, 1909. 157 (35)

GOLDBERG, Jonathan. *James I and the Politics of Literature: Jonson, Shakespeare, Donne and Their Contemporaries*. The Johns Hopkins University Press, Baltimore, 1983. 27 (54)

GOLDGAR, Bertrand A. *Walpole and the Wits, The Relation of Politics to Literature, 1722–42*. University of Nebraska Press, Lincoln and London, 1976.

GOLDSCHMIDT, E. P. *Medieval Texts and Their First Appearance in Print*. Oxford University Press, Oxford, 1943. 52 (116)

GOLDSMITH, Oliver. *New Essays by Oliver Goldsmith*. Ed. R. S. Crane. University of Chicago Press, Chicago, 1927. 17 (135)

GOODY, J. R., ed. *Literacy in Traditional Societies*. Cambridge University Press, Cambridge, 1968.

GOSSMAN, Lionel. "Literary Education and Democracy." *Modern Language Notes*, 86 (1971), 761–89. 72 (773)

GRAY, Thomas. *Correspondence*. Eds. Paget Toynbee and Leonard Whibley. 3 vols. Clarendon Press, Oxford, 1935.

GREENE, Donald J. *The Politics of Samuel Johnson*. Yale University Press, New Haven, 1960.

—— *Samuel Johnson's Library, An Annotated Guide*. English Literary Studies Monograph, Series 1. University of Victoria, Victoria, 1975. 212 (5)

GROSS, John. *The Rise and Fall of the Man of Letters, A Study of the Idiosyncratic and the Humane in Modern Literature*. Weidenfeld and Nicolson, London, 1969.

GUILLÉN, Claudio. *Literature as System, Essays toward the Theory of Literary History*. Princeton University Press, Princeton, 1971.

HAGSTRUM, Jean H. *Samuel Johnson's Literary Criticism*. University of Chicago Press, Chicago, 1952.

HARBAGE, Alfred. *Shakespeare's Audience*. Oxford University Press, London, 1941.

HARRIS, John, De Bellaigue, Geoffrey, and Millar, Oliver. *Buckingham Palace*. Nelson, London, 1968. 24 (23)

HARRIS, Michael. "Newspaper Distribution during Queen Anne's Reign: Charles Delafaye and the Secretary of State's Office." In *Studies in the Book Trade, In Honour of Graham Pollard*, eds. R. W. Hunt, I. G. Philip *et al*. Oxford Bibliographical Society, Bodleian Library, Oxford, 1975.

—— "The Structure, Ownership and Control of the Press, 1620–1780." In *Newspaper History from the Seventeenth Century to the Present Day*, eds. George Boyce, James Curran, and Pauline Wingate, pp. 84–97. Constable, London, 1978.

HARRIS, Roy. "The History Men." *TLS* (Sept. 3, 1982), 935–36. 196 (935), 198 (936)

—— *The Language Myth*. St. Martin's Press, New York, 1981. 185 (75)

HARTMAN, Geoffrey. *Wordsworth's Poetry, 1787–1814*. Yale University Press, New Haven, 1964.

HAVELOCK, Eric A. *Preface to Plato*. Belknap Press of Harvard University Press, Cambridge, 1963.

HELGERSON, Richard. *Self-Crowned Laureates: Spenser, Jonson, Milton and the Literary System.* University of California Press, Berkeley, 1983.

HILL, G. B. See Boswell, *Life of Johnson.*

HOLLADAY, Gae, and Brack, O. M., Jr. "Johnson as Patron." *Greene Centennial Studies.* Eds. Paul J. Korshin and Robert Allen. University Press of Virginia, Charlottesville, 1984, pp. 172–99.

HOWE, Irving. "George Gissing: Poet of Fatigue." In *Collected Articles on George Gissing,* ed. Pierre Coustillas, pp. 119–25. Case and Co., London, 1968.

HUGHES, Peter. "Allusion and Expression in Eighteenth-Century Literature." In *The Author in his Work, Essays on a Problem in Criticism,* eds. Louis L. Martz and Aubrey Williams, pp. 297–318. Yale University Press, New Haven, 1978. 43 (302)

HUME, David. "Of the Standard of Taste." In *Essays, Moral, Political and Literary,* pp. 253–77. London, 1742.

IRWIN, George. *Samuel Johnson: A Personality in Conflict.* Oxford University Press, Oxford and Auckland, 1971.

JACK, Ian. *The Poet and his Audience.* Cambridge University Press, Cambridge, 1984.

JACKSON, Sidney L. *Libraries and Librarianship in the West.* McGraw-Hill, New York, 1974.

JOHNSON, Samuel. *The Works of Samuel Johnson in Nine Volumes.* Oxford University Press, London, 1825. All Johnson references are to this edition unless otherwise specified.

—— "An Account of the Harleian Library." *Works,* vol. 5, pp. 180–89.

—— "The Adventurer." *Works,* vol. 4. 256 (180), 258 (189), 265 (188)

—— "A Compleat Vindication of the Licensers of the Stage." *Works,* vol. 5, pp. 329–44. 29 (344)

—— *Diaries, Prayers and Annals.* Ed. E. L. McAdam, Jr. with Donald and Mary Hyde. *The Yale Edition of the Works of Samuel Johnson,* vol. 1. Yale University Press, New Haven, 1958.

—— *The History of Rasselas, Prince of Abyssinia.* Ed. G. B. Hill, rev. J. P.

Hardy. Clarendon Press, Oxford, 1929, 1968. 32 (20), 113 (63), 114 (158)

—— *The Letters of Samuel Johnson.* Ed. R. W. Chapman. 3 vols. Oxford University Press, Oxford, 1952. 25 (1:218), 101 (1:398)

—— *The Lives of the English Poets.* Ed. G. B. Hill. 3 vols. Oxford University Press, Oxford, 1905. 29 (1:108), 32 (1:399), 78 (2:399), 79 (2:367), 81 (2:357, 429), 91 (1:2), 92 (1:329), 113 (2:116), 154 (1:410), 155 (1:366), 179 (1:418; 3:94), 180 (3:220, 221, 430, 126), 181 (3:127), 273 (1:59, 312), 274 (1:206, 271, 82), 276 (1:224, 20, 293, 469, 221), 277 (3:390, 417, 440, 337, 251), 281 (3:441, 242, 38), 282 (3:49)

—— "The Plan of an English Dictionary." *Works*, vol. 5, pp. 1–22. 200 (19)

—— "Preface to the English Dictionary." *Works*, vol. 5, pp. 23–51. 182 (42), 184 (25), 185 (51), 186 (50), 187 (23), 188 (27, 31, 23, 26, 25), 189 (30, 40, 34, 35, 35), 190 (37), 192 (44), 193 (48, 47, 43, 37), 194 (46, 27, 29), 195 (33, 33), 196 (40, 27), 197 (43)

—— "Preface to Harleian Miscellany" and "Proposals." In *Catalogus Bibliothecae Harleianae.* 2 vols. Thomas Osborne, London, 1743.

—— "Preface to Shakespeare." In *Johnson on Shakespeare*, ed. Arthur Sherbo. *The Yale Edition of the Works of Samuel Johnson*, vol. VII, 59–113. Yale University Press, New Haven, 1968. 166 (95), 169 (97, 97, 106), 170 (108), 171 (106), 229 (66), 235 (70), 236 (60), 248 (59)

—— "Proposals for Printing, by Subscription, the Dramatick Works of William Shakespeare." In *Johnson on Shakespeare*, ed. Sherbo, pp. 51–58. 167 (52), 170 (51)

—— *The Rambler.* Eds. W. J. Bate and Albrecht B. Strauss. *The Yale Edition of the Works of Samuel Johnson*, Vols. III, IV, V. Yale University Press, New Haven, 1969. 222 (3:120), 278 (4:284)

—— "Review of Jenyn's *Free Inquiry*." *Works*, vol. 6, pp. 64–65.

KAMES, Henry Home, Lord. *Elements of Criticism* (1762). Ed. Abraham Mills. Huntington and Savage, New York, 1851. 266 (13)

KAUFMAN, Paul. *Libraries and Their Users.* The Library Association, London, 1969. 69 (215)

KEAST, W. R. "The Theoretical Foundations of Johnson's Criticism." In *Critics and Criticism, Ancient and Modern*, ed. R. S. Crane, pp. 389–407. University of Chicago Press, Chicago, 1952. 227 (397, 391), 238 (397)

KEATS, John. *Letters of John Keats*. Ed. M. Buxton Forman. Oxford University Press, Oxford, 4th ed., 1952. 43 (272)

KERNAN, Alvin. *The Imaginary Library: An Essay on Literature and Society*. Princeton University Press, Princeton, 1982.

KINSLEY, William. "*The Dunciad* as Mock Book." *Huntington Library Quarterly*, 35 (1971–72), 29–47.

KNOBLAUCH, Cyril H. "Samuel Johnson and the Composing Process." *Eighteenth-Century Studies*, 13 (1980), 243–62. 223 (245)

KORSHIN, Paul J. "Types of Eighteenth-Century Literary Patronage." *Eighteenth-Century Studies*, 7 (1973–74), 453–73.

KRISTELLER, Paul O. "The Modern System of the Arts." In Kristeller, *Renaissance Thought II*, Harper Torchbooks, pp. 163–227. Harper and Row, New York, 1965. 266 (226)

KRUTCH, Joseph Wood. *Samuel Johnson*. Henry Holt, New York, 1944. 142 (143)

LACKINGTON, James. *The Confessions of James Lackington, Late Bookseller at the Temple of the Muses*. Ezekiel Cooper *et al.* Eds. and General Book Stewards for the Methodist Connection in America, Brooklyn, N.Y., 1806.

—— *Memoirs of the Forty-Five First Years of the Life of James Lackington*. London, 13th ed., 1810. 231 (92)

LAMY, Bernard: see Hughes, Peter.

LEED, Jacob. "Patronage in the *Rambler*." *Studies in Burke and his Time*, 14 (1972), 5–21.

—— "Johnson and Chesterfield: 1746–47." *Studies in Burke and his Time*, 12 (1970), 1,677–90.

LIPKING, Lawrence. *The Life of the Poet, Beginning and Ending Poetic Careers*. University of Chicago Press, Chicago, 1981.

—— *The Ordering of the Arts in Eighteenth-Century England*. Princeton University Press, Princeton, 1970. 110 (456)

LOCKE, John. *An Essay Concerning Human Understanding* (1690, 5th ed. 1706). Ed. John W. Yolton. 2 vols. J. M. Dent, Everyman's Library, London, 1961.

LONSDALE, Roger. *Dr. Charles Burney, A Literary Biography*. Clarendon Press, Oxford, 1965. 265 (64)

LOWRY, Martin. *The World of Aldus Manutius, Business and Scholarship in Renaissance Venice*. Basil Blackwell, Oxford, 1979.

LUKÀCS, Georg. *Studies in European Realism*. Intro. Alfred Kazin, no trans. The Universal Library, Grosset and Dunlap, New York, 1964.

MCADAM, E. L., Jr. "Dr. Johnson as Bibliographer and Book Collector." In *New Light on Dr. Johnson*, ed. F. W. Hilles, pp. 163–76. Yale University Press, New Haven, 1959. 211 (173)

MCCARTHY, William. *Hester Thrale Piozzi, Portrait of a Literary Woman*. University of North Carolina Press, Chapel Hill and London, 1985.

MACAULAY, T. B. "Croker's Edition of Boswell's Life of Johnson." In Macaulay, *Critical and Miscellaneous Essays*, vol. 2, pp. 13–56. D. Appleton and Company, New York, 1896. 30 (36)

MCFADDEN, George. *Dryden the Public Writer 1660–1685*. Princeton University Press, Princeton, 1978.

MCFARLAND, Thomas. *Originality and Imagination*. The Johns Hopkins University Press, Baltimore, 1985.

MCKENZIE, D. F. *The London Book Trade in the Later Seventeenth Century*. Sandars Lectures, Cambridge, 1976.

MCLUHAN, Marshall. *The Gutenberg Galaxy*. University of Toronto Press, Toronto, 1962; reprinted 1966. 15 (255), 50 (244, 250), 51 (245, 217, 248), 52 (144, 244, 156), 297 (269)

MACHLUP, Fritz. *Knowledge: Its Creation, Distribution, and Economic Significance*. Vol. II, Machlup, *The Branches of Learning*. Princeton University Press, Princeton, 1982.

MACK, Maynard. *Alexander Pope, A Life*. Yale University Press in assoc. with W. W. Norton, New Haven and New York, 1986. 10 (110), 212 (85)

MALONE, Edmond: *see* Boswell, *Correspondence*.

MARX, Karl, and Engels, Friedrich. *The Communist Manifesto*. Intro. A.J.P. Taylor, trans. Samuel Moore (1888). Penguin Books, Harmondsworth, 1967. 296 (83)

MAUROIS, André. *Prometheus, The Life of Balzac*. Trans. Norman Denny. Harper and Row, New York, 1965. 311 (254)

MAXTED, Ian. *The London Book Trades, 1775–1800*. Dawson, Folkestone, Kent, 1977.

MILLER, Edward. *Prince of Librarians, The Life and Times of Antonio Panizzi of the British Museum*. Andre Deutsch, London, 1967. 252 (108)

MITCHELL, C. J. "The Spread and Fluctuation of Eighteenth-Century Printing." *Studies on Voltaire and the Eighteenth Century*, 230 (1985), 305–21. 60 (306), 61 (318)

MORRIS, John N. *Versions of the Self*. Basic Books, New York, 1966. 125 (175, 193)

MUMBY, F. A. and Norrie, Ian. *Publishing and Bookselling*. Jonathan Cape, London, 5th ed., 1974.

MUNBY, A.N.L. *Sale Catalogues of Libraries of Eminent Persons*. 7 vols. Mansell with Sotheby Parke Bernet Publications, London, 1973.

MURRAY, Katherine E. M. *Caught in the Web of Words, James H. Murray and the OED*. Yale University Press, New Haven, 1977.

NEUBERG, Victor E. *Popular Education in Eighteenth Century England*. The Woburn Press, London, 1971.

OLNEY, James. *Autobiography: Essays Theoretical and Critical*. Princeton University Press, Princeton, 1980.

ONG, Walter J., S.J. *Orality and Literacy, The Technologizing of the Word*. Methuen, London, 1982.

—— "Reading, Technology, and the Nature of Man: An Interpretation." *Yearbook of English Studies*, 10 (1980), 132–49. 206 (142), 221 (133), 225 (136, 134)

—— "Romantic Difference and the Poetics of Technology." In Ong, *Rhetoric, Romance, and Technology*, pp. 255–83. Cornell University Press, Ithaca, 1971. 296 (282, 279, 279)

—— "The Writer's Audience Is Always a Fiction." In Ong, *Interfaces of*

the Word: Studies in the Evolution of Consciousness and Culture, pp. 53–
81. Cornell University Press, Ithaca, 1977.

PARKINSON, R. N. *Edward Gibbon*. Twayne Publishers, New York,
1973. 16 (34)

PARRINDER, Patrick. *Authors and Authority: A Study of English Literary
Criticism and Its Relation to Culture 1750–1900*. Routledge and Kegan
Paul, London, 1977.

PINKUS, Philip. *Grub Street Stripped Bare*. Archon Books, Hamden, Ct.,
1968.

PIOZZI, Hester Lynch. *Anecdotes of Samuel Johnson*. In *Johnsonian Mis-
cellanies*, ed. G. B. Hill. 2 vols. Oxford University Press, New York,
1966. 142 (106, 111)

PIPER, David. *The Image of the Poet, British Poets and Their Portraits*. Oxford University Press, New York, 1982.

PLANT, Marjorie. *The English Book Trade, An Economic History of the
Making and Sale of Books*. George Allen and Unwin, London, 3rd ed.,
1974. 68 (235)

POPE, Alexander. *The Correspondence*. Ed. George Sherburn. Oxford
University Press, Oxford, 1956.

——— *The Poems of Alexander Pope*. Ed. John Butt; one-volume collection
of Twickenham edition. Yale University Press, New Haven, 1963.
(Book and line numbers to *Dunciad* are given) 11 (344; 1:42), 12
(3:193), 13 (2:19; 1:274), 14 (4:101, 157, 249)

POTTLE, Frederick A. *James Boswell, The Earlier Years, 1740–1769*.
McGraw-Hill, New York, 1966. 126 (87)

——— *Pride and Negligence: The History of the Boswell Papers*. McGraw-
Hill, New York, 1982. 126 (6)

PRICE, Martin. *To the Palace of Wisdom: Studies in Order and Energy from
Dryden to Blake*. Doubleday, New York, 1964.

PYNE, W. H. *The History of the Royal Residences*. 3 vols. A. Dry, London,
1819.

RAWSON, Claude. "Gothic without Gloomth." *TLS* (Dec. 23, 1983),
1,427.

REICHARD, Hugo M. "Boswell's Johnson, the Hero Made by a Committee." *PMLA*, 95 (1980), 225–33. 92 (225), 241 (227)

—— "Pope's Social Satire: Belles Lettres and Business." In *Essential Articles for the Study of Alexander Pope*, ed. Maynard Mack, pp. 683–703. Archon Books, Hamden, Ct., 1964. 10 (694)

SAMMONS, Jeffrey L. *Literary Sociology and Practical Criticism, An Inquiry*. Indiana University Press, Bloomington, 1977.

SAUNDERS, J. W. "From Manuscript to Print: A Note on the Circulation of Poetic MSS in the Sixteenth Century." *Proceedings of the Leeds Philosophical and Literary Society* (vol. 6, pt. 8), 507–28.

—— *The Profession of English Letters*. Routledge and Kegan Paul, London, 1964. 34 (34)

—— "The Stigma of Print: A Note on the Social Bases of Tudor Poetry." *Essays in Criticism*, 1 (1951), 139–64.

SAVAGE, Richard. *The Poetical Works of Richard Savage*. Ed. Clarence Tracy. Cambridge University Press, Cambridge, 1962.

SCHOLES, Robert E. "Dr. Johnson and the Bibliographical Criticism of Shakespeare." *Shakespeare Quarterly*, 11 (1960), 163–71. 167 (169)

SELLS, A. L. Lytton. *Thomas Gray: His Life & Works*. George Allen and Unwin, London, 1980.

SHELLEY, P. B. *A Defense of Poetry*. In *Critical Theory Since Plato*, ed. Adams, pp. 498–513.

SHERBO, Arthur. *Samuel Johnson, Editor of Shakespeare*. University of Illinois Press, Urbana, 1956.

SIDNEY, Sir Philip. *An Apologie for Poetrie*. In *Elizabethan Critical Essays*, ed. G. Gregory Smith, I, 148–207. Clarendon Press, Oxford, 1904. 41 (194, 196)

SITTER, John. *Literary Loneliness in Mid-Eighteenth-Century England*. Cornell University Press, Ithaca, 1982. 224 (9)

SLEDD, James H., and Kolb, Gwin J. *Dr. Johnson's Dictionary, Essays in the Biography of a Book*. University of Chicago Press, Chicago, 1955. 183 (111), 190 (29)

SMART, Christopher. *The Collected Poems*. Ed. Norman Callan. 2 vols. Routledge and Kegan Paul, London, 1949. 84 (stanza 4)

SMITH, Adam. *An Inquiry Into the Nature and Causes of the Wealth of Nations.* Ed. Edwin Cannan. Random House, New York, 1937. 76 (315)

SMITH, H. Clifford. *Buckingham Palace.* Country Life Ltd., London, 1931.

STRAUS, Ralph. *Robert Dodsley, Poet, Publisher and Playwright.* John Lane, The Bodley Head, London, 1910. 63 (117), 66 (101), 67 (148)

SWIFT, Jonathan. *The Poems of Jonathan Swift.* Ed. Harold Williams, 3 vols. Clarendon Press, Oxford, 2nd ed., 1958. 75 (2, line 253ff.)

TAYLOR, Archer. *General Subject-Indexes Since 1548.* University of Pennsylvania Press, Philadelphia, 1966.

TAYLOR, F. "Johnsoniana from the Bagshawe Muniments in the John Rylands Library: Sir James Caldwell, Dr. Hawkesworth, Dr. Johnson, and Boswell's Use of the 'Caldwell Minute.' " *Bulletin of the John Rylands University Library of Manchester,* 35 (1952), 211–47. 45 (235, 238, 239)

TEMPLE, William. "A Sketch of the Character of the Celebrated Mr. Gray." *The London Magazine,* 1772. 35 (XLI, 140).

THOMAS, Donald. *A Long Time Burning, The History of Literary Censorship in England.* Routledge and Kegan Paul, London, 1969.

THRALE, Mrs. Hester Lynch: *see* Piozzi.

TOMPKINS, Jane P. "The Reader in History: The Changing Shape of Literary Response." In *Reader-Response Criticism, From Formalism to Post-Structuralism,* ed. Jane P. Tomkins, pp. 201–32. The Johns Hopkins University Press, Baltimore, 1980. 223 (214, 203, 205)

TRACY, Clarence R. *The Artificial Bastard, A Biography of Richard Savage.* Harvard University Press, Cambridge, 1953.

—— "Johnson and the Common Reader." *Dalhousie Review,* 57 (1977), 405–23. 234 (410)

VALÉRY, Paul. *Aesthetics.* Trans. Ralph Manheim. Bollingen Series, XLV.13. Pantheon Books, New York, 1964. 174 (183), 176 (185)

WAINGROW, Marshall: see Boswell, *The Correspondence.* . . .

WALKER, Keith. "Images of Intellect." *TLS* (Aug. 3, 1984), 870.

WALPOLE, Horace. *The Yale Edition of Horace Walpole's Correspondence.* Ed. Wilmarth S. Lewis, 48 vols., Yale University Press, 1937-83. 16-17 (35-244).

WARTON, Thomas. *History of English Poetry.* Ed. W. C. Hazlitt. 4 vols. Reeves and Turner, London, 1871. 269 (1:3)

WATT, Ian. "Publishers and Sinners: The Augustan View." *Studies in Bibliography.* Ed. Fredson Bowers. Bibliographical Society of the University of Virginia, vol. 12, pp. 3–20. University Press of Virginia, Charlottesville, 1959.

—— *The Rise of the Novel.* University of California Press, Berkeley, 1959.

WATZLAWICK, Paul, ed. *The Invented Reality . . . Contributions to Constructivism.* W. W. Norton, New York, 1984.

WEINBROT, Howard, ed. *New Aspects of Lexicography.* Southern Illinois University Press, Carbondale, 1972.

WELLEK, René. *The Rise of English Literary History.* University of North Carolina Press, Chapel Hill, 1941. 242 (132), 269 (132)

—— "What is Literature?" In *What is Literature?*, ed. Paul Hernadi, pp. 16–23. Indiana University Press, Bloomington, 1978. 259 (19), 263 (19), 264 (19)

WILES, R. M. *Serial Publication in England before 1750.* Cambridge University Press, Cambridge, 1957.

WILLIAMS, Aubrey. *Pope's "Dunciad."* Yale University Press, New Haven and London, 1955.

WILLIAMS, Raymond. *Culture and Society, 1780–1950.* Chatto and Windus, London, 1958. 294 (36)

—— *The Long Revolution.* Chatto and Windus, London, 1961.

WILSON, Edmund. "The Boys in the Back Room." In Wilson, *Classics and Commercials*, pp. 19–56. Farrar Straus, New York, 1950. 73 (56)

WIMSATT, W. K., Jr. "Johnson's Dictionary." In *New Light on Dr. Johnson*, ed. F. W. Hilles, pp. 65–90. Yale University Press, New Haven, 1959. 186 (70)

—— *Philosophic Words, A Study of Style and Meaning in the "Rambler" and "Dictionary" of Samuel Johnson.* Yale University Press, New Haven, 1948.

—— *The Prose Style of Samuel Johnson.* Yale University Press, New Haven, 2nd printing, 1963.

WOODRING, Carl. *Wordsworth*. Harvard University Press, Cambridge, 1968.

WORDSWORTH, William. "Preface" to the second edition of *The Lyrical Ballads*. In *Critical Theory Since Plato*, ed. Adams, pp. 433–43. 264 (433, 436, 437 n.1)

—— *The Prelude, A parallel text*. Ed. J. C. Maxwell. Penguin Books, Harmondsworth, 1971. Citations are to the 1805 text unless otherwise specified, and line numbers are those of the "A" text as given by Maxwell. (Book and first line number given) 288 (4:441; 11:271), 289 ([1850] 1:88; 7:149), 290 ([1850] 7:722), 291 (13:70), 292 (12:301; 13:446)

YUNG, Kim Kai. *Samuel Johnson 1709–1784*. Herbert Press, London, 1984. Based on catalogue of 1984 exhibition of Johnson portraits at National Portrait Gallery.

INDEX

A

Abbott, John, 94

Abrams, M. H., 292

Addison, Joseph, 113, 123, 154, 229, 275, 281, 305

advertising cost for *Idler*, 68

Aeneid, see Virgil

Aesop, 156

Akenside, Mark, 64, 277

Aldus Manutius, 41, 304

Allen, Edmund, 83, 173

Altick, Richard, xiii, 69

ancients, quarrel with the moderns, 153, 154, 243, 280; hacks choose to be ancients, 88; in *Battle of the Books*, 156

Annual Register, The, 66

anonymity: eighteenth-century, 71; Gray, 64-65; medieval, 52, 71; Shakespeare, 114; Swift, 42, 71

Arber, Edward, 72

Arbuthnot, John, 196

Arendt, Hannah, 77, 95

Ariosto, Lodovico, 33, 275

Aristotle, 154, 172, 246, 258

art: and mechanical reproduction, 152–53; as cultural system, 279; book design as, 63; fine arts grouped, 262; first histories of, 268; fostered by old order, 28; history of changing systems of, 238, 266–67; in eighteenth-century knowledge trees, 261; Johnson on various arts, 264–66; Kames'

grouping of, 266

Aubrey, John, *Brief Lives*, 268

audience: eighteenth-century readers, 68, 204, 311; fictional, 232; listeners in Dryden's *Essay*, 4, 68, 204; Milton's, 69; of Thomson's *Seasons*, 234; *Prelude*'s, 292; print separates from author, 218; Shakespeare's, 223, 281; struggle for control of, 270–71. *See also* common reader

aura, 153–59; Benjamin's definition, 152; Gissing's, 157; source of in printed works, 157, 165, 172, 198, 203

Austen, Jane, 38, 123

author: death of, 72; eighteenth-century flood, 74; film unmakes, 73; image of fixed by Johnson and Boswell, 148; in eighteenth-century France, 302; made real by print, 52, 74; metaphysical right to his work, 101; print separates from audience, 218; romantic (*see* romantic poet), 149; source of true language, 197; unknown in earlier times, 71

Ayling, Stanley E., 25

Ayscough, Samuel, 259

B

Bacon, Sir Francis, 175, 186, 198, 260

Bailey, Nathaniel, 182

Walpole, Horace, 16, 85, 125, 268
Walton, Izaak, 166
Warburton, William, 26, 169
Ward, Ned, 74
Warner, Jack, 73
Warton, Thomas, 101, 268
Watt, Ian, xii, 68
Watts, Dr. Isaac, 196, 271
Weber, Max, 94
Weinbrot, Howard, xiii
Wellek, René, 242, 259, 263, 268, 269
Wesley, John, 128, 205
West, Nathanael, 73
Whitefield, George, 205
Whitman, Walt, 127, 296
Wilde, Oscar, 38
Wilkes, John, 29, 128
Williams, Mrs. Anna, 207
Williams, Raymond, xiv, 294
Wilson, Edmund, 73
Wimsatt, William K., Jr., xiii, 175, 186, 196
Wither, George, 99
Wood, Anthony à, *Athenae Oxionensis*, 268
Woodring, Carl, 296

Woolf, Virginia, 199
Wooton, William, 156
Wordsworth, Dorothy, 292
Wordsworth, William, 22, 108, 125, 127; contrasted to Johnson, 288; "literature" for all imaginative writing, 264; poetry opposite of science, 264;
— *Prelude*: as paradigm of romanticism, 287–94; definition of romantic poet, 108, 288; prefers nature over city, 289, 306; spots of time, 291
work as opposite of labor, 77, 86
writers: become center of letters in eighteenth century, 46, 273; factory workers in publishing, 74ff., 91–97, 298–99, 310, 311; necessity of meeting deadlines, 67; become owners of copyright, 99; in France, 299–303
Wyatt, Sir Thomas, 34, 42
Wycherley, William, 79, 274

Y

Yalden, Thomas, 271
Young, Edward, *Night Thoughts*, 277

Library of Congress Cataloging-in-Publication Data

KERNAN, ALVIN B.

PRINTING TECHNOLOGY, LETTERS, & SAMUEL JOHNSON.

BIBLIOGRAPHY: P.

INCLUDES INDEX.

1. JOHNSON, SAMUEL, 1709–1784—AUTHORSHIP.

2. PRINTING—ENGLAND—HISTORY—18TH CENTURY.

3. AUTHORS AND READERS —ENGLAND—HISTORY—18TH CENTURY.

4. LITERATURE AND SOCIETY—ENGLAND—HISTORY—18TH

CENTURY. 5. BOOK INDUSTRIES AND TRADE—ENGLAND—HISTORY

—18TH CENTURY. 6. BOOKS AND READING—ENGLAND—HISTORY—

18TH CENTURY. I. TITLE. II. TITLE: PRINTING TECHNOLOGY,

LETTERS, AND SAMUEL JOHNSON.

PR3537.A9K47 1987 828'.609 86–42842

ISBN 0–691–06692–2 (alk. paper)

Alvin B. Kernan is Avalon Foundation Professor of the Humanities and Professor of English at Princeton University. Among his several works are The Playwright as Magician *(Yale, 1979) and* The Imaginary Library *(Princeton, 1982).*